Reimagining Dialogue on Identity, Language and Power

NEW PERSPECTIVES ON LANGUAGE AND EDUCATION

Founding Editor: Viv Edwards, *University of Reading, UK*

Series Editors: Phan Le Ha, *University of Hawaii at Manoa, USA* and Joel Windle, *Monash University, Australia.*

Two decades of research and development in language and literacy education have yielded a broad, multidisciplinary focus. Yet education systems face constant economic and technological change, with attendant issues of identity and power, community and culture. What are the implications for language education of new 'semiotic economies' and communications technologies? Of complex blendings of cultural and linguistic diversity in communities and institutions? Of new cultural, regional and national identities and practices? The New Perspectives on Language and Education series will feature critical and interpretive, disciplinary and multidisciplinary perspectives on teaching and learning, language and literacy in new times. New proposals, particularly for edited volumes, are expected to acknowledge and include perspectives from the Global South. Contributions from scholars from the Global South will be particularly sought out and welcomed, as well as those from marginalized communities within the Global North.

All books in this series are externally peer-reviewed.

Full details of all the books in this series and of all our other publications can be found on http://www.multilingual-matters.com, or by writing to Multilingual Matters, St Nicholas House, 31–34 High Street, Bristol, BS1 2AW, UK.

NEW PERSPECTIVES ON LANGUAGE AND EDUCATION: 117

Reimagining Dialogue on Identity, Language and Power

Edited by
Ching-Ching Lin and Clara Vaz Bauler

MULTILINGUAL MATTERS
Bristol • Jackson

DOI https://doi.org/10.21832/LIN4723
Names: Lin, Ching-Ching, editor. | Vaz Bauler, Clara, editor.
Title: Reimagining Dialogue on Identity, Language and Power/Edited by Ching-Ching Lin and Clara Vaz Bauler.
Description: Bristol; Jackson: Multilingual Matters, 2024. | Series: New Perspectives on Language and Education: 117 | Includes bibliographical references and index. | Summary: "This book reimagines dialogue as a tool to drive inquiries, encourage reflection and develop meaningful collaborations. It aims to foster public conversations surrounding identity, language and power that inspire criticality, innovation and multimodal engagement"—Provided by publisher.
Identifiers: LCCN 2023028057 (print) | LCCN 2023028058 (ebook) | ISBN 9781800414716 (paperback) | ISBN 9781800414723 (hardback) | ISBN 9781800414730 (pdf) | ISBN 9781800414747 (epub)
Subjects: LCSH: Dialogue. | Intercultural communication. | Language and languages—Usage. | Identity (Philosophical concept) | Power (Philosophy) | Communication in education. | LCGFT: Essays.
Classification: LCC P95.455 .R45 2024 (print) | LCC P95.455 (ebook) | DDC 303.48/2—dc23/eng/20230802
LC record available at https://lccn.loc.gov/2023028057
LC ebook record available at https://lccn.loc.gov/2023028058
Library of Congress Cataloging in Publication Data
A catalog record for this book is available from the Library of Congress.

British Library Cataloguing in Publication Data
A catalogue entry for this book is available from the British Library.

ISBN-13: 978-1-80041-472-3 (hbk)
ISBN-13: 978-1-80041-471-6 (pbk)

Multilingual Matters
UK: St Nicholas House, 31–34 High Street, Bristol, BS1 2AW, UK.
USA: Ingram, Jackson, TN, USA.

Website: https://www.multilingual-matters.com
Twitter/X: Multi_Ling_Mat
Facebook: https://www.facebook.com/multilingualmatters
Blog: https://www.channelviewpublications.wordpress.com

Copyright © 2024 Ching-Ching Lin, Clara Vaz Bauler and the authors of individual chapters.

All rights reserved. No part of this work may be reproduced in any form or by any means without permission in writing from the publisher.

The policy of Multilingual Matters/Channel View Publications is to use papers that are natural, renewable and recyclable products, made from wood grown in sustainable forests. In the manufacturing process of our books, and to further support our policy, preference is given to printers that have FSC and PEFC Chain of Custody certification. The FSC and/or PEFC logos will appear on those books where full certification has been granted to the printer concerned.

Typeset by SAN Publishing Services.

Contents

	Contributors	vii
	Foreword *Suresh Canagarajah*	xv
	Introduction *Ching-Ching Lin and Clara Vaz Bauler*	xix

Part 1: Dialogic *Testimonio*

1	*Ni de Aquí, Ni de Allá*: Reflections on Trying to Fit into a Box *Sandra Rodríguez-Arroyo, Laura C. Walls and Ferial Pearson*	3
2	On the (Constant) Process of Becoming a Critical Language Educator in the Brazilian Context *Priscila Fabiane Farias, Leonardo da Silva and Litiane Barbosa Macedo*	17
3	Unpacking Raciolinguistic Ideologies and Power Dynamics in Teacher Education through Intersectionality *Sumeyra Gok and Angelina Gillispie*	31
4	Black Women's *Ibasho:* Creating a Space of Belonging in Japan *Kinsella Valies and Lisa M. Hunsberger*	45
5	Negotiating Identity, Language and Power: Dialogic Reflections on Non-Native English-Speaking Writing Instructors in the US Composition Classroom *Lan Wang-Hiles, Ekaterina Goodroad, Tong Zhang and Judith Szerdahelyi*	60

Part 2: Digitally-Mediated Public Scholarship

6	Twitter/X as Thinking Communities: Responding, Reacting and Acting on Linguistic Discrimination *Clara Vaz Bauler and Vanja Karanović*	77

7   Forming Performative Space through Legitimate
    Peripheral Participation: Digitally-Mediated Dialogic
    Inquiry of Four BIPOC TESOL Professionals   91
    *Ching-Ching Lin, Derek Baylor, Yasmeen Coaxum
    and Shuzhan Li*

8   Professional Communities in the Making: Critical
    Dialogues in the ELT Field   107
    A.R. Shearer and Clara Vaz Bauler

9   Escaping the H-Index: On the Value and Voice
    of Public Engagement for Racialized Scholars   125
    JPB Gerald and Clara Vaz Bauler

Part 3: Through a Critical Incident Lens

10 When Daily Uses of Language, Identity and 'Power'
    Intersect with the Global (Center) versus Local (Periphery)
    Power Relations: An Interdisciplinary Study   141
    Ribut Wahyudi and M. Faisol

11 A Critical Dialogue Among Participants in a Professional
    Learning Community   158
    *Luciana C. de Oliveira, Destini Braxton,
    Jia Gui and Tara Willging*

12 Ebbs, Flows, What's New is Old: A Collaborative
    Autoethnography of Three EFL Educators in Turkey   173
    *Edmund Christopher Melville, Rasha Ashkar and Nicholas
    Douglas*

13 Critical Listening: A Teacher-Scholar Dialogue
    on the Challenges of Linguistically- and
    Culturally-Centered Coursework   189
    Julia E. Kiernan, Joyce Meier and Xiqiao Wang

14 Curiosity Matters: Envisioning Intercultural
    Dialogue in Qualitative Research Practice   204
    Wing Shuen Lau and Kristine Mensonides Gritter

    Index   219

Contributors

Rasha Ashkar, MA, is a primary school classroom teacher and English language coordinator at Bilkent Laboratory and International School in Ankara, Turkey. She completed her master's degree at the University of Bath in the UK.

Suresh Canagarajah is the Edwin Erle Sparks Professor and Director of the Migration Studies Project at Pennsylvania State University. He teaches World Englishes, Second Language Writing, and Postcolonial Studies in the departments of English and Applied Linguistics. His early education and teaching was in the war-torn region of Jaffna, Sri Lanka. He has taught before in the University of Jaffna and the City University of New York. His book *Resisting Linguistic Imperialism in English Teaching* (OUP, 1999) won the Modern Language Association's Mina Shaughnessy Award for the best research publication on the teaching of language and literacy. His subsequent publication *Geopolitics of Academic Writing* (UPittsburgh Press, 2002) won the Gary Olson Award for the best book in social and rhetorical theory. His study of World Englishes in writing pedagogy won the 2007 Braddock Award for the best article in the College Composition and Communication journal. His most recent publication is *Translingual Practice: Global Englishes and Cosmopolitan Relations* (Routledge, 2013), which won the 2014 BAAL best book award and MLA's Mina Shaughnessy Award. He is a former editor of *TESOL Quarterly* and a past President of the American Association of Applied Linguistics.

Litiane Barbosa Macedo holds a degree in English (2010), an MA (2014) and a PhD (2018) in language studies. She is currently a professor of the English program at the Federal University of Santa Catarina (UFSC), Brazil. She has developed investigations with the perspectives of Critical Discourse Analysis, Systemic Functional Linguistics, Multimodality, and Decolonial Studies to analyze race and gender representations in several media publications and institutional spaces. Her most recent publications discuss discourse and gender dynamics in Cape Verdean contexts; contributions of Afroperspectivism to decolonize Critical Discourse studies; the role of images in the meaning constructions of fake news posts in Brazil; and the analysis of anti-vax discourses on Twitter/X.

Clara Vaz Bauler has a PhD in Education from the University of California, Santa Barbara. She is a sociolinguist and critical discourse analyst, and is interested in unveiling unjust and often hidden educational practices that propagate language shaming and discrimination. She investigates language used in news media, social media and classrooms inquiring on the contexts, purposes and consequences of using certain terms and enacting specific policing practices associated with migration flows and linguistically diverse populations. As a language educator, she is interested in pedagogical practices that validate and affirm minoritized and racialized multilingual students' funds of knowledge and linguistic-semiotic resources. She advocates for the naturalization of multimodality in language teaching and learning spaces via digital media technology.

Derek Baylor, MA, is currently a doctoral student at Rutgers University. He was also a member of the TOC fellowship at Teachers College. His research interests lie in examining how a 'linguistic reconstructionist' approach to language learning and teaching might allow educators and institutions to better navigate the range of complexities that invariably arise from SLA pedagogies based upon deficit language ideologies, perspectives, and teaching practices.

Destini Braxton is a K-12 special education Mathematics teacher for Richmond Public Schools and a PhD candidate in Education, with a concentration in Educational Psychology at Virginia Commonwealth University (VCU). As a special education teacher, she works closely with students who are dually identified as English Language Learners and students with a disability. She served two years as a Holmes Scholar at VCU, which provided research mentorship for minority graduate students. Her research examines how teacher-student relationships impact students' motivational, engagement, academic emotions, and teacher trust among minoritized students in STEM, using an asset-based approach.

Yasmeen Coaxum, MA, has taught ELLs in national and international contexts for more than 13 years, specializing in English for Academic Purposes and Business English at language schools, universities and corporations in Japan, Turkey, Germany, Spain and the US. Her research interests include CALL, MALL, vocabulary acquisition, and pedagogical grammar.

Leonardo da Silva is a professor of the English program at the Federal University of Santa Catarina (UFSC), Brazil. His main research interests include critical pedagogy, task-based language teaching and Teaching of English and Portuguese as Additional Languages. He holds a master's degree in Cultural Studies and a PhD in Language Studies and his most recent publications focus on critical perspectives and emancipatory practices in language education.

Luciana C. de Oliveira is Associate Dean for Academic Affairs and Graduate Studies in the School of Education and a Professor in the Department of Teaching and Learning at Virginia Commonwealth University, Richmond, VA, USA. Her research focuses on issues related to teaching multilingual learners at the elementary and secondary levels. She served in the presidential line of TESOL International Association (2017–2020) and was a member of the Board of Directors (2013–2016). She was the first Latina to ever serve as President (2018–2019) of TESOL.

Nicholas Douglas, MA, is a former teacher at Bilkent Laboratory and International School in Ankara, Turkey.

M. Faisol, MA, is the Dean of Faculty of Humanities, Universitas Islam Negeri Maulana Malik Ibrahim Malang, Indonesia. He teaches undergraduate degree for Arabic Literature Department and Approaches to Islamic Study for Postgraduate Level. He was an invited speaker at the ASEAN level. He has published books and articles in Islamic and Qur'anic Studies.

Priscila Fabiane Farias is a professor at the Teaching Methodologies Department in the Federal University of Santa Catarina (UFSC), in Brazil. She teaches courses for the English program which involve teacher professional development in EFL contexts. Her main research interests include critical language pedagogy, task-based language teaching and additional language teacher professional development. She holds a master's degree and a PhD in language studies and her most recent publications focus on critical perspectives towards language education and on the use of critical tasks as pedagogical tools for English as an Additional Language learning and critical consciousness development.

JPB Gerald is a graduate of the EdD program at CUNY – Hunter College in Instructional Leadership and a theorist seeking justice for the racially, linguistically, and neurologically minoritized. He identifies as Black and neurodivergent, though he spent most of his life unaware of the latter. He hosts a podcast called Unstandardized English and has published his writing in academic journals, practitioner magazines, and national newspapers. His first book, on the harm caused by the centering of Whiteness in language education, was published by Multilingual Matters in 2022. He works in education management for Momentus Capital. He lives with his wife, young son, and dog in New York on stolen Munsee Lenape and Canarsie territory.

Angelina Gillispie is a middle school EL teacher in Virginia. She graduated from the University of New Hampshire with a MAT degree in Secondary Education and previously worked as a high school EL teacher in Massachusetts. She is dual certified in the fields of ESL and ELA. She has spent time serving students in marginalized communities and previously worked as a teacher for GEAR UP and Breakthrough, two programs whose missions centered around increasing the number of low-income students' success in postsecondary education.

Sumeyra Gok is an assistant teaching professor at Iowa State University. She earned her PhD in Education from the University of New Hampshire and previously worked as an ESL teacher in Massachusetts and New Hampshire. Her introduction to teaching was as an English as a foreign language instructor in Turkey, which is where she is from. Her research interests include translingual and transnational educator identities, culturally sustaining pedagogies, and decolonizing teacher education.

Ekaterina Goodroad is an Assistant Professor of Russian at Defense Language Institute in Monterey, California. As a Russian-born English instructor who has formal training in two different systems of education, and who has taught academic English in US colleges and universities – the discipline which is traditionally dominated by native English speakers in US higher education, she has experienced challenges NNESWIs face in US higher education institutions and has developed strategies to overcome these challenges. Her area of expertise is languages and cultures. Her research interests are related to NNESWIs in US higher education institutions. She was the Vice Chair of the NNESWIs Standing Group at the Conference of College Composition and Communication (CCCC). (Author's DISCLAIMER: This presentation has been approved for public release by the Defense Language Institute Foreign Language Center's Public Affairs Office. For verification please e-mail: mpao@dliflc.edu. Contents of this presentation are not necessarily the official views of the Defense Language Institute Foreign Language Center, nor are they endorsed by the Department of the Army, the Department of Defense, or the U.S. Government. All third party products /materials featured in the presentation remain the intellectual property of their respective authors/ originators. Use of outside materials is done under the fair use copyright principle, for educational purposes only. The content of this presentation is the sole responsibility of the author(s)).

Jia Gui is a graduate research assistant and PhD candidate in Education, with a concentration in Curriculum, Culture, and Change at Virginia Commonwealth University. Her research interests include TESOL, foreign language teaching and learning, and teacher education.

Lisa M. Hunsberger is a full-time lecturer at Kyushu Sangyo University in Fukuoka Prefecture, Japan. She has an MA in linguistics and has been an educator for over 15 years. Lisa has taught in Jamaica, France, and from kindergarten to retirees in Japan. She is an Apple Distinguished Educator, and she is active in professional TESOL communities in Japan and South Korea. Lisa regularly delivers presentations and workshops on effective presentation design at TESOL organizations in Japan and Korea.

Vanja Karanović has a PhD in Linguistics and is a Year 1 Subject Leader, and an A-Level English Language subject tutor at the Sixth Form College,

Farnborough. Her research focuses on the maintenance and shift of heritage languages, as well as bilingual language development and, more specifically, bilingualism as a first language. She advocates against linguistic discrimination and monolingual ideologies. She is a proud Bosnian and multilingual.

Julia E. Kiernan is an assistant professor of communication at Lawrence Technological University. Her research and teaching are intimately linked, and regularly examine the shifting impacts of pedagogical and curricular design in the digital humanities, translingual and transnational writing, environmental humanities, and health humanities. Her work has appeared in a number of peer-reviewed edited collections as well as the journals- *Composition Forum, Interdisciplinary Humanities, Communication and Language at Work* and *Composition Studies*.

Shuzhan Li, PhD, is an assistant professor in the Education Department at Ithaca College. He was an English teacher in Qingdao and Beijing, China before receiving his MEd at Vanderbilt University and PhD at the University of Florida. His teaching and research focus on preparing culturally and linguistically responsive educators for students from diverse backgrounds.

Ching-Ching Lin,EdD, has extensive experience working with culturally and linguistically diverse populations. Her most recent research interests mainly focus on engaging diversity as a strategic action plan for social change. She is a co-editor and contributing author of the following two edited volumes, *Inclusion, Diversity and Intercultural Dialogue in Young People's Philosophical Inquiry* (Brill Publishers, 2017) and *Internationalization in Action: Leveraging Diversity and Inclusion in the Globalized Classroom* (Peter Lang, 2020).

Joyce Meier is an associate professor of Michigan State University's Writing, Rhetoric, and Cultures Department, where she also serves as associate director of the first-year writing program. Her WPA work focuses on teaching multilingual learners; she has published in *Composition Forum, English Education, The Reading Matrix* and the *Journal of Global Literacies, Technologies, and Emerging Pedagogies*, along with multiple essays within larger collections.

Edmund Christopher Melville is the Director of the American School of Baghdad @ the American University Iraq-Baghdad and began the write-up of this chapter while working as the Director of Teacher Residency at Touro Graduate School of Education. He holds a doctorate in education from the University of Sussex (Brighton, UK) and dual master's degrees from Mercy College, the first in urban education and the second in educational supervision. Furthermore, he holds two bachelor's degrees: one in dance and another in educational studies.

Kristine Mensonides Gritter is a professor of literacy at Seattle Pacific University. She is a former middle school English teacher. She has a PhD in Curriculum, Teaching, and Educational Policy from Michigan State University.

Ferial Pearson is an Assistant Professor of Teacher Education at the University of Nebraska at Omaha. She was a high school teacher in Omaha for over a decade while simultaneously earning her Master's degree in Curriculum and Instruction. Dr Pearson earned her EdD in Educational Leadership at the University of Nebraska at Omaha. She created the Secret Kindness Agents Project with her high school students; it now exists in over 500 schools globally, and it has been featured at Lady Gaga's Born This Way Foundation, Hallmark, *Parents Magazine*, Learning for Justice website and magazine, *Midwest Living Magazine*, and more. As a Kenyan Indian Muslim immigrant queer disabled woman of color, she is passionate about working towards diversity, equity, inclusion, accessibility and kindness. She has received national and local awards for her work in education and social justice, authored two books, and was featured as a speaker at TEDx Omaha.

Sandra Rodríguez-Arroyo is an Associate Professor of ESL/Bilingual Teacher Education and a faculty member with the Office of Latino/Latin American Studies (OLLAS) at the University of Nebraska at Omaha. After earning her Bachelor's degree in Secondary English Education from the Universidad de Puerto Rico en Cayey, Dr Rodríguez-Arroyo began her career as an English as a Second Language (ESL) educator in public and private schools on her island. She received her Master's in Education (MEd) in Bilingual/Multicultural Education and a Doctorate in Education (DEd) in Curriculum and Instruction from Penn State University. Dr Rodríguez-Arroyo directs the University of Nebraska at Omaha's ESL and bilingual teacher education programs and researches translanguaging perspectives in bilingual education teacher preparation, asset-based service-learning experiences with diverse learners and families, and Latina faculty *testimonios*.

A.R. Shearer (she/her) is a sudden cardiac arrest (SCA) survivor and loves to tell her death story. She is uncovering ways to incorporate trauma-informed lenses and abolitionist frameworks into any future academic work she does. She holds an MA TESOL from The New School and a Bachelor of Science in Oceanography from Cal Poly Humboldt, and wants to one day investigate the intersection of ELT and the ocean sciences. She is also working on a CAS in Disability Studies and Woman & Gender Studies with a Master of Science in Cultural Foundations of Education from Syracuse University. She is a Community College in France Bootcamps alumni at the Université Grenoble Alpes. School is cool and all, but her true passion is sitting on the couch with the dogs watching the rabbits destroy the kitchen and each other.

Wing Shuen Lau has a PhD in Education from Seattle Pacific University. She holds a Master's degree in Teaching English to Speakers of Other Languages (TESOL) and a Bachelor's in Translation. Her most recent research work has connected perspectives in culturally responsive practices and social-emotional learning. She is particularly interested in promoting access to equitable literacy instruction.

Judith Szerdahelyi earned her PhD from The University of North CarolinaGreensboro with an emphasis on Rhetoric and Composition. After teaching for 20 years at Western Kentucky University, she retired in 2021. At WKU, she taught a variety of writing courses both face-to-face and online. Her research interests include non-native English-speaking writing instructors, creative non-fiction theory and pedagogy, and composition theory and pedagogy. In addition to a co-authored textbook on writing issued in Hungary, her publications include book chapters and academic articles published by IGI Global, Cambria Press and *Computers and Composition Online*. She is the founder and immediate Past Chair of the Non-Native English-Speaking Writing Instructors (NNESWIs) Standing Group at the Conference on College Composition and Communication (CCCC). She served as the Creative Non-fiction Standing Group's workshop facilitator for three years at CCCC. Her creative non-fiction essay was published in *Griffel*. Additionally, she edited *The Kentucky English Bulletin* for four years.

Kinsella Valies is an assistant professor at Jissen Women's University in Tokyo, Japan. Kinsella received her Master's in Applied Linguistics from the University of Limerick. During her twenty years as an educator, she has lived and taught in five countries. She is active in several international educational organizations and volunteers as the JALT Peer Support Group Chair. Research interests include formative speaking assessment and TBLT. Most recent publications include *Rubric Design and Development for English Speaking Practice and Performance in the First-year University Classroom* (2023).

Laura C. Walls is an Associate Professor of Spanish in the Department of Foreign Languages & Literature and the Office of Latino/Latin American Studies (OLLAS) at the University of Nebraska at Omaha. She earned her BA in Spanish and international relations from the University of California, Davis, before completing her MA in Spanish at Stanford University. Dr Walls earned her PhD in applied linguistics at UCLA. She teaches courses in Spanish as a heritage language, second and heritage language pedagogy, composition, bilingualism, and sociolinguistics. Dr Walls' scholarship bridges the fields of sociolinguistics, second language acquisition, and heritage language pedagogy.

Lan Wang-Hiles is an Associate Professor of English at West Virginia State University, where she also directed the English as a Second Language

(ESL) Program. Her research interests include L2 writing, writing center theories and tutoring practices, multilingualism, and non-native English-speaking teacher identity. Her research has been published as peer-reviewed journal articles and book chapters by *NYS TESOL Journal*, MLA, the Michigan University Press, Springer, Multilingual Matters and IGI Global. Currently, she is the Chair of the Non-Native English-Speaking Writing Instructors (NNESWIs) Standing Group for the Conference of College Composition and Communication (CCCC), and a Higher Education Representative of the West Virginia TESOL Board.

Ribut Wahyudi (PhD, Victoria University of Wellington, New Zealand) is the Head of English Literature Study Program at Faculty of Humanities, Universitas Islam Negeri Maulana Malik Ibrahim Malang, Indonesia. He has published book chapters with Palgrave Macmillan (2016, 2017), Routledge (2018, with Chusna), Multilingual Matters (2021), Springer (2021), Sunway University Press (2021) and Routledge (2022)and is a regular invited reviewer for *Asian Englishes*. In 2020 and 2021, he was invited by the Editor of English Language and Linguistics, Routledge New York to review book proposals in Critical Applied Linguistics studies and an invited reviewer for American Association of Applied Linguistics Conference 2023.

Xiqiao Wang is an assistant professor in the University of Pittsburgh's Composition, Literacy, Pedagogy, and Rhetoric program. Her research on multilingual writing process in the context of global migration has appeared in professional journals such as *Research in the Teaching of English*, *College Composition and Communication*, *Journal of Second Language Writing*, *Journal of Basic Writing* and *Composition Studies*.

Tara Willging is a graduate research assistant and doctoral student at VCU's School of Education, with a concentration in Curriculum, Culture, and Change. She is also a full time ESOL Specialist for Chesterfield County Public Schools. Her research interests include family engagement with multilingual learners, language use in schools, and student-teacher relationships.

Tong Zhang is an Assistant Professor of English language at Duke Kunshan University. Her research interests include second language writing, TESOL pedagogy and theory, and teacher identity. She has presented her research at the Conference of College Composition and Communication (CCCC), TESOL Convention & English Language Expo, and American Association for Applied Linguistics. Her publications include book chapters and academic articles published by *ELT Journal* and Routledge. Now Tong serves as an Online Coordinator in the Executive Committee of the Non-native English Writing Instructors (NNESWIs) Standing Group at CCCC.

Foreword

Suresh Canagarajah

Critic: So, why this glorification of talk? Is it all connected to the 'language turn' in diverse fields these days? Isn't talk simply instrumental to conveying our thoughts? Language is a tool to convey what's in our minds already. Thinking is more important; talk comes later. That's why whenever someone goes on talking, I say, 'Blah blah blah.'

Fan: I think that's a very poor understanding of the significance of talk. I think of talk as an activity. The notion of activity is best captured by the term 'languaging' as coined by some linguists. That is talk is a verb, not a noun. And when we talk or engage in languaging, we also explore, question, reformulate, and regenerate ideas. Talk clarifies and engenders thinking, rather than being disconnected from cognition or serving only as a pliable tool for the mind.

Critic: Okay, but talk can do nothing to change social life. That's why when some scholars start theorizing, I cut them short by saying, 'Just talk, and no action.' Talk can't accomplish anything practical.

Fan: A lot of action is happening between participants during talk. Consider that when people from two language or cultural groups are talking, the effort to negotiate their diversity is already social action. It involves a lot of work. Through such negotiation, they might be developing better social understanding, they might establish new relationships, they might initiate new social networks which bring their other acquaintances into an expanding relationship, and

Critic: No, I am not referring to things happening in interpersonal relationships. I am talking about wider social and structural changes.

Fan: We cannot disconnect language or talk from social structures. It is a bias to consider language as non-material. Structures, institutions and environments are considered material and, therefore, more durable and significant. However, talk and language, together with diverse other semiotic resources, participate in constructing social structures and practices. Consider how the capacity of two people to negotiate their differences and generate shared values and norms can serve as a model or template for democratic deliberation and co-existence in the wider society. Consider how words travel, and discourses proliferate, influencing and reconstructing other places and times. Consider what happens when the visions, identities, and experiences of the authors travel through this book to motivate social change. Consider the creative construction of new worlds and realities through such mobile discourses. Consider how talk develops critical orientations on social structures and institutions we already have by allowing people to pool their diverse experiences together and reimagine change. Consider how

Critic: But the notion of dialogue as research and representation in this book is going too far. Exploring knowledge through talk is subjective. I prefer the objective observation or recording of empirical realities and facts.

Fan: However, even in the observation of real-life conditions, language is implicated. The articles we read, the lectures we have listened to, and the conversations we have had with students and colleagues shape what we observe out there and how we interpret them. In many of our observations, other people are talking. Students in our classrooms or conversationalists in society are talking as they are being recorded for (or during) our study. As researchers, we participate in this conversation with them as we analyze and interpret their talk. The notion of dialogue as research brings into clearer focus that language and dialogue are always part of the research experience.

Critic: But allowing the dialogue to serve as the whole research article? That's going too far. If just dialogue is the research report, who will interpret that dialogue for the findings, results, or generalizations for readers? Dialogue as research writing is simply because of the laziness of scholars who don't want to offer us their analysis and conclusions. They don't have the intellectual capacity or writing skills to write a fully-fledged article. An article as dialogue is a half-hearted or incomplete article.

Fan: Even in articles written in a single author's voice, or constructed in the traditional objective genre of the IMRD research articles (i.e. Introduction, Methods, Results, Discussion), there is considerable dialogue involved. Dialogue with the readers, dialogues among other authors cited, dialogue with the research participants. Here we have to also consider the other word related to 'dialogue' – i.e. dialogical. I am told that the etymology of dialogue is as follows: i.e. dia: through or across; logos: word, knowledge, meaning. 'Discourse' similarly means running between two points. This etymology reminds us that dialogue is not a mere instrumental representation of preconstructed thought, but the negotiation of diversity and construction of new knowledge. In fact, even in a single-authored (and what you called fully-fledged) research article, we shouldn't (and don't) stop with the author's words on the research findings and conclusions. We should run between, across, and through the words on the page, read between and behind the lines, and construct new and critical knowledge. So a researcharticleas dialogue is simply inviting us to perform this dialogical activity by bringing the need for critical engagement and knowledge construction out into the open. Meanings can never be offered on a platter!

Critic: Okay, hold it. Are you saying that the defense you are making for dialogue in this book also has to be taken with a pinch of salt? That we shouldn't take your word? That the truth lies behind and beyond our dialogue on dialogue here? You are cutting the branch you are sitting on!

Fan: You got me there! But I agree with you. What you say demonstrates the power of language, dialogue, discourse. Meanings exceed the words we both are uttering now. There are both limits to dialogue, and also diverse new possibilities. What does this dialogue say about new academic writing, alternate forms of knowledge formation, diverse ways of writing the foreword as a genre, contrasting ways of interpreting research studies, multiple ways of engaging in research? And there are new questions. Who signs this dialogue as the author when current publishing conventions require the ownership of words by individuals? Or on the other hand, some might be thinking of the limits to dialogue at a point when new technologies are both muzzling talk and endlessly proliferating it to create a situation where texts are difficult to get a handle on, and no one is ever able to participate in all the conversations? What happens when people occupy their own talk bubbles, choose their own conversational partners to the exclusion of others, and start constructing their own realities? Our talk in this book is part of an expanding chain of intertextual links, and we can only hope to nudge the conversation in liberatory directions so that the conversation will proceed in more ethical and inclusive pathways. We have to let our words travel free, but we can make sure we have framed them for an ethical and democratic flight.

Introduction

Ching-Ching Lin and Clara Vaz Bauler

This edited volume aims to be an enactment of sociological reimagination, as a way to reimagine public conversations that inspire criticality, innovation and multimodality around the intersection of identity (self), language (mediating mechanism) and power (sociocultural domain). In response to an existential crisis in today's political climate in which the entangled history of racial colonialism, monolingual ideologies and other geopolitical forces continue to perpetuate prejudice and social injustice in and around the way we use languages social practices, this edited volume is a call to rethink the personal as the political and vice versa. In the past decades, we have experienced grand challenges facing ourselves and society within the shifting cultural landscapes, in various forms of segregation, fragmentation and exclusivity. While these political and epistemological breakdowns make us wonder where our future society is heading, the advent of social media presents opportunities where counter discourses can be designed, deployed and orchestrated to challenge the status quo and dominant narratives in public spheres. Hence a reimagination of dialogue is needed in order to support new ways of seeing, feeling, encountering and envisioning the world.

So, what is dialogue and why does it matter to the research, teaching and social practices of academics and the communities we are part of? Can dialogue be captured in writing? Are we truly creating spaces and participating in dialogue as researchers and professionals in academia? What is the role of power, language and identity in the act of dialogue and vice versa? This edited book is an attempt to engage with these questions in centering dialogue as the method used to conduct research and texture our inquiry. We believe that dialogue can be leveraged as a participatory research tool, not just to collect and analyze data, but also as a way of sharing knowledge and growing understanding. Dialogue, according to Paulo Freire (1996), is an existential requirement, an encounter that allows us to pronounce and enact the world with others. To Bakhtin (1986), dialogue is knowledge construction in itself as all texts are responsive, dialogically interrelated to other texts and other voices in the chain of communication. This idea implies that all acts are dialogic in nature because our ideas, including what many people would consider individual ideas, are constantly in the process of interaction, in agreement or in controversy with other people's and groups' ideas and discourses (Bakhtin, 1986). If we take these nuanced understandings of dialogue seriously, dialogue approaches to research embody 'knowledge in action' and make it unique as a generator of new knowledge, insight as well as opportunities for social intervention. Consequently, dialogue not only provides an extraordinarily rich and generative data source but also opens up new possibilities of interpretation and serves as an excellent medium for critical reflection.

As humans, we yearn deeply to dialogue, for a sense of belonging. Dialogue is a constitutive element of human experience. While dialogue may not capture the full range, nuances and extent of human experience, it helps illuminate our hidden psychological and social traps through a shared meaning making process. Drawing on diverse theoretical perspectives in the tradition of critical theories, we envision dialogue as a method and process of knowing and inquiry that prioritizes the perspectives of others, and allows for further exploration of the possibility of the cohabitation and interference of different perspectives, and hence more likely to bring closer attention to the fuller scope of human experience. Traditional research and educational practices, however, often rely on methodological solipsism, which tends to perpetuate the status quo by neutralizing meaning and decontextualizing discourse. To disrupt the cycle of knowledge production and oppression, this edited volume calls for methodological innovation and epistemological pluralism. Dialogue, by amplifying 'the propensity for participative listening - ultimately the inevitability of responsiveness/responsibility toward the other' (Petrilli, 2016) – provides a relational space of openness, tolerance and understanding.

The need for dialogue is particularly evident in the context of academia, where the 'solo' paper, presenting 'original ideas" with the goal of filling perceived research gaps, is the most esteemed prize; the meaning and importance of dialogue can get lost, misrepresented and, frequently, dismissed. However, a dialogical approach to research, teaching, learning and knowledge construction would reject this more conventional individualistic understanding of research. All texts come from determined perspectives and ideologies (Volochinov, 2004; Foucault, 1975) and are located and constructed within socio-historical moments and power relations. In this sense, Bakhtin (1986) aptly argues that:

> The topic of the speaker's speech, regardless of what this topic may be, does not become the object of speech for the first time in any utterance; a given speaker is not the first to speak about it. The object, as it were, has already been articulated, disputed, elucidated, and evaluated in various ways. Various viewpoints, world views, and trends cross, converge, and

diverge in it. The speaker is not the biblical Adam, dealing only with virgin and still unnamed objects, giving them names for the first time. (1986: 93)

The proposal of this book is to center dialogue as method as well as writing style and strategy to understand the depth and complexity of individuals' and shared lived experiences, particularly how they intersect with identity, language and power. In doing so, we resist and reimagine academic writing, social inquiry and educational practice within multilingualism and multimodality. We operate on the premise that dialogic approaches to identity, language and power, where two or more people from diverse cultural, racial, ethnic, ability, and/or linguistic trajectories jointly engage in an exploratory talk of how language learning, teaching and embodiment play a role in identity development when sharing, critically reflecting and examining their experiences, self-concepts, texts, pedagogies and other equity related issues. Dialogue becomes a vehicle for public engagement, social interaction and knowledge construction.Each chapter will implement concrete instances of dialogue among diverse researchers to engage in constructive critical conversations centering the intimate relationship among identity, language and power. The organization of each chapter is intentionally designed to support a variety of dialogic modalities that can be enregistered via the use of digital media technology or captured in narratives of critical incidents that happened outside of the moment of analytical reflection. For example, authors have recorded and used transcripts of their conversations on Zoom or used speech-to-text technology to capture the very language(ing) they were embodying during the interpretive and texturing phases of their research. This use of digital media technology, for instance, allowed dialogue to not only be the medium for idea generation during conversation, but the writing itself. The result is extraordinary as the texts become hybridized, expressing the natural tension between the diverse strategies of accommodation and resistance researchers engage in in the act of writing academic texts and doing research (Canagarajah, 2021). In this work, dialogue becomes a vehicle to challenge purist and standardized norms that serve as gatekeepers of multilingualism, linguistic variation and creativity.

Indeed, many of the authors of this volume are multilingual writers whose thinking, expression and perceived 'deficient' texts have often been denied entry in publications deemed prestigious. This edited book attempts to disrupt this vicious cycle by providing a dialogic platform as the main medium for academic research. We bring back calls for the questioning of the hegemony of standardized written varieties, especially English monolingualism, in global publications. Although we acknowledge that we are far from achieving this goal as most of the chapters in this book utilize English as the main medium of dialogic reflection and writing, we attempted to make space to address inequalities in academic communication in affirming ways authors and their research are positioned vis-à-vis their dialogue in practice (Canagarajah, 2021). Dialogue in practice, with its potential to mesh oral, written, and semiotic media, provided authors with an opportunity to actively embody hybridity, blurring artificial, restrictive and imposed linguistic and modality borders of conventional academic writing.

This edited volume, hence, represents a joint venture, where we explore dialogue not so much as a practice of egalitarian compromise, but as an invite to further the discourse through critical partnership and collaborative inquiry. In our selection process, we especially favor proposals who are committed to dialogue in diverse cultural environments, aiming to cross disciplinary, institutional and role boundaries in their scholarly collaboration. We are in awe of what has transpired in front of us. While the traditional format remains to have a strong hold on our imagination, through shared accountability, we envision a new level of intellectual endeavors and mutual engagement. Consequently, we identify three emerging themes from the chapters, which do not exhaustively capture what we have learned and experienced through this shared journey but signal a rare insight into the shifting and overlapping landscapes of related fields.

Dialogic *Testimonio*: Identity, Language and Power

It is not surprising that many contributing authors have resorted to the use of collaborative autoethnography as a method of inquiry from the respective perspective of self and communal sharing. We refer to it as dialogic *testimonio*, borrowing a term from a narrative research methodology rooted in Latin American history. Dialogic *testimonio* utilizes the shared perspective of first-person accounts by multiple narrators who shared their instances of social and political inequality, oppression, or any specific form of marginalization. Dialogic *testimonio*, as a multivocal research approach is relevant for us to understand the entangled relationship between self and society, since it allows participants to work collaboratively to share their personal stories and reflect on the pooled autoethnographic data. It provides an open invitation to engage in challenging dialogue and reflection with cultures, communities and individuals whose experience and voices have historically been marginalized. Dialogic *testimonio* can act as a pathway for transformative learning since it fosters a participatory activist stance by dealing directly with identity development.

Digitally Mediated Public Scholarship: Language, Identity and Power

Through social media, people have discovered new ways to communicate and collaborate. Many authors from this edited volume explore talking about controversial issues over social media as a form of political engagement and social activism. Digital media invites us to rethink physicality, interaction and dialogue. In their chapters, by reflecting on their experience targeting bias in social media and their struggle to represent their own stories, beliefs, opinions and identities navigating social media, they help us gain understanding of the way we perceive, dialogue, interact and behave toward each other through the mediating mechanism of language.

Specifically, since many of them are BIPOC (Black, Indigenous, People of Color) scholars, the major findings of their studies include examples and information related to racial microaggressions and the impacts as it relates to our self-concepts and relations with others. This reflexivity quality of identity talk over social media has important methodological implications. The digital media settings invite us to investigate both how social media shapes our identity as well as the formative role played by language and social media in the enactment of their identity development. These authors agree that digital networked media open up important opportunities for reimagining a new social research method, in a fine-grained, real-time, and participatory form of analysis. At the same time, there arises a need to reconcile the tension within these approaches, that is, between their effort to harness digital media *instrumentally*, to map issues unfolding beyond these settings, and their desire to capture *sui generis* dynamics which are congenial to the nature of digital spheres.

Through a Critical Incident Lens: Power, Language and Identity

Many authors have chosen to explore their reflective practices and professional knowledge through the lens of critical incidents in their professional settings. The discussion of critical incidents helps promote reflection on teaching practices and prompt insights into the intricate dynamics beyond the normal school process, especially those power relationships that cannot be named or verbalized. Analyzing critical incidents enables educators to revisit their incidents critically, by examining underlying biases and assumptions that influence many important aspects of educational practices and processes.

Critical dialogue about critical incidents, however, requires educators to collaborate with colleagues for mutual examination of their educational practices. Specifically, educators will need to go beyond solitary reflective practice. True reflective practices can only be collaborative acts in which peers assist each other in mutual examination of biases. Therefore, collaborative and exploratory talk is necessary because biased practices are often too easily overlooked in solitary reflection, especially when applied to personal experience and relations to each other.

With the assistance of objective peers, the influences of cultural bias and personal experience can be explored through interaction and dialogue. Consequently, dialogue provides educators the opportunity to examine the power relationship in professional and social contexts and to reinterpret critical incidents in ways that allow for new approaches.

Through this edited volume, we hope to drive home the idea and act of reimagining dialogue as a new methodology that highlights academic pursuits as political acts. Dialogic approaches to investigating the intersection of identity, language and power, therefore, represent an integrative model of self-inquiry and social activism and provide a valuable standpoint to understand the participatory nature of our very effort to question and investigate our sense of self in the world.

We are very proud of this edited book. We thank authors for the many rounds of revisions, but above all, for reimagining the role of dialogue in academic writing and research. We are charting new ground together. And, for that, we are extremely hopeful. We invite readers to join us in dialogue. As you read the chapters, inquire, question, analyze, converse and contact us for further conversations. As any dialogue, the work presented here provides one instance or moment of reflection and texture. It is not supposed to be a finished product, but a provocation, an opportunity to think together, a chance for further critical conversation. We welcome your participation.

References

Bakhtin, M.M. (1986) *Speech Genres and Other Late Essays*. Austin: University of Texas Press.
Canagarajah, S. (2021) Diversifying academic communication in anti-racist scholarship: The value of a translingual orientation. *Ethnicities* https://doi.org/10.1177/14687968211061586
Foucault, M. (1975) *Surveiller et punir* (Les Editions de Minuit). Paris: Gallimard.
Freire, P. (1996) *Pedagogy of the Oppressed* (revised edn). New York: Continuum.
Petrilli, S. (2016) Dialogue, responsibility and literary writing: Mikhail Bakhtin and his Circle. *Semiotica* 2016 (213), 307–343.
Volochinov, V. (2004) *Marxismo e filosofia da linguagem*. Sao Paolo: Hucitec.

Part 1
Dialogic *Testimonio*

1 *Ni de Aquí, Ni de Allá*: Reflections on Trying to Fit into a Box

Sandra Rodríguez-Arroyo, Laura C. Walls and Ferial Pearson

> '*Nosotros los* Chicanos straddle the borderlands …. Being Mexican is a state of soul – not one mind, not one of citizenship. Neither eagle nor serpent, but both. And like the ocean, neither animal respects borders.'
> (Anzaldúa, 1987: 43–44)

The myth of borders and belonging to a country is one that authors like Gloria Anzáldua have explored for decades. The quote above, along with the saying *ni de aquí, ni de allá* (neither from here nor there), reflects this feeling of not being one thing or the other, but both, while constantly navigating these borders. We are a society of binary thinking, male or female, gay or straight, from this place or that place, etc. However, life is more nuanced and complicated. Many of us live at intersections and borders, identifying as neither and both simultaneously. As educators, we bring these intersections into our work and must reflect on this. Brazilian critical pedagogue Paulo Freire encouraged teachers to engage in praxis, which he defined as 'reflection and action upon the world to transform it' (2002: 51). Freire emphasized the importance of dialogue to 'transform the world.' He described dialogue as 'the encounter between men, mediated by the world, in order to name the world' (2002: 88). For Freire, dialogue could not exist in 'the absence of a profound love for the world and for the people' (2002: 89). Through dialogue, 'whoever teaches learns in the act of teaching, and whoever learns teaches in the act of learning' (Freire, 1998: 31). Freire encourages us to engage in praxis and dialogue. Because of our desire to learn from one another, we, three multilingual and minoritized women, decided to explore the borders and intersections of our experiences and how they manifest themselves in our lives through dialogue.

Framing our Dialogues

The frameworks of intersectionality, raciolinguistics, and community cultural wealth guide our analysis in this chapter. We understand deeply that our personal, professional, and communal identities are inextricably intertwined. Delgado Bernal describes this perspective as a *trenza* (braid): 'When we are able to weave our personal, professional, and communal identities, we are often stronger and more complete ... at the same time, weaving together these and many other identities is fraught with complexity, tensions, and obstacles' (2008: 135).

The way we experience oppression at the intersections of our nuanced identities is what American feminist legal scholar, critical race theorist, and civil rights advocate Dr Kimberlé Williams Crenshaw (1989) defines as *intersectionality*. Our identities are the lenses through which we see our personal and professional lives; the various aspects of our humanity – such as class, race, sexual orientation, disability, faith, language of origin and gender – cannot be separated. When we stand at the intersection of two streets, we are not on one street or another; we are on both simultaneously. Instead of thinking of prejudice and bigotry targeting a collection of separate identities, intersectionality allows us to understand that pieces of our identities are interlocked. We exist as whole people who struggle with all these pieces together, not just as individuals.

Although negative statements about a person's skin color or ethnicity are sometimes called out as reflecting racist ideologies, language is discussed less often. Nevertheless, judgments about language are judgments about people, whether they be about class, race, gender, etc. Here, we draw on *raciolinguistic ideologies*, the process of racialization through language (Flores & Rosa, 2015), as an analytical framework. Flores and Rosa explain that the standard language variety is tied to monolingual Whiteness. Speakers who do not reflect this normative standard are racialized. Language can also normalize racialized people through what Bucholtz (2016) terms *indexical bleaching* – the mispronunciation or anglicization of ethnic names. She describes the process of naming, de-naming and renaming individuals with what are perceived as difficult-to-pronounce names. Because names index identities and social meanings, indexical bleaching strips away these meanings. Thus, this process serves to deracialize individuals and further normalize Whiteness.

Tara Yosso's *community cultural wealth* model helps explain the 'array of knowledge, skills, abilities, and contacts possessed and utilized by Communities of Color to survive and resist racism and resist macro and micro-forms of oppression' (2005: 77). The community cultural wealth model includes six types of capital: aspirational, navigational, social, linguistic, familial, and resistant capital. As we acknowledge our community cultural wealth, we uplift each other and recognize individuals and communities that give us forms of capital that influence our personal and professional journeys.

Answering Questions through *Testimonio* and *Reflexión*

We questioned how our experiences as minoritized women who identify as Boricua, Chicana, and Kenyan Muhindi, recognizing that our ethnic and cultural backgrounds influenced our experiences. Sandra identifies as Boricua, which comes from the Arawak (Taíno) Indian name for Puerto Rico, Borinquén, which means 'land of the Brave Lord' (Santiago, 1995: xviii). In the words of Roberto Santiago, '*Boricua* is what Puerto Ricans call one another as a term of endearment, respect, and cultural affirmation … . *Boricua* is a powerful word that tells the origin and history of the Puerto Rican people' (Santiago, p. back cover). Laura identifies as a Chicana, a term stemming from the Nahuatl word *mexitli* (me-shee-tlee), which references the historical migration of the *Mexica* indigenous people out of Aztlán, the homeland, and into what is today the southwestern part of the United States. Although it was initially used as a derogatory term to refer to individuals of Mexican heritage, it was appropriated by Mexican-Americans during the 1940s and has come to symbolize an identity that straddles two worlds, that of being of Mexican descent and that of being American. Ferial identifies as a Kenyan Muhindi, now officially the 44th recognized tribe in Kenya, referring to Kenyans who have Indian ancestry and who have been Kenyan citizens for generations. As we started our dialogues, we asked these research questions:

(1) How do our intersectional identities affect our interactions and experiences in different contexts as minoritized women?
(2) What can we learn from engaging in dialogue and reflexión to understand our experiences?
(3) What similarities and differences appear in our lived experiences as minoritized women from different backgrounds?

Our work is based on collective *testimonios* (Cervantes-Soon, 2012; Delgado Bernal, 2008), harvested from a dialogical approach through Zoom interactions. *Testimonio* is an approach that focuses on narratives in oral, written, and digital forms involving participants in critical reflection 'within particular socio-political realities' (Delgado Bernal *et al.*, 2012: 364). Scholars in the field 'embrace the use of counterstories and other methodological and pedagogical approaches that view the community and family knowledge of communities of color as a strength' (Delgado Bernal, 2002: 121). Through sharing and reflecting on narratives of survival and resistance, *testimoniantes*, those of us telling our experiences, can critically assess them to reclaim, transform and emancipate ourselves from these oppressions (Alemán, 2012; Caldas & Heiman, 2021). As we theorized these practices, we drew from Espino's *et al.* (2012: 444) suggestion of *reflexión* as 'an innovative methodological technique for bridging *testimonios* across lived experience'.

Reflexión 'allows us to analyze and interpret our *testimonios* as part of a collective experience that reflects our past, present, and future, thus moving us toward a collective consciousness' (Espino *et al.*, 2012: 445). In *reflexión*, partners engage in dialogues that 'move beyond self-reflection and self-inquiry toward a shared experience' (2012: 445). The authors emphasize that *reflexión* is a complement of *testimonio* 'that focuses not only on the telling of lived experience but the (re)telling of those experiences to a trusted dialogue partner' (2012: 446). Caldas and Heiman (2021: 60) state, 'the inclusion of *reflexión* under-scores the dialogic nature of sharing collective histories that encourages critical observations across identity borders, survival strategies, and stories of success in oppressive spaces'. Engaging in *reflexión* guided us to name everyday personal and professional experiences, (re)tell lived experiences, and find themes from our dialogues.

Interactions and reflections

We met online six times from May to December 2021. Each session took different directions, from the personal to the professional, the interactions and reflections continuing without pause. We shared issues about the proposed topics: the interplay of language, culture and power with our personal, professional and communal identities to engage in *reflexión*. In the spirit of *reflexión*, we asked questions, connected them to our intersectional identities, recognized raciolinguistic ideologies in our interactions with others, and described our community cultural wealth. Sandra recorded the significant themes that emerged.

Data from the transcribed video-recorded interactions were analyzed for overarching themes. As we reflected at one point, 'It is interesting, we did not know at the beginning ... that when it comes to languages, we are all passionate about language, but it has so much history and everything involved with it' (November 20, 2021). The subsequent dialogues demonstrate how our *reflexión* allowed us to 'situate and explain how our lived experiences exist within a broader set of social and institutional structures' (Espino *et al.*, 2012: 445).

Our Dialogues

Our findings are divided into dialogues to emphasize the conversational nature of our interactions as we moved back and forth from individual to collective experiences.

Dialogue: Where are you from?

Throughout our meetings, we reaffirmed the need not to be labeled and assigned a 'category.' Towards the beginning, Laura was emphatic about hating the 'Where are you from?' question. We laughed, but we also needed to reflect on why we all have a strong defensive reaction when someone asks this question. Laura feels that 'people want to put me into a box. I hate it because they are not asking me where I am from; they are asking me what my ethnicity is. So just ask me my ethnicity and stop asking me where I am from. Why don't you just outright make your racism, put it on the table, and do not pretend it is an innocent question when it is not.'

Ferial reflected on how she gets that same reaction when she tells people she is from Kenya: 'I have faced profound rejection of my multiracial identity and experiences. I keep needing to justify my identity as a Kenyan and as a multiethnic person.' Even other Africans from smaller towns in Kenya refuse to believe that Ferial is Kenyan. At an African Leadership Summit in Omaha, some Kenyans refused to believe she is from Nairobi based on her lighter skin color: 'No! You are from Coast!' They did not believe she was from inland and must be from Mombasa, where more people have mixed ancestry. When Ferial mentioned the last time she was home in Kenya to a Togolese woman, the woman laughed, saying it was 'a good joke.' She did not believe Ferial could be Kenyan. These interactions make Ferial hesitant to attend African celebrations as she is not accepted as a true Kenyan despite having Swahili ancestry. However, Indian ancestry goes back five generations in Kenya, Kenyan Indians are officially called the 44th tribe of Kenya (Verjee, 2017), and she has dual Kenyan and American citizenship.

Sandra sometimes feels that people ask her, 'Where are you from?' to say they have a Puerto Rican friend or request information about going on vacation to the island. She is rarely asked about her experiences growing up in a low middle-class family in Puerto Rico in a town surrounded by mountains and not a beach. Like Ferial's experiences, Sandra learned that a White staff assistant had identified her as Black on the university database. It was not until a new staff assistant, who is Black, noticed it years later that Sandra learned about this mislabeling. It was problematic that another person chose the race 'label' to meet a quota, which was not Sandra's choice.

Our dialogues have highlighted how inextricable the different pieces of our identities are from each other. Not only did all three of our stories weave together like Delgado Bernal's *trenza*, but our identities as women, academics, and multi-language speakers also intersected within those stories. We know that our personal, professional, and communal identities come together to make us stronger, as do our cultural, ethnic, and linguistic identities. This intersectionality, revealed by our dialogue, reinforced our understanding of how we cannot separate our academic selves from our personal selves, just as we cannot omit parts of our linguistic abilities, ethnic heritage, and gender identities from academia and our lives (Crenshaw, 1989). The result has been that we find we are *ni de aquí, ni de allá* (neither from here nor there); our skin is not the right color; our accents are unexpected, or our intersectional identities do not fit into existing boxes, so, we are forced into spaces that are uncomfortable and do not feel right.

Ferial has had to defend her intersectional identities the most. When applying for her marriage certificate, there was no space to put 'Indian African' as her ethnicity. The closest was 'Asian.' Ferial does not identify as South Asian only; this was a complete erasure of a whole section of her ancestry and lived experiences, which underscores why intersectionality is essential. When she interviewed for American Citizenship, the immigration officer said, 'It says here you are from Kenya, but …' and then reached out to make a circle over Ferial's face with his palm, miming erasure of her skin. When she asked if he meant that she was not dark enough to be from Kenya, he said yes. He could not understand that Indian Africans exist and did not have an intersectional understanding that Ferial does not have to be either Indian or Kenyan; she can be both/and. These situations harken back to the question, 'Where are you from?' as the answer is nuanced, something that people with uncomplicated, dominant, and hegemonic identities have never had to consider.

Laura's experiences growing up in a bilingual household with an American father and a Mexican mother are strengths when she interacts with heritage speakers with similar experiences. Sandra would like others to see beyond the tourist view of Puerto Rico and ask deeper questions about her experiences. For example, it was not until recently that some colleagues learned that she lived in Boston and attended bilingual education programs as a child. Ferial should not have to explain her origins or who she is constantly. She says, 'I am a Kenyan woman; my people have history. I did not learn about Kenyan Indians like Pio Gama Pinto (Durrani, 2018) and Suleman Verjee (Jamal, 2017). They were both instrumental in fighting for Kenyan independence until I had been living away from Kenya for more than 20 years. I was trained as an English teacher and taught English for over a decade, but I did not get to pick my area of research or teach in my area of expertise. Because of my multilingualism and brown skin, I was immediately pigeonholed. I was a practicum coach for Social Studies teacher candidates (which I had never studied or taught). I served on every diversity committee while only teaching classes that counted for our "diversity" credits. This work is important to me, but so is my expertise, experience, and training as an English teacher; I was not given a choice.'

We are more than our appearance. We should define our identities, and others should acknowledge them instead of questioning our responses to the 'where are you from' question.

Dialogue: Linguistic discrimination and privilege

As multilingual speakers, it is no surprise that language is often a topic of conversation. We spoke about linguistic discrimination and linguistic privilege, our names, the colonization of our languages and identities, and how our languages and language experiences translate into our classrooms. Ferial tells of her experience as an undergraduate international student in the United States.

> I emailed my advisor to request a meeting to create a plan of study. Despite the email being in [standard] English, she greeted me extremely loudly and slowly when I came to her office. When I answered in [standardized American] English, she was shocked and commented on how wonderfully I spoke English.

The advisor expected that Ferial's English would match her expectation of otherness of her as an immigrant, that otherness being the racialized speaker of English whose accent and grammar do not match that of her own. However, when Ferial showed up with a different accent and spoke 'standard' American English, she challenged those expectations. We use 'standard' in quotes here to emphasize that this language variety is an imagined standard not only as a variety (Mena & García, 2020), but as the only appropriate variety. Additionally, compliments themselves served to index Ferial's otherness, which the advisor herself would have perceived as inappropriate and offensive had Ferial been a white native speaker of English. This is an example of what Flores and Rosa (2015) call the racialization of 'non-native' speakers.

Ferial's experience contrasts with Sandra's as Sandra's otherness is displayed for everyone to hear. Sandra described when she stopped to talk to a colleague meeting with a student. Upon hearing Sandra speak, the student remarked that her accent was 'cute.' Rather than understand this comment as the condescending remark Sandra understood it to be, the student likely considered it a compliment. Nevertheless, despite the social hierarchy between a professor and a student, the student breached that social order to point out Sandra's otherness, labeling her as someone that does not belong. As Lippi-Green (1997) has highlighted, Sandra's accent helps sustain and perpetuate the racialization of speakers such as herself, thus perpetuating social and power structures that diminish Sandra's expertise.

The discrimination Laura describes stems from her experience as a heritage speaker of Spanish. Having grown up in California, she speaks a US Spanish variety, strongly influenced by Mexican Spanish. As a contact variety, US Spanish is often seen as 'incorrect' and 'impure' and heritage speakers' bilingual repertoires in English and Spanish are often seen as deficient. Therefore, she often spoke of being ridiculed by family members in Mexico who recognize their own Spanish as superior. She recounted an incident of linguistic bullying in which a cousin enlisted her classmates as participants. She describes her cousin asking her, '¿Te gusta Ana?' (Do you like Ana?). Given the look on her and the other classmates' faces, Laura understood it was a trap, but could not see where it was or how to escape it. Clearly, she would have to say yes, and so she did. As all the girls laughed, she asked her cousin, '¿A ti no te gusta Ana?' (You don't like Ana?), to which she replied, 'No, a mi me cae bien' (No, I like [different verb] her). Laura's cousin was able to ridicule her because she knew that Laura would be unaware of the subtle difference in Mexican Spanish between the verbs *gustar* (to be attracted to) and *caer bien* (to be liked platonically) when referring to people.

Although we have experienced linguistic discrimination, we have benefited from linguistic privilege and capital (Gallagher-Geurtsen, 2007; Yosso, 2005). Ferial and Laura, for example, speak normative American English with no perceived 'deviant' accent. Ferial describes herself as an 'accent chameleon,' because she can subconsciously mimic the accents of people around her. This ability means that her language is not racialized. Ferial's skill with accents and her married last name (Pearson) hides the fact that she is an immigrant. Therefore, immigrant communities see her as an outsider. Laura's English language privilege is similarly compounded by her white last name, 'Walls.' These have allowed her English to go unnoticed as a racialized variety. For the most part, her Spanish is accepted by native speakers as normative and congruent with the monolingual 'standard,' or privileged variety. This acceptance is likely due to her lifelong interaction with Mexican speakers, and her career and research focus on Spanish as a heritage language. In a conversation she had with the very cousin who used to bully her, the cousin admitted to not being an expert in Spanish and relinquished that authority to Laura, whose PhD is in Applied Linguistics. That was a moment of empowerment for Laura from a lifetime of bullying from the woman who once diminished her bilingualism.

Sandra's linguistic capital also arises from her expertise as a former English as a Second Language (ESL) teacher and her current role as an ESL and bilingual teacher educator. Her bilingualism and accent are seen as assets rather than 'language interference' (Weinreich, 1953). Her history as an English learner in Boston and Puerto Rico gives her more credibility with colleagues, students, and teachers. When she returns to Puerto Rico, she is consulted as the English language authority. Sandra sometimes wonders whether her accent or bilingualism would have been seen as an asset had she chosen another profession or a different teacher education field (ex., Math).

We must acknowledge how our linguistic discrimination, privilege, and capital have affected us. We reflected on moments where we experienced both, how it depends on context, and its impact on our lives.

Dialogue: Racialization through naming

As our dialogues focused on language and identity, names became a subject of conversation. Our names are often anglicized as speakers of languages other than English and members of a non-dominant culture. This anglicization is an example of indexical bleaching, which aligns our names with American normativity and Whiteness (Bucholtz, 2016). Sandra and Ferial discuss this whitening when reflecting upon their names.

People try to anglicize Sandra's name to 'Sandy' or ask her whether it is 'San-dra' or 'Son-dra.' As a second language speaker of English, she cannot distinguish between the two pronunciations, so she finds it difficult to explain the difference. In our conversation on the topic, Ferial recommended she use the song 'Look at me, I'm Sandra Dee' from *Grease* as a reference. While a helpful recommendation for an American audience, not growing up in the dominant American culture, Sandra did not understand the reference, so Ferial and Laura played a video clip of the movie with the song.

The problem for Sandra is not always with pronouncing her name; others often find it appropriate to change the spelling. She recently received an email where her name had been changed to 'Sondra.' Likewise, in an article about her award-winning work with service-learning, her name was listed as 'Dr Arroyo' despite numerous corrections on Sandra's part before its publication. This last example stems from the writer's lack of knowledge about Spanish last names and how he disregarded her explanations. Ferial also has a complicated relationship with the pronunciation of her name.

> My mom doesn't know how to pronounce my name, and her father couldn't pronounce her name either because there is no 'z' sound in his language, and her name is Fiza. This was a result of them both speaking multiple languages while still choosing names for their children from languages they understood, but did not speak (Persian for my name and Urdu for my mother's).

Until Ferial was in graduate school, everyone had anglicized her name. However, when a professor asked her, 'How do you pronounce it at home?' she felt comfort, acceptance, and catharsis for the first time since leaving Kenya.

The pronunciation of Laura's first name in English or Spanish has never bothered her because it is a '[r]eflection of the fact that my whole life is in English and Spanish.' Growing up in a bilingual home where her father spoke English and her mother spoke Spanish has always felt natural. She explains that 'Omaha is the only place I am *Laura* (Spanish), not *Laurita*, not Laura (in English).' In other areas of her life, friends and family pronounce Laura in English. Any Spanish pronunciation has always been modified into a nickname by adding a diminutive, *Laurita*, or by manipulating the name entirely, *Lorecas*. Instances of misnaming have always been with her last name, which is ironically English. Rather than Walls, she is often called 'Wells,' 'Wall,' 'Wallis' or 'Waltz' but never Walls.

Our names and pronunciation give us the sense of belonging needed as minoritized women in academia.

Dialogue: Language and colonization

Our dialogues on identity, whiteness, and racism eventually led to a deeper discussion of colonialism and its effects on our language practices. As we are all tied either directly or through ancestry to colonized countries (i.e. Puerto Rico, Mexico and Kenya) and a colonizer (i.e. the United States, Spain and Great Britain), it is by no accident that we speak the colonizers' language. Ferial is Kenyan, and one of the two official languages is English. People from India have been in Africa for over 200 years due to colonialism, racism, Islamophobia, classism and indentured slavery, and unfortunately, much of the world is unaware of this. Although English is not a native language for most of Kenya's inhabitants, it remains dominant due to its colonial ties to Great Britain and its importance globally. In Puerto Rico, both Spanish and English are rooted in the island's past and present. Furthermore, were it not for the Spanish presence in North America, Spanish would not be the dominant language of Mexico and Puerto Rico.

Our dialogues on the importance of knowing the colonial language led Ferial to share the devastating consequences of not speaking English.

> My maternal grandmother, who had both African and Indian ancestry, died in her 50s because of linguistic discrimination in her own country of Kenya. She had diabetes and did not understand what the doctor said about insulin use. He had been practicing in Kenya yet had never learned the multiple languages my grandmother and other Kenyans spoke. My grandmother thought she should inject herself with insulin every time she ate sugar; this caused her heart to enlarge dangerously, and she died of a massive heart attack. Furthermore, many professionals, including expat teachers, never learn the local languages, and to this day, the most prestigious schools in Kenya are taught in English by 'native' English speakers. Language discrimination is racist and classist.

This linguistic oppression is difficult for Ferial to reconcile with her love of the English language, which allowed her to escape to different worlds through literature and even become a high school English teacher.

Sandra, too, has a complicated relationship with English. Only when she participated in an AERA (American Educational Research Association) panel with Dr Luis Moll as a fellow discussant did she question her assumptions. In her presentation, Sandra explained her 'love affair' with English, the importance of teaching English, and preparing others to do so. Moll problematized those thoughts and pointed to the dangers of not recognizing the colonial history of English in Puerto Rico. Then, she began investigating the language policies implemented on the island at the beginning of the US occupation. She reflected on not learning this history during her secondary English teacher education program in Puerto Rico. It took Moll's critique to acknowledge how English was more than just a second language; it was *imposed* to make Puerto Ricans more 'American' (Rodríguez-Arroyo, 2013).

Through trying to explain our language learning experiences to each other, we realized the political nature of those experiences. We asked each other: 'How do we break away from the structures we grew up with? How do we use it in our personal and professional lives?' Laura realizes that she must continue sending a clear message to her heritage learner students that their linguistic traits should never be described as 'bad.' Ferial commits to a humanizing pedagogy that holistically embraces the experiences of all her students and intentionally includes many languages daily, for example, through music as students enter and work in the classroom, her greetings, talking with students, and assigned content. She makes it a point to drive home the importance of embracing her students' familial and social capital, never putting down how students or communities speak instead of celebrating it. Sandra ensures that her students and family members know why we speak the colonizer's language and its ties to oppression. She wants to continue questioning why specific languages are the 'standard' or the 'prestige variety,' who decided it, and who benefits. Sandra uses resistant capital to challenge the inequalities in teaching English as a second or foreign language (Yosso, 2005).

Breaking from colonial structures requires us to tap into our community cultural wealth. It is a 'commitment to conduct research, teach, and develop schools that serve a larger purpose of struggling toward social and racial justice' (Yosso, 2005: 82). We take this commitment seriously, because racial and social justice struggle is essential for minoritized communities to survive and thrive.

Not So Different

On the surface, we appear to be incredibly different; a Boricua, a Chicana, and a Kenyan Muhindi. However, we found through dialogue and *reflexión* that language, identity and power played significant roles in our lives professionally and personally. We are more similar under the surface than at first glance. We explored the nuance inherent in our identities, discovering that while some were empowering in some contexts, they were the reason for discrimination in others. The pride in our linguistic abilities was mixed with shame, sadness and anger. Furthermore, all three – language, identity and power – affect how we move in the world, including how we teach and interact with colleagues and every community we are part of.

In our meetings, we witnessed one another's stories, and at times, we were angry and frustrated with the *testimoniante*. Simultaneously, we were reminded of our communal cultural wealth and how we are 'part of a legacy of resistance to racism and the layers of racialized oppression' and become 'empowered participants, hearing their own stories and the stories of others' (Yosso, 2005: 75). Sharing our *testimonios* made us grow as a community of scholars and as friends and gain the strength to continue our journeys while sustaining our identities and those of our students in academia. Yosso (2005) will call this strength to continue our personal and professional lives, our aspirational and navigational capital. Freire's advice of sharing praxis to transform the world truly works for us. We believe engaging in dialogue and *reflexión* can be similarly transformative for others and confirms what other scholars have experienced (Alemán, 2012; Espino *et al.*, 2012; Caldas & Heiman, 2021; Delgado Bernal, 2002).

Monthly, we discovered our differences and similarities despite being born and raised in different lands. As we finished one of our meetings, we asked, 'How did we all end up in Omaha, Nebraska?' We laughed as we realized our families had no clue where Nebraska was. Sandra's mother thought she was moving to Alaska, not Nebraska. It was not until she visited Sandra that she realized that Nebraska and Alaska were not close geographically, and it was not as cold. Laura said her *Tía* (Aunt) Chelo would tell everyone: *Laurita vive en Alaska* (Laurita lives in Alaska). Tía Chelo now knows Nebraska's location as she was reminded that her father had worked in the state. Ferial's parents needed a reference point; they felt better knowing that Malcolm X was born in Omaha. This shared experience led to a follow-up question, 'Why do we stay?'

Our reasons vary. Laura finally feels settled, because she had always felt temporary in the places she had lived before. She also likes her freedom in what and how she teaches and researches. Omaha is just the right size for her. It is more complicated for Ferial, as her children have roots in Nebraska. Unlike Laura and Sandra, she is pre-tenured and has to be careful about a lot; she constantly asks permission to do what is right for her students and the community; she does not feel Laura's sense of freedom. Like her children, Ferial's students energize her and give her reason to stay, as do colleagues like Sandra and Laura, whose company and dialogue are healing and strength-giving. Homesickness is as present and intense as when she first immigrated as an undergraduate student; she hopes to be where the other half of her heart is someday. Sandra also has conflicted feelings about staying. She enjoys the ESL teacher candidates and bilingual education teachers she interacts with through her teaching. However, her homesickness for her family in Puerto Rico continues after over two decades of being away from her island. Job opportunities in Puerto Rico for her expertise are non-existent. For now, her Omaha friends are her family.

This type of honest exchange made us excited for each meeting. Our dialogues allowed us to speak truth to power with women who respected, encouraged and lifted us. We are committed to continue learning, growing, healing and transforming through ongoing dialogues.

Critical Discussion Questions

(1) Have you ever experienced having to fit your identities into ill-fitting boxes? How did you negotiate it?
(2) What pieces of your identity have you had to mute when entering academic spaces? What would it take for you to feel comfortable bringing your whole self to those spaces?
(3) Despite being raised in three different contexts, we discovered common experiences through dialogue. How might you encourage students to dialogue and explore their similarities, considering theoretical concepts like intersectionality, raciolinguistics, and community cultural wealth?
(4) Which languages exist in your community context? Do they exist in your community's academic spaces? Which languages need to be lifted more, and how could you do that?
(5) How might you intentionally create space for your students and colleagues to show up without muting pieces of their identities?

References

Alemán, S. (2012) Testimonio as praxis for a reimagined journalism model and pedagogy. *Equity & Excellence in Education* 45 (3), 488–506. https://doi.org/10.1080/10665684.2012.698175
Anzaldúa, G. (1987) *Borderlands/La frontera: The New Mestiza*. San Francisco: Aunt Lute.
Bucholtz, M. (2016) On being called out of one's name: Indexical bleaching as a technique of deracialization. In H.S. Alim, J. Rickford and A. Ball (eds) *Raciolinguistics: How Language Shapes Our Ideas About Race* (pp. 273–289). Oxford: Oxford University Press.
Caldas, B. and Heiman, D. (2021) Más allá de la lengua: Embracing the messiness as bilingual teacher educators. *Journal of Language, Identity & Education* 20 (1), 58–70. https://doi.org/10.1080/15348458.2021.1864209
Cervantes-Soon, C.G. (2012) Testimonios of life and learning in the Borderlands: Subaltern Juárez girls speak. *Equity & Excellence in Education* 45 (3), 373–391. https://doi.org/10.1080/10665684.2012.698182
Crenshaw, K. (1989) Demarginalizing the intersection of race and sex: A Black feminist critique of antidiscrimination doctrine, feminist theory and antiracist politics. *University of Chicago Legal Forum* (1), Article 8. http://chicagounbound.uchicago.edu/uclf/vol1989/iss1/8
Delgado Bernal, D. (2002) Critical race theory, Latino critical theory, and critical race and gendered epistemologies: Recognizing students of color as holders and creators of knowledge. *Qualitative Inquiry* 8 (1), 105–126. https://doi.org/10.1177/107780040200800107
Delgado Bernal, D. (2008) La trenza de identidades: Weaving together my personal, professional, and communal identities. In K.P. Gonzalez and R.V. Padilla (eds) *Doing the*

Public Good: Latina/o Scholars Engage Civic Participation (pp. 135–148). Sterling, VA: Stylus.

Delgado Bernal, D., Burciaga, R. and Flores Carmona, J. (2012) Chicana/Latina testimonios: Mapping the methodological, pedagogical, and political. *Equity & Excellence in Education* 45 (3), 363–372. https://doi.org/10.1080/10665684.2012.698149

Durrani, S. (2018) *Pio Gama Pinto: Kenya's Unsung Martyr. 1927–1965*. London: Vita Books.

Espino, M., Vega, I., Rendón, L., Ranero, J. and Muñiz, M. (2012) The process of reflexión in bridging testimonios across lived experience. *Equity & Excellence in Education* 45 (3), 444–459. https://doi.org/10.1080/10665684.2012.698188

Freire, P. (1998) *Pedagogy of Freedom: Ethics, Democratics, and Civic Courage*. Lanham, MD: Rowman and Littlefield.

Freire, P. (2002) *Pedagogy of the Oppressed*. London: Continuum.

Flores, N. and Rosa, J. (2015) Undoing appropriateness: Raciolinguistic ideologies and language diversity in education. *Harvard Educational Review* 85 (2), 149–171. https://doi.org/10.17763/0017-8055.85.2.149

Gallagher-Geurtsen (2007) Linguistic privilege: Why educators should be concerned. *Multicultural Perspectives* 9 (1), 40–44. https://doi.org/10.1080/15210960701334094

Jamal, K. (2017) *Indian Settlers in Africa: The Legacy of Suleman Verjee and Sons*. CreateSpace Independent Publishing Platform.

Lippi-Green, R. (1997) *English with an Accent: Language, Ideology, and Discrimination in the United States*. New York: Routledge.

Mena, M. and García, O. (2020) 'Converse racialization' and 'un/marking' language: The making of a bilingual university in a neoliberal world. *Language in Society* 50 (3), 343–364. https://doi.org/10.1017/S0047404520000330

Rodríguez-Arroyo, S. (2013) The never-ending story of language policy in Puerto Rico. *Revista Comunicación, Política y Cultura* 4 (1), 79–98.

Santiago, R. (1995) *Boricuas: Influential Puerto Rican Writings-An Anthology*. London: One World.

Verjee, Z. (2017, August 7) *Kenya's 44th Tribe: Why I'm Finally a First-class Citizen of My Country*. CNN. https://edition.cnn.com/2017/08/04/africa/kenya-asian-community/index.html

Weinreich, U. (1953) *Languages in Contact: Findings and Problems*. The Hague: Mouton.

Yosso, T.J. (2005) Whose culture has capital? A critical race theory discussion of community cultural wealth. *Race, Ethnicity and Education* 8 (1), 69–91. https://doi.org/10.1080/1361332052000341006

2 On the (Constant) Process of Becoming a Critical Language Educator in the Brazilian Context

Priscila Fabiane Farias, Leonardo da Silva and Litiane Barbosa Macedo

Educators in Brazil have encountered different challenges throughout history, being the last decade marked by several threats (Duboc & Ferraz, 2021; Pessoa & Freitas, 2021). In the last few years, more specifically, Brazilian teachers have been silenced in many different ways by proposals or movements like *Escola Sem Partido*, which have been accusing teachers of indoctrinating students according to a 'leftist' agenda (Frigotto, 2017). In a similar trend, neoliberal perspectives towards education in Brazil have contributed to the revision of important national guidelines towards a so-called neutral education (Farias & Silva, 2020), mostly focused on the job market. In this context, practicing what Freire called an emancipatory education has been not only difficult but also threatening, which can be perceived as evidence of the urgent need for critical educational practices (Farias & Silva, 2021).

When it comes to research, the situation is not different: Brazilian researchers have faced enormous challenges over the last few years, such as budget cuts (Mckie, 2021) or even lack of investment and the dismissal of human and social sciences (when compared to the hard sciences, for example) (Paula, 2019). In this scenario, critical perspectives to research seem to find less space in Brazil. Moreover, it is also relevant to consider the hierarchical status research has in the Brazilian scientific community. From a colonial perspective of western knowledge production, there seems to be a common understanding that research is not supposed to be political or based on personal narratives, since it should be 'neutral' and based on empirical evidence. It is also supposed to make use of hegemonic methodologies of research if one wants their voices to be considered as scientifically valid (Macedo, 2021). In this sense, doing critical research in Brazil is going against the grain, since it entails challenging hegemonic understandings of science that help sustain coloniality in contemporaneity.

This is the context that motivated this chapter. We, the authors, are three Brazilian teacher-researchers who work with English as an additional language and with teacher development in a Brazilian university in the south. Besides being close friends, we share a belief in autonomous, emancipatory, collective, and democratic learning, so our teaching and research practices are based on critical perspectives towards language and society (Crookes, 2021). We also claim that critical education is imperative in Brazil. By critical education we mean 'a profound, ongoing commitment to social justice' (hooks, 2010: 14), which moves beyond philanthropy, focusing on political, historically anchored, socially situated pedagogical projects that aim at transformation (Gounari, 2020).

Additionally, drawing on the idea of praxis, it is our mutual understanding that to do critical education one must constantly work on developing their own critical consciousness (Freire, 1970). Moreover, as hooks (2010) states, we are what we are because our story is the way it is. So, in this chapter, departing from critical perspectives on education (Freire, 1970; hooks, 2010) and on additional language teaching and learning (Pennycook, 2001; Crookes, 2021; Souza & Monte-Mor, 2018), we focus on collaboratively and dialogically analyzing a set of short personal narratives. Thus, we look at our own path as critical beings in an attempt to understand what may have contributed (and still contributes) to our critical development as educators, reflecting on challenges to be faced by those who dare to do critical work in Brazil. Hence, we hope this piece may contribute to a robust understanding of the interplay of identity, language, and power (Queiroz, 2020) – concepts perceived here from a critical and decolonial perspective – in the Brazilian additional language teaching scenario, specially because we side with Hall (1990: 222) who says that identity is a production, 'which is never complete, always in process, and always constituted within, not outside, representation'.

Becoming a Critical Educator: The Concept of Critical Consciousness

Gounari (2020: 3) denounces that 'language as a site of power, ideological tensions, political and financial interests, hierarchies, and symbolic and material violence, is most definitely a war zone'. In this sense, as Brazilian language teacher-researchers, we are part of this war. But what position do we occupy and what position do we want to occupy? Additionally, how do we get there and, in that matter, how do we make ourselves heard?

By collectively looking at their own narratives and individual experiences, Häusler *et al.* (2018) make a case for transgressive writing and research practices as a way to decolonize research and practice, opening a safe space for voices to be heard while promoting self-understanding. Inspired by Häusler *et al.* (2018) and by other authors who have engaged with story-telling in the fields of education and applied linguistics (see Kumaravadivelu, 2016; hooks, 2010; Freire, 1997), we attempt to exercise agency in the established war zone by considering our own experiences as a starting point. For that purpose, we look specifically at our critical consciousness development.

According to Freire (1970), since teaching and learning is always a political act, education should contribute to the awakening of critical consciousness. Such a process encompasses being able to understand how power and oppression operate in society, and also being able to critically act upon reality. It is a nonlinear and never-ending process, as we are always engaged in critically interpreting and acting upon ever-changing contexts. That means that not only students but also teachers are engaged in this movement, especially since in order to be a critical teacher, one needs to constantly work on their critical consciousness as well (Silva *et al.*, 2017).

Leal (2021) explains that even though in his early work Freire theorized critical consciousness 'as a process with a set of stages' (2021: 2), the concept is not to be seen as serial, as if one progresses through fixed steps aiming at a standard achievable goal. As she points out, critical consciousness, 'as theorized by Freire, contains a broad spectrum of attitudes and behaviors' (2021: 3). Drawing on works of Freire and other authors such as Smith (1976), Leal (2018) indicates some of these attitudes and behaviors, stating that critical consciousness involves awareness, reflection, and action in/upon the world while it is a process that is agentive, discursive, dialogic, dynamic, emotional, enacted and social. In this sense, developing critical consciousness is an individual but also a social/collective process.

In Freire's view, personal experience is as important as scientific knowledge. We reinforce, thus, that critical consciousness can be developed through what Freire has termed pedagogical praxis, considering that, as indicated by Tagata (2018: 257), 'practice without theory is thoughtless activism; on the other hand, theory without practice may lead to idealistic and empty verbalism'. But what are some elements/experiences within praxis that may contribute to teachers' critical development? With this question in mind, we attempt to understand our own path as critical educators.

Transgressive Research Practices for Emancipatory Education

Inspired by Häusler *et al.* (2018: 3), we have drawn 'on the productive tension between harmonizing our experiences and continuing individual struggles to experiment with unconventional and possibly transgressive writing practices'. For this purpose, we engaged in movements guided by collaborative autoethnography (Blalock & Akehi, 2018).

Autoethnography (Ellis *et al.*, 2011) focuses on first-person narratives in which specific moments of one's trajectory are examined. In collaborative autoethnography, this movement takes place collectively. As Blalock and Akehi (2018: 94) highlight, among several possibilities for researchers to engage in collaborative autoethnography, it 'may begin as an intentional discussion focused on similar experiences'. In this study, we collectively analyze the narratives of (i) our own paths in becoming critical educators, (ii) our own practices in critical language classrooms, and (iii) our perceptions of the role we have as critical educators in Brazil, hoping to contribute to informing possible paths of Brazilian teachers within their critical consciousness development.

According to Ellis *et al.* (2011: 3), 'when researchers do autoethnography, they retrospectively and selectively write about epiphanies that stem from, or are made possible by, being part of a culture and/or by possessing a particular cultural identity'. Thus, we started our study by meeting online to discuss our own critical consciousness development. At that moment (April of 2020), we were at the beginning of the pandemic in Brazil and our professional positions were somewhat recent. Hence, our interest in understanding our own critical consciousness process derived from the challenges and difficulties faced by us (and by other teachers) in such critical times while also trying to understand our identities, roles, and responsibilities within this scenario.

As a suggestion brought by Priscila (the first author), we first read Häusler *et al.* (2018). Then, motivated by the collaborative reflections proposed in their article, we decided to write our own stories guided by the following questions, which represent the most pressing issues we wanted to approach: (1) Which experiences in our lives have contributed to our development as critical educators? (2) What do we do in our practice to promote learners' critical [language] development? (3) What is our role as critical educators in the Brazilian context, especially in face of so many challenges? We wrote our narratives individually and in Portuguese, as it felt more natural to use our mother tongue to describe our personal experiences.

Even though personal narratives are not very common in conventional academic research, 'perhaps reflective of the suspect status of this kind of knowledge' (Windle, 2017: 372), we side with Windle (2017: 373) when he states that 'it opens up some rich possibilities for reflection and allows for an important part of scholarly practice to become visible'. Ellis *et al.* (2011) elucidate that, in autoethnography, narratives are not important simply because they are meaningful personal accounts of one's experiences engaging with cultural aspects of collective experiences, but this writing style is also a way to produce accessible texts, 'a move that can make personal and social change possible for more people' (2011: 4).

The next step was to share the narratives with each other. As Blalock and Akehi (2018: 94) emphasize, 'the subjective and personal nature of autoethnography combined with a collaborative element also illuminates how partners or groups work together'. In this sense, we asked one another questions about aspects that were not clear and reflected on our own individual voices based on the collective voices that emerged from our discussions. It is relevant to highlight at this point that, by asking and answering questions about the narratives written individually, we had the opportunity to revisit our own experiences and reflect on how our stories were being told, which resulted in new, clearer and more detailed versions of these stories, thus giving us the opportunity to engage in the process of collaborative narrative construction. After that, we read each other's narratives again, this time attempting to name aspects that seemed salient in each story. The purpose of this thematic analysis (Yukhymenko *et al.*, 2014: 96) was to identify important elements of our critical consciousness development. In order to avoid generalizing individual experiences and erasing authorial voices, we engaged in this thematic analysis individually at first. Subsequently, another meeting took place in which the narratives and the topics identified by each author were compared and contrasted dialogically. As we can see, thus, collaboration and critical dialogue guided not only data generation – since we shared and discussed our personal narratives - but also data analysis. In the following section, we focus on translated extracts of our personal accounts, grouped together according to the themes we identified as paramount to this discussion. Due to space constraints, only the most relevant or illustrative extracts for each theme are presented.

Discussing Narratives of Critical Consciousness Development

When looking at our personal narratives, similarities could be found. Although we are aware that each one of us has a different story, which carries intersectional marks we do not intend to erase or ignore, we were also moved by hooks (2010: 49) when she says that 'telling stories is one of the ways that we can begin the process of building community'. Therefore, we explore five different aspects that seemed to collectively resonate from our individual accounts. In order to preserve and validate our authorial voices, we begin each subsection by presenting excerpts from the narratives and then move on to discuss them in light of the literature.

The feeling of not belonging

'In a certain way, I felt displaced where I was born. I liked to read, study, I loved cinema and literature. I wanted to have friends who shared similar interests. On the one hand, my context presented me with a "single story" of who I could be; on the other hand, books and movies presented me with other worlds and possibilities.' – Leonardo.

'At school, the race/gender intersectionality didn't give me a break: I was the funny one in the class. This is what was left for a black and overweight girl most of the time, especially in a crucial moment for our identity formation and self-esteem that is adolescence. Unconsciously, this was the way I found to be accepted. I wished I could fit in, I knew somehow the physical traits that were considered as beautiful were the white ones. My idols were all white. My standard of beauty was white. I desired to slim my nose. I used to straighten my hair and lied that it was natural for several years (due to my indigenous heritage, I used to say that I took after my grandmother).' – Litiane

'I grew up in a small town where the perception of the world seemed quite homogeneous. People thought alike, acted alike, there were similar social expectations that I repeatedly didn't fit into. I felt an internal conflict: I was proud of my roots, my city, my history. And I felt that every time I identified problems in the actions or perceptions naturalized there, I was somehow betraying these roots, being ungrateful. The impulse of questioning was often silenced by myself in an attempt to belong.' – Priscila

The three narratives started with memories from our childhoods. In doing so, we described the beginning of our critical consciousness development process with a feeling of non-adjustment. Leonardo – who defines himself as a White gay man – expressed that he felt displaced in the small city he was born in because there seemed to be one single story (Adichie, 2009) of who he could be. This feeling, for Leonardo, seemed to motivate him to find contexts to belong to other than the one he was in. Litiane – who is a Black woman born in Southern Brazil – described the relation of the intersectionality (Crenshaw, 2018) of gender and race in her identity formation, highlighting that even though these were painful marks for her while growing up, she made attempts to be accepted among her peers. Priscila described her experience growing up in the countryside, where worldviews/behaviors seemed mostly homogeneous, pointing out that she often felt disadjusted but found it hard to question the established norms because, like Litiane, she wanted to belong. Still, in spite of the fact that Priscila did not feel contemplated by gender norms – which dictated how girls should behave, for instance – she looked for approval and acceptance.

In this sense, the narratives highlight how social location and identity categories seemed to shape personal experience, creating a feeling of dissatisfaction/discontent. It is possible to observe instances of awareness and reflection triggered by personal experiences, which could indicate levels of naive transitive consciousness among the three of us. As Leal (2021: 2) signals, naive transitive consciousness is one of the Freirean stages of the critical consciousness process, in which 'individuals are able to perceive unjust social power structures, investigate their causes, and begin to be able to visualize alternatives'. Still, one thing that must be highlighted is the different emphasis given to these experiences when comparing Leonardo's story to Litiane's and Priscila's. Whereas Leonardo emphasized events that describe how he tried not to accept his feeling of non-adjustment, Litiane and Priscila focused on their search for acceptance. We wonder if this may be an implication of gender dynamics, since women are, since early childhood, commonly taught to silence their thoughts and to tame their impetus in order to adapt to gender and social norms through performativity (Butler, 1999).

The role of education

'When I finished high school, I entered a public university. Maybe I was expecting to learn a profession, but I learned much more than that. I could better understand the world around me and, consequently, better understand myself. I already had a sense of justice (I knew I could/should dance if I wanted to, I stood up for my mother when I believed she was not being treated fairly because of her gender), but I couldn't quite articulate it. Academic knowledge, together with the diverse academic environment allowed me to reflect upon issues that were part of my identity.' – Leonardo

'Even though I could feel it, I could not name it. It was at the university that the process of critical thinking began; both professionally and personally.' – Litiane

'As a university student, I had access to texts, reflections, and knowledge that contributed greatly to my process of becoming a critical educator. But the human relationships that I experienced in that space showed me the complexity and cruelty that shape our society, helping me to make sense of what bothered me as a child. Because I got to know people very different from me, their stories and their experiences, I went through a transformation of my own.' – Priscila

As it can be seen, the three narratives call attention to the university as a space that allows for awareness and transformation. We make reference to knowledge as a tool for action, describing entering the university [and, more specifically, the English language program] as a hallmark in our paths since we could reflect on ourselves, name and understand feelings, and even engage in transformation.

It is also clear from our narratives that this knowledge we got in contact with/developed because of the university was not purely theoretical: although the theory was important because it helped us name the world (Freire & Macedo, 1987), equally (or more) important was the knowledge we shared and built with peers, professors and students as we began to better understand our previous experiences and the world around us.

Crookes (2021) highlights the power of dialogue in education as a tool for students to name the world in such a way that others may review their own perspectives of reality, initiating possible changes. In this sense, it is important to clarify: critical dialogue is not about indoctrination; on the contrary, it is about being open to listen, understand and become aware of the perspectives and positions of others instead of finding a consensus or agreement. As Shin and Crookes (2005: 114–115) stress, 'through the awareness of the link between their life issues and the macro sociopolitical, cultural context, they [students] learn to make decisions in and outside the classroom and can eventually take actions outside the classrooms'. Hence, for the three of us, being in the university and exercising critical dialogue was perceived as a chance to move forward into our individual/collective critical consciousness process. It is important to highlight that the three of us were students in the English language program – in this sense, it can be argued that the different classes we took, combined with an academic environment that valued diversity, seem to have favored the promotion of critical dialogue.

The role of teaching

'Maybe my biggest challenge was to start teaching at the Federal Institute, where I worked for seven years. I had to leave my academic bubble and move to a campus in which promoting discussions on gender was seen as innovative since there were no projects approaching such topics. Because of this challenge, I decided to conduct my PhD research in the same context where I worked.' – Leonardo

'During college, I started my career as a teacher. At first, I would notice some problems, such as stereotypes present in textbooks. I would also notice that many students reproduced beliefs. I would not problematize these issues, nor would I take these moments as an opportunity for discussion, because I felt that I was not yet prepared to deal with such responsibility. With time, experience and reading, I noticed that my attitude changed, specifically at the end of the undergraduate program when I had contact with my area of study: critical discourse analysis.' – Litiane.

'My experiences as a school teacher gave me the chance to grow as an educator. First, because I did much more than teach, I learned. Like when I had the opportunity to supervise student-teachers, teaching and learning in a collective and democratic way. Later, as an English teacher in two state schools, I was also deeply changed. In one of these schools, together with other teachers and students themselves, I co-coordinated an interdisciplinary project where students produced a documentary about their own neighborhood – perceived as a dangerous and marginalized community – rescuing their own history and the voice of people who were part of that place.' – Priscila

As it can be seen, language teaching was an opportunity to make sense of what we were learning in university while also learning by doing (Dewey, 1938). More than that, for the three of us, teaching was an opportunity for action.

Gounari (2020: 12) highlights that the process of critical reflection 'becomes part of our human existence, when as members of different social groups we are called to understand our sociocultural location at different moments and make important decisions'. Hence, our path in the university contexts – first as student-teachers and later as teacher-researchers – allowed us to build over our critical consciousness, experimenting with moments of awareness, reflection, and action as the political system also became pedagogical (Giroux, 2004).

Hence, we argue that teacher education programs should offer opportunities for teachers' critical consciousness development. As Greggio and Gil (2010) call attention to, critical reflection is often overlooked by teacher education programs while technical and practical reflection is favored. While the critical level of reflection does not negate the technical and practical ones, 'it moves a step further in the reflection process since it incorporates the understanding of society, its structuring forces, and their connection to the educational process' (2010: 59).

Principles of a critical educator

'(...) critical education is much more than presenting critical contents or promoting moments of reflection in the classroom. The pedagogical process needs to be critical as well. My role is not to bring ready-made truths and present them to the students. Instead, my role is to create opportunities for students to be able to reflect by themselves. But to do so they need to have access to trustworthy information, they need to be instigated and motivated to think and reflect, they need to learn to consider different arguments, to propose counter-arguments, and to develop critical dialogue.' – Leonardo

'I believe that what makes our pedagogical practice critical is providing opportunities for students to not only learn a language and its linguistic structures, but also to raise their consciousness on how language reflects social norms that can propagate exclusion and inequalities. It is understanding that there is no position or a way of thinking that is not free of ideologies and, therefore, communicating through an additional language is not an exception to that: learning a language can also be a transformative and emancipatory act.' – Litiane

'My experiences as a school teacher prepared me to work at the university, as a teacher educator, mainly because they allowed me to perceive the relevance of horizontal and democratic student-teacher relationship as well as the importance of co-constructing knowledge in education so that students are perceived as agents of the teaching and learning process.' – Priscila

As we approached the end of our narratives, the three of us discussed some principles that we believe to guide our practice as teacher-researchers. For us, 'a critical teacher is someone who: (1) considers the context and their learners for their pedagogical actions/choices; (2) creates opportunities for awareness, reflection and transformation through their practice; and (3) is focused on the learning process, not the product.'

As it is a set of principles and not a methodology, there is no recipe for critical teaching (Silva *et al.*, 2017; Crookes, 2021). In this sense, by identifying some principles in our practice, we continue our critical consciousness development, learning from/with each other. Moreover, by advancing our own processes, through research and pedagogical practice, we begin to find possibilities for collective critical consciousness development in Brazilian education.

Critical education as a path for social transformation

'*As an educator and researcher in the area of critical perspectives for additional language teaching, my role is to not only promote students' critical development, but also to contribute to my peers' development (including teachers in other areas). I guess this is the only path to transform education in Brazil.*' – Leonardo

'*We urgently need to educate citizens who understand the importance of their roles for a democratic and fair society and this starts with collective conscience and empathy. For that, I believe that the critical development of individuals is the way out for the social transformation we so desperately need.*' – Litiane.

'*There is no teaching without people. Human relationships are at the core of teaching and learning. It is our duty to teach critically so that students can understand their immediate reality and have the means to act upon it with the aim of transforming it.*' – Priscila

There seems to be a consensus among us that critical [language] education is the path towards the transformation of our society. In this sense, we cannot help but wonder: is this an echo of a common concern for Brazilian teachers/researchers? We certainly hope so.

Freire (1997) talks about *esperança*, which can be translated as hoping and believing in a better future. The author uses the noun as a verb, *esperançar*, explaining that it does not entail naive hope, since it means 'recognizing the given conditions as socially constructed, but seeking possibilities so that these same conditions can be modified. So here, being hopeful is also a form of resistance' (Clasen & Farias, 2021: 252, our translation). In this sense, because we hope, we resist. Because we act to promote critical language education, we continue our path towards individual and collective critical consciousness development.

(In)concluding Remarks: Challenges for Brazilian Critical Educators

Built individually and rebuilt collectively through this writing process, our stories are, like Hausler *et al*'s (2018: 14), 'always shaping and never finished'. Drawing on Leal (2018), the narratives seem to be made of non-static moments of awareness, reflection, and action that were guided by attempts of agency, enactment, and social transformation and shaped by discourse, critical dialogue, and emotions. Hence, we were able to identify common aspects in the narratives – such as the feeling of non-belonging, the role of higher education, the importance of teaching experiences, and a commitment to critical education and social justice – which are elements that seem(ed) to contribute to our identity formation and to our practice as critical educators.

Our main goal was to open space for discussing possible venues for critical teaching in current Brazil, especially considering that critical education results from a complex relationship between power relations and individual/collective identities, all constitutive and constituted by language. In this sense, because our narratives (and our future as a nation) are not fixed/finalized, we decided to end our piece by continuing to tell our stories, focusing on some of the challenges we highlighted when trying to promote critical education. We do so because we agree with Häusler et al. (2018: 1) when they say that 'political work cannot be done by individuals acting independently', since we learn and transform collectively. By explicitly acknowledging/denouncing some of the challenges Brazilian educators have been facing, we raise our individual/collective voices, hoping to contribute to collective awareness that may lead to collective critical consciousness and transformation.

'Critical educators often feel threatened for being fragilized. During my PhD research, a councilman tried to pass a law that prohibited discussions on gender at schools located in the city where I worked. And that was the topic of my study. So this created and intensified students' rejection of the topic. Later, when we organized a movie session with films that dealt with themes such as gender and sexuality, my teacher peers and I were harassed online and reported to the council that oversees the rights of children in the city on the basis of false allegations.' – Leonardo

'I affirm that teaching with a critical perspective is very difficult, especially in our recent socio-political scenario. Being a teacher with this approach in Brazil has become an act of courage but necessary. This is because the ultraconservative supremacy is strongly present in our society and it is so violent that questioning social injustice might cost our personal relations, our dignity, our income, and even our lives.' – Litiane

'My biggest challenge is to balance fear and insecurity, while working towards emancipatory education in Brazil. I seek to promote daily opportunities for critical education in my practice. This is what moves me and what gives me hope. Even though, as Brazilian teachers, our minds and actions are haunted by fear, we challenge oppression and injustice. We are not fearless, but we go on.' – Priscila

Critical Discussion Questions

(1) The narratives in this paper highlighted the impact of several aspects of the teacher-researchers' paths to their critical consciousness development. When you consider your own trajectory as a learner/educator/researcher, can you identify similar aspects central to your development? Which experiences would you highlight in your own narrative of critical development?
(2) Considering that the chapter you read highlighted important elements in the authors' critical consciousness development, what do you believe we, as educators, should do in order to create spaces for students to develop both linguistic and critical skills?
(3) What is the relevance of including narrative inquiry or narrative-based reflection in teacher-education programs? How can we make teacher education more critical (moving beyond the technical and practical levels of reflection to include a perspective that is indeed committed to social transformation)?
(4) How can we make narrative-inquiry research (or even classroom research) more visible? Also, how can we stand up against positivist and western perspectives of research that erase personal and localized perspectives in education?
(5) Paulo Freire was exiled during the Brazilian dictatorship due to his critical pedagogy postulations. In critical times in which teachers are falsely accused of indoctrination or even persecuted by movements that try to erase the political nature of education, how can we exercise our agency to continue doing our work with a focus on social justice?

References

Adichie, C.N. (2009) *The Danger of a Single Story*. Retrieved December 28, 2021, from https://www.ted.com/talks/chimamanda_ngozi_adichie_the_danger_of_a_single_story

Blalock, A.E. and Akehi, M. (2018) Collaborative autoethnography as a pathway for transformative learning. *Journal of Transformative Education* 16 (2), 89–107.

Butler, J. (1999) *Gender Trouble: Feminism and the Subversion of Identity*. New York: Routledge.

Clasen, S. and Farias, P.F. (2021) Entre A Esperança E As Condições Materiais: Relato De Experiência Sobre O Estágio Supervisionado Em Inglês Em Tempos De Ensino Remoto E Pandemia. *Revista Sobre Tudo* 12 (2), 245–270.

Crenshaw, K. (2018) Demarginalizing the intersection of race and sex: A black feminist critique of antidiscrimination doctrine, feminist theory, and antiracist politics [1989]. *Feminist Legal Theory* 57–80. https://doi.org/10.4324/9780429500480-5

Crookes, G. (2021) Critical language pedagogy: An introduction to principles and values. *ELT Journal* 75 (3), 247–255.

Dewey, J. (1938) *Experience and Education*. New York: Kappa Delta Pi Publications.

Duboc, A.P. and Ferraz, D. de. (2021) Language, literacy, and education in times of crises: 'Introductory' notes. *Revista Brasileira De Linguística Aplicada* 21 (2), 295–309.

Ellis, C., Adams, T. and Bochner, A.P. (2011) Autoethnography: An overview. *Forum: Qualitative Sozialforschung Social Research* 12 (1).

Farias, P.F. and Silva, L. (2020) I'm gonna leave you with the backlash blues: Uma análise acerca da concepção do ensino de língua inglesa na base nacional comum curricular sob o viés da pedagogia crítica. *Revista e-Curriculum* 18, 137–157.

Farias, P.F. and Silva, L. (2021) Doing critical language teaching through tasks: Insights from the Brazilian context. *Education Sciences* 11, 223. https://doi.org/10.3390/educsci11050223

Freire, P. (1970) *Pedagogy of the Oppressed*. New York: Continuum.

Freire, P. and Macedo, D. (1987) *Reading the Word and the World*. Boston: Bergin & Garvey Publishers.

Freire, P. (1997) *Pedagogia da esperança: um reencontro com a pedagogia do oprimido*. São Paulo: Paz e Terra.

Frigotto, G. (2017) *Escola 'Sem' Partido*. Rio de Janeiro: Laboratório de Políticas Públicas UERJ.

Giroux, H.A. (2004) Cultural Studies, public pedagogy, and the responsibility of intellectuals. *Communication and Critical/Cultural Studies* 1, 59–79.

Gounari, P. (2020) Critical pedagogies and teaching and learning languages in dangerous times: Introduction to the Special Issue. *L2 Journal* 12 (2), 3–20.

Greggio, S. and Gil, G. (2010) O conceito de professor reflexivo na formação de professores. In S.M. Barros and M.A. Assis-Peterson (Orgs.) *Formação crítica de professores de línguas: Desejos e possibilidades* (pp. 55–68). São Carlos, SP: Pedro e João Editores.

Hall, S. (1990) Cultural identity and diaspora. In K. Woodward (ed.) *Identity and Difference* (pp. 222–237). London: SAGE Publications.

Hausler, A.H., Leal, P., Parba, J., West, G.B. and Crookes, G.V. (2018) 'How did you become political?': Narratives of junior researcher-practitioners in applied linguistics. *Critical Inquiry in Language Studies* 15 (4), 282–301.

hooks, b. (2010) *Teaching Critical Thinking: Practical Wisdom*. New York: Routledge.

Kumaravadivelu, B. (2016) The decolonial option in English teaching: Can the subaltern act? *TESOL Quarterly* 50 (1), 66–85.

Leal, P. (2021) The development of teacher attitudes to discrimination in language education scale: A measurement tool of critical consciousness for language teachers. *Education Sciences* 11, 200.

Leal, P. (2018) Becoming and Being a Critical English Language Teacher: A Mixed-Methods Study of Critical Consciousness. PhD thesis, University of Hawai'i, Manoa, HI, USA.

Macedo, L.B. (2021) Enegrecendo os Estudos Críticos Discursivos: Contribuições Epistemológicas Afroperspectivistas para o campo da análise crítica do Discurso no Brasil. *Trabalhos Em Linguística Aplicada* 1–14. https://doi.org/10.1590/0103181395 61411520210310

McKie, A. (2021, November 11) Brazilian Science in Danger: President cuts federal science budget by 90 percent. Researchers fear a brain drain. *Inside Higher Ed*. Retrieved December 25, 2021, from https://www.insidehighered.com/news/2021/11/11/brazil-cuts-federal-science-spending-90-percent

Pennycook, A. (2001) *Critical Applied Linguistics: A Critical Introduction*. Mahwah, NJ: Lawrence Erlbaum.

Pessoa, R.R., Freitas, M.T.U. (2021) 'Resistindo Na Boca Da Noite Um Gosto De Sol': Pedagogia Da Pergunta Como Resistência Democrática Na Educação Linguística. *Trabalhos em Linguística Aplicada* 60 (1), 217–232.

Paula, R.F.S. (2019, June 5) Brazilian universities fear Bolsonaro's plan to eliminate humanities and slash public education budgets. *The Conversation*. Retrieved December 25, 2021, from https://theconversation.com/brazilian-universities-fear-bolsonaro-plan-to-eliminate-humanities-and-slash-public-education-budgets-117530

Queiroz, L. (2020) *Decolonialidade e concepções da língua: uma crítica linguística e educacional*. Campinas: Ponte Editores.
Shin, H. and Crookes, G. (2005) Exploring the possibilities for EFL critical pedagogy in Korea - A two-part case study. *Critical Inquiry in Language Studies: An International Journal* 2 (2), 113–138.
Silva, L., Farias, P., D'Ely, R.C.S.F. (2017) Doing critical English language teaching: Designing critical tasks to promote critical media literacy. *Revista A Cor das Letras* 18, Especial, 99–121.
Silva, L., Silva, M., Rocha, N.V. (2017) 'Let's not forget we are language teachers!': Investigating critical teaching and critical reflection in the practicum of an English undergraduate program. *Fórum linguístico* 14 (1), 1866–1879.
Souza, L.M.T.M. and Monte Mór, W. (2018) Afterword still critique? *Revista Brasileira de Linguística Aplicada* 18, 445–450.
Tagata, W.M. (2018) Post-critique in contemporary ELT praxis. *Revista Brasileira de Linguística Aplicada* 18 (2), 255–280.
Windle, J.A. (2017) Social identity and language ideology: Challenging hegemonic visions of English in Brazil. *Gragoatá* 22 (42), 370– 392.
Yukhymenko, M.A., Brown, S.W., Lawless, K.A., Brodowinska, K. and Mullin, G. (2014) Thematic analysis of teacher instructional practices and student responses in middle school classrooms with problem-based learning environments. *Global Education Review* 1 (3), 93–109.

3 Unpacking Raciolinguistic Ideologies and Power Dynamics in Teacher Education through Intersectionality

Sumeyra Gok and Angelina Gillispie

Teacher identities are formed by our experiences. They are constructed, maintained, and negotiated in relation to the cultural, social and political contexts around us (Varghese *et al.*, 2005). This construction and negotiation of identity is dynamic. In spaces that are dominated by ideologies that give power to certain racial, ethnic, cultural and linguistic groups, renegotiation of identities from non-dominant backgrounds may occur in the form of silence, assimilation, or loss of connection to cultural backgrounds. Therefore, we argue that the dominant racial, ethnic and linguistic identities in teachers' social and professional spaces perpetuate a power dynamic which ultimately determines who has privilege and who is disserviced. This power dynamic is also present in teacher education. Consequently, the voices and perspectives of educators from underrepresented backgrounds are often left out of the conversations. Exclusion of these voices secures the norm of Whiteness and undermines the principles of multicultural education (Montecinos, 2004).

One of the biggest reasons for the underrepresentation of the voices and perspectives of teachers of color is the Whiteness lens that is prevalent in most teacher educator programs. In the phenomenon called Whiteness as property through which 'preservice teachers that possess the experiences, perspectives, knowledge and dispositions aligned with and valued by the dominant White society find reinforcement and success' (Brown, 2014: 337). As a result, the voices of teachers of color become othered. This is the same lens that frames teachers of color as role models for students of color, but not necessarily for all students. However, as Ladson-Billings (2005) argues, a lack of diversity within a predominantly White teacher educator workforce limits the possibilities of 'richer and more complex perspectives' that can inform teacher preparation and student learning (Pham, 2018).

It is crucial to include the voices and perspectives of preservice teachers from underrepresented backgrounds and create a curriculum outside of the Whiteness lens in order to reimagine teacher education programs to be culturally and linguistically just spaces. This restructuring should increase opportunities for meaningful participation, recognize and value the experiences and backgrounds of educators from non-dominant racial, cultural, and linguistic backgrounds, and be culturally responsive to the communities they serve (Pham, 2018). With this study, we aim to highlight these voices through our experiences, navigating the different professional and social spaces within the predominantly White institutions where we work and study. This study aims to answer the following questions:

(a) How do predominantly White spaces in education affect the way educators from minoritized backgrounds negotiate and present their teacher identities?
(b) How do our identities as language teachers from minoritized backgrounds influence our pedagogies and interactions with our students?
(c) What can teacher education programs do to encourage and make space for these critical dialogues around identity and power to disrupt deficient ideologies?

Framing Our Critical Dialogue Through a Raciolinguistic Lens

Raciolinguistics constitutes our theoretical framework for this study. Raciolinguistic ideologies explain that racialized bodies are often associated with linguistic deficiency and they privilege dominant White perspectives on the linguistic practices of racialized communities (Flores & Rosa, 2015). This happens because race and language are closely linked as ethnic and racial identities are styled, performed and constructed through language (Alim *et al.*, 2016). Therefore, language often serves as a proxy for racial and linguistic identities. As a result, practices of language users from non-dominant backgrounds can be racialized. Racialization occurs through the creation, occupation, and transformation of racial categories within specific political, social, and economic contexts based on one's cultural identities (Selod, 2015).

We used a raciolinguistics lens to analyze our narratives because raciolinguistics helps us examine our racialized experiences in relation to our minoritized identities as language teachers. In this study, we used the term 'minoritized' to refer to our racial, ethnic, and linguistic identities. For Angelina, this refers to her African American and White biracial identity and her linguistic identity as a speaker of African American Vernacular

English (AAVE). On the other hand, for Sumeyra, minoritized identity refers to her ethnicity as a Turkish and Middle Eastern immigrant and her linguistic identity as a multilingual speaker. Although Sumeyra's White racial identity is in the dominant racial group and grants her certain privileges, she mainly drew from her racialized ethnic and linguistic identities in order to make sense of how she negotiated her language teacher identity. Thus, raciolinguistics provided us with a lens to understand why we both considered our linguistic practices to be deficient and attempted to present ourselves differently in order to attain the competent language teacher persona that we internalized.

Creating a Dialogic Space

Our way of creating a dialogic space to have the conversation around identity and pedagogy was through counter-narratives. Counter-narratives are used for telling the stories of people whose experiences are often overlooked or silenced. They serve 'as a tool for analyzing and challenging the dominant stories of racial privilege' (Solorzano & Yosso, 2002: 32). They are also a means to document and share how race, ethnicity, and language influence the educational and professional experiences of people from non-dominant backgrounds, whose stories counter the stories of the privileged that are considered normal and neutral (Milner et al., 2020). Therefore, our critical dialogue was conducted as counter-narratives of our raciolinguistic and ethnolinguistic experiences in White monolingual spaces.

Critical incidents were our starting point of discussion. We started with the question 'can you think about a moment while teaching that highlighted some aspect of your identity in relation to power?' These were one of the moments that either became a turning point for us in terms of defining our identities or strongly influenced our pedagogies moving forward. After we both chose and wrote our critical incidents, we shared them with each other and created discussion points for our dialogue highlighting the similarities and differences between our narratives. We conducted this conversation in a recorded virtual meeting as we wanted the discussion to flow naturally. Upon identifying our themes, we made additional comments on a shared document to clarify and elaborate on the excerpts we have chosen. As a result, our counter-narratives were created in a storytelling format, and they tell our stories of becoming.

Who Are We?

Sumeyra is a Turkish woman, who first immigrated to the US with her family at 14. She was placed in English language services when she arrived. She later returned to Turkey and completed a bachelor's program in English. Her first introduction to teaching was through language schools in Turkey, where she taught English as a foreign language. She later returned to the US for a master's program in Education. Upon graduation, she started to work as a high school ESL teacher at an urban school. After a year, she started her doctoral program in Education, during which she visited high schools, taught adult English learners, and worked with pre-service teachers. She now works at a public university in the Midwest. She identifies as a translingual and transnational woman.

Angelina is a biracial woman of African American, White and Lebanese ancestry, who grew up in a predominantly White town in New England. Having been raised by her White mother, conversations regarding her race were not very common growing up. Being a first generation college student, she completed her teaching education program with an accelerated master's in Education and a dual certification in ESL and ELA (English Language Arts). During her college program, she began to reflect and take part in conversations regarding race and to connect with the African American students she served. She is now working in an urban school in Massachusetts and preparing to transition to work as a middle school ESL teacher in Virginia where she will be working with newcomers.

Our connection was through a course at a public university in New England. Sumeyra was the instructor of the course as part of her graduate assistantship during her doctoral program and Angelina was a pre-service teacher taking it. Our non-dominant racial, ethnic, and linguistic backgrounds at a predominantly White institution and our mutual interest in working with multilingual learners drew us together. Angelina was one of the few pre-service teachers interested in an ESL certification and during our time together; she worked on projects that were similar to Sumeyra's dissertation topic. After Angelina finished her program and became a teacher, we started to work together as an interviewer and participant for Sumeyra's study. It then evolved into a collaboration, which set the premise for this critical dialogue.

Critical Incidents

Sumeyra's critical incident:

In 2016, I was hired as an ESL teacher at an urban high school in Massachusetts. I was one of the five ESL teachers in the building. The overwhelming majority of the students in this school were non-White and multilingual. However, most of the teachers were White, US American, and monolingual English speakers. On my first day of teaching, I introduced myself as Ms G. Although my last name was already very short, I wanted to appear less foreign. I was paying close attention to my accent and was not sharing my background yet. Most of my students had been in ESL services for many years and some even considered English to be their dominant language. As I was going over the attendance, one of my students asked '*Miss, don't get offended but why are YOU teaching this class?*' I immediately got offended. I responded '*because I like teaching*' but I got frustrated with myself for not being able to handle the question better by asking him to elaborate on what he meant by that. I could have explained to them that I also used to be an English learner in high school and that I could relate to their language learning experiences. Instead, I shut him down with a simple remark and moved on because what if he was right and I was not competent or qualified enough for that position? That question set the tone for how I chose to present myself to my students.

Angelina's critical incident:

Being a biracial young woman growing up and living in predominantly White spaces, I have learned how to dilute my Blackness and conform to the socially accepted norms found in the dominant White community. This meant speaking AAVE, or African American Vernacular English, was off the table in the majority of spaces. In 2021 during my time as a student teacher in an urban school district, I divided my time between two different high schools. I taught ESL and English Language Arts classes. Although the student population in both schools were diverse, the staff at both schools was predominantly White. In fact, at one of the schools, I was the only staff member of color. The students I served knew me as Ms G. One February morning, I was working with one of my students of Afro-Latino descent, and we began to talk about his life experiences connected to his writing assignment. One thing led to another, and we ended up both conversing in AAVE. This student turned to me at the end of our conversation and said, '*I feel like I can just kick it back and talk to you about whatever, Ms G. There ain't a lot of other teachers that understand us or connect with us like you do.*' This pivotal moment changed the way I approached teaching and how I connected with my students for the remainder of that school year and the school years to come. I was so worried about not being seen as a professional that I did not realize that I had this ability to tap into and connect with my students in a way other teachers were unable to.

Becoming Critical Educators: Analysis of Our Experiences

Coming from different racial, ethnic, and linguistic backgrounds, we shared experiences that were similar during our first year of teaching/student teaching. There were common threads in our critical incidents such as trying to blend in and creating a competent teacher persona in our minds. The discussions that came out of our critical incidents showed us that we both went through the process of hiding parts of our identities, then learning to embrace those parts, and lastly, using them as assets in our teaching. However, these processes looked different and happened at different times for us. Another similarity from our critical incidents was the demographics of the schools where we taught: student populations were racially, ethnically and linguistically diverse; however, the overwhelming majority of the teachers were White and monolingual. In our critical dialogue, we talked about how these demographics affected the way we presented our identities at the time, then we went deeper into the reasons behind our attempts to blend in and uncovered that we had preconceived notions of what a competent and a professional teacher looked like. Sumeyra shared:

> I had not initially shared my background with my students. I didn't know how much I should share and what would be professional. I did not tell them that I also used to be an English learner when I was at their age. I tried to present a professional identity and in my mind, that meant being a native English speaker, someone who has been educated in the US, and an American citizen. Though I was partially educated in the US and only had a slight accent when speaking English, I felt the urge to hide my linguistic background and my immigration story from my students and colleagues.

For Sumeyra, the pressure of not fitting in came from her international status. She was questioning her own competency as a language teacher because she was worried that her students wouldn't want to be taught by someone who was not an American citizen or a native English speaker. This comes from the native speaker fallacy, which is the notion that the ideal teacher of English is a native speaker of that language as defined by Phillipson (1992) and it stems from Noam Chomsky's linguistic concept that established the native speaker as the authority on the language and the ideal informant (Canagarajah, 1999). This notion gives an advantage to the native speaker as the expert of the target language. By doing so, it also creates a hierarchy among languages and dialects while positioning non-native speakers as outsiders. This was the ideology Sumeyra had internalized at the time. Therefore, during her first week of teaching, when a student questioned why she was teaching that class, Sumeyra did not feel comfortable sharing her linguistic and educational journey, even though it could help other students connect with her more.

This hierarchy of languages can also exist within the same language. As a biracial American woman, Angelina spoke AAVE in some of her social circles. But she was hesitant to use AAVE in school as she was worried that it would not be regarded as professional. Angelina shared:

> It wasn't up until college that I even knew there was a name for African American Vernacular English. I remember feeling so cheated, and frankly, upset that I wasn't aware about this integral part of my identity. The way I would see myself professionally or how I wanted others to see me was somebody who speaks proper English, not somebody who is speaking in slang, because people tend to look down upon people who speak AAVE. So, I was really kind of diluting it and just pushing it to the side so I could conform.

Angelina's attempts to blend in were also fueled by years of trying to highlight her White identity over her African American roots in the predominantly White schools that she attended. Although she always considered herself to be a biracial woman, she was not aware that her AAVE linguistic resources could be an asset. In raciolinguistics, this is explained by the lingering effects of colonization, which positioned non-European populations as inferior and perceived these groups as linguistically deficient (Rosa & Flores, 2017). Furthermore, linguistic identities are perceived to be closely linked to racial identities and Whiteness becomes an intrinsic element of 'standard' or 'mainstream' English (Motha, 2006). Thus, Angelina, as a biracial woman, has grown up not recognizing AAVE as a legitimate dialect because it was often looked down upon both by the dominant community and the African American community, who internalized this positioning.

As a result of our positionings as the linguistic other, we tried to blend in during our first years of teaching. However, blending in looked different for both of us as our tensions around identity differed. For Angelina, blending in meant being cautious about who heard her talking in AAVE. This is a result of AAVE often being reduced to slang, which affects people's perceptions of racial identity. AAVE is positioned as inferior because standard English often defines the 'social norms, prejudices, attitudes, and expectations as decided by social groups in power' (Haddix, 2015: 4). Angelina explains:

> As I was conversing with one of my students in AAVE, I was quieter and more unsure of myself. It was almost like I didn't want others to hear the conversation. I thought they would think differently of me or think that I wasn't competent enough to teach them. I didn't want them to think 'you're teaching us about grammar and then here you are speaking this AAVE slang.' And, honestly, I don't know if I would have had the ability to really fully explain myself back then and get into that conversation of AAVE being a whole dialect with grammar systems.

These prejudices towards AAVE cause educators of color to question their professional identities. Haddix (2015) explains that being the only teacher of color and constantly feeling the need to monitor her language made her feel like she did not have a right to teach English when she was non-native to mainstream American English. Similar feelings were shared by us. That is because Whiteness and standardized English are closely linked. Together they define what are legitimate forms of speech and the bodies that can legitimately speak and be heard (Daniels & Varghese, 2020). The strong influence of Whiteness and standard English on one's identity and positioning as the insider versus outsider may cause people from non-White and/or non-standard English speaking backgrounds to try to hide or change parts of their identities. This was the case for both of us. Sumeyra attempted this by trying to sound less foreign and Angelina felt more comfortable presenting her White identity over her African American one.

One of the ways we attempted to fit into the Whiteness and standard English frames was through our names. We both referred to ourselves as Ms G in school, but for different reasons. Angelina was grappling with the fact that her foreign looking last name coupled with her racially and ethnically ambiguous appearance caused others to question her identity as an American. Therefore, she wanted to clarify the confusion by making it easier for her students. On the other hand, Sumeyra's reasoning for choosing Ms G was connected to her attempts to hide her foreignness. Sumeyra shared:

> I called myself Ms G even though my last name is only three letters long. That was a decision I made before going into teaching. It was a small yet significant attempt to seem less foreign. For the same reason, I introduced myself as Sue during my master's program because I thought it was on me to make it easier for others. I think names are a good indication of how we feel about our identities. Now I definitely teach people how to pronounce it, even if it takes time.

Talking about our experiences of changing our names and being mindful about who is listening made us realize that we were putting on a façade. When having this conversation, we both agreed that having that façade was exhausting and keeping it up required a lot of effort. Over time, we learned how to be vulnerable with our students and share about our own backgrounds. This vulnerability helped us form stronger connections with our students, and in turn, helped us embrace our identities. Angelina shared:

> Students were very welcoming, and our connections became more meaningful. Students began to open up more to me about their personal lives and I felt like I could really embrace myself authentically. So, in a way the students actually gave me the permission to open up to them more. My cooperating teacher at the time, who was White, told me once *'these kids tell you things they never have and never would never share with me in my over twenty years of teaching. I've never seen this type of connection before. They see you and they see themselves.'* It really changed my approach to teaching and connecting with students.

Similarly, Sumeyra was also able to open up to her students more after she saw how enthusiastic some of her students were to know more about her background. Recognizing the significance of connecting with our students and embracing our identities as assets in our teaching now, we questioned our internalized oppression and feelings of disempowerment. Internalized oppression occurs when we internalize constant messages that we and our group are inferior to the dominant group such as believing that the dominant group members are more qualified for their positions (Sensoy & DiAngelo, 2017). We uncovered that the internalized oppression started taking roots in the predominantly White monolingual spaces in which we were educated and started teaching. Angelina was often the only person of color in these spaces and Sumeyra was often the only non-American and/or multilingual person. We both agreed that having spaces or communities consisting of people from similar backgrounds as ours would have helped us embrace our identities sooner. Although Sumeyra consciously sought communities of support during her doctoral program, she did not find those spaces during her master's program or her first year of teaching. She explains:

> There was only one person of color in my teacher education program and no multilingual teacher candidates or international students. So even if they didn't explicitly say it, I got the message that a teacher looks and talks a certain way. And then, you go into teaching and again the demographics are similar. So, you find yourself trying to work hard to look like them and behave like them.

This brings forth the issue of how teacher education programs as predominantly White monolingual spaces implicitly support the dominant notions of power and legitimacy when it comes to teacher identity. As a result, after completing these programs and starting to teach, misconceptions about what constitutes a competent teacher become almost inevitable.

Reflecting on Our Critical Dialogue

Going back to our critical incidents, we both shared moments in which there were interactions with our students. Although our self-journeys and our interactions with our colleagues are equally important when learning to negotiate the tensions surrounding our identities, our biggest concerns were about our students; how they would perceive us and how we could best work with them. We internalized misconceptions about what a competent teacher looks like. We also believed that our students would have the same misconceptions having been through the same education system. Our critical dialogue helped us think about how we could have implicitly supported those misconceptions by not showing who we really were and not working towards helping them unlearn these biases. Angelina shared:

> I would want my students to know I'm a professional. I have my master's degree as a first-generation college graduate. And as you can see, I'm perfectly capable of doing so. Don't let anybody tell you that the language or the dialect you speak at home with your families is lesser than the

"standard". That represents who you are. I know there are going to be a lot of people that look down on those who are speaking AAVE. I know that that message is out there, and it can cause a lot of damage. I am working to change that narrative.

Sumeyra adds that:

When I refrained from sharing my journey learning English or my immigration story with my students, I was doing it to look like a competent teacher but the message it sent to students was that my background is not important. What is important is that I'm here in the US teaching English and I think that message is really harmful. It's saying that our only target is for you to learn English and sound more American. And look at me trying my best to blend it and sound like a native English speaker.

These negative messages are out there and can be internalized by students. We had also internalized some of these messages and had to work to unlearn them. One of those messages told us that our professional and social identities had to be separate, therefore, we felt hesitant to use our linguistic, racial and ethnic resources in our professional spaces. However, our social and pedagogical identities are inseparable even though we are often forced to conceptualize them as apart (Peercy *et al.*, 2019).

We both went through different processes in terms of unlearning these internalized oppressive ideologies and breaking through the deficit lenses through which we were seeing ourselves. For Sumeyra, it was not until halfway into her doctoral program that she started to view her linguistic identity as a resource, rather than looking at it through a deficient lens. This change, albeit slowly, was prompted by her introduction to the field of translingualism and to the autoethnographies of numerous translingual and transnational language teachers and teacher educators, who have navigated through similar tensions (Canagarajah, 2012; Yazan, 2019; Solano-Campos, 2014; Jain, 2021). Translingualism challenges the monolingual ideology, which defines linguistic difference as a problem and a characteristic of those who are different and outside of the 'norm' (Lu & Horner, 2013). Therefore, translingualism helped Sumeyra view her linguistic resources through an asset-based lens, which was further reinforced after her research interests shifted towards raciolinguistics. Looking back at her critical incident where she felt the urge to hide her accent, ethnic and linguistic background, and even her foreign name, Sumeyra is able to see how she internalized ideologies that favored Whiteness and mainstream English over the language practices of minoritized groups and this had a strong influence on how she viewed and presented her identities.

On the other hand, what contributed to how Angelina reconceptualized her identities as an asset was a combination of different factors, including some of the college courses she participated in that helped her tap into the words and experiences of her African American ancestors, the students she served and connected with during her student teaching at a racially and linguistically diverse district, and the political climate at the time. The year of 2020 was a pivotal moment for her. She remembers being triggered by the violent death of Ahmaud Arbery and began to use her voice, even using AAVE in her speech at a Black Lives Matter rally. She felt pulled to use her voice and finally claim it as *her* community. Her journey started from rejecting her African American roots and only presenting herself as White, and resulted in feeling as part of the African American community and embracing her linguistic resources to support them. Raciolinguistics also helped her re-evaluate her experiences as a student that caused her to blend in for the sake of abandoning a part of her identity. As a teacher, she wants to challenge the ideologies that silence AAVE and uphold the assumption that standard English is racially neutral (Motha, 2006).

Another noteworthy outcome of our conversation was regarding how the tensions around identity are not fully resolved. For Angelina, embracing her racial and linguistic backgrounds also came with the realization that she would like to educate her students about AAVE, however, this brought up other tensions. She shared:

> As a biracial woman attempting to confront and untangle my identity, I continuously felt pressured to ask myself the question: 'Am I even Black enough to speak AAVE, let alone educate my students about it?'

Similarly, Sumeyra's negotiation of her linguistic identity has evolved. Though she learned to embrace her linguistic resources as an asset, she started to question her ethnoracial identity:

> Getting into this field of raciolinguistics and identity work made me realize that I still feel that in-betweenness but in a different context. We talked about how Whiteness and standard English were intrinsically connected. I identify neither as a person of color nor as a White American who speaks standard English. I find myself in the dominant racial category, but I feel as though I don't belong there due to my ethnic and linguistic backgrounds.

These tensions around identity have taught us that we are still learning to negotiate and reconceptualize our identities, but we have come a long way. Motha (2006) explains that race or linguistic minority statuses are not clear-cut categories and their meanings are both subjective and negotiable. Therefore, as we are reflexively looking back on our experiences, we are learning to renegotiate our positionings and the meanings we make of our identities and experiences. We have started to do that 'by claiming and leveraging our identities to empower ourselves' (Peercy *et al.*, 2019) and as educators, we would like to support our multilingual, multicultural students in doing the same.

Conclusion

Our pedagogies continue to evolve as we learn to embrace our identities, use them as assets in our pedagogies, and continue to negotiate and reconceptualize our identities in our social and professional spaces. Conducting this critical dialogue helped us dive deeper into our experiences and think about what we internalized about what it means to be a competent teacher and our conscious and unconscious choices to blend in. During this critical dialogue, we have found that we have shared similar experiences, even though we come from very different backgrounds. For Sumeyra, tensions around identity were centered on her linguistic background and her sense of belonging due to her immigration status/nationality, whereas for Angelina, they were about embracing her racial identity as a biracial woman and her dialect as a linguistic asset. However, despite experiencing different tensions, we agreed that when studying and working in predominantly White monolingual spaces, it becomes crucial to find spaces that are not centered on Whiteness and monolingualism to connect with others who are going through similar journeys.

In a field where it is of utmost importance to be reflective practitioners, it is imperative that we focus on decentering Whiteness and monolingual ideologies in our educational spaces. The disproportionate racial, ethnic, and linguistic representation found in the majority of US schools and teacher education programs is alarming, so we must think about ways to support teacher candidates from minoritized backgrounds, who, like us, may form distorted conceptions of what it means to be competent. We both had misconceptions about being a competent teacher. We associated standard American English with a professional identity, and we did not want to stand out. Sumeyra was immediately positioned as the linguistic other due to her accent and language learning history, which made her self-conscious about teaching English when she wasn't native to it herself. Angelina did have access to the standard American English as she grew up with her White family members. However, she had a whole other linguistic resource (AAVE) she could tap into but initially had trouble associating it with her professional identity. These struggles are not new, and they go back to the colonial mentality, which 'positioned colonized populations as inferior to idealized European populations' and still continues to 'shape the world order in the postcolonial era by framing racialized subjects' language practices as inadequate' (Rosa & Flores, 2017: 627).

Therefore, if we want to make teacher education programs and schools safe places for educators from diverse backgrounds, we need to start by decolonizing these spaces and question the implications of allowing the dominant groups to claim raceless, cultureless, and languageless identities by positioning racially and linguistically diverse people as the other (Haddix, 2015).

Critical Discussion Questions

(1) How can our racial/ethnic/linguistic backgrounds as educators be used as assets in a classroom setting?
(2) Can opening up about our social identities help our students be open about theirs?
(3) Can this be a source of empowerment for students?
(4) Can we begin to dismantle dominant and harmful assumptions related to race/ethnicity/language when it comes to power?
(5) How are we able to or what can we do to rewrite the professional educator narrative?

References

Alim, S., Rickford, J.R. and Ball, A.F. (2016) *Raciolinguistics: How Language Shapes Our Ideas About Race*. Oxford: Oxford University Press.

Brown, K.D. (2014) Teaching in color: A critical race theory in education analysis of the literature on preservice teachers of color and teacher education in the US. *Race, Ethnicity and Education* 17 (3), 326–345. doi:10.1080/13613324.2013.832921

Canagarajah, S. (1999) Interrogating the 'native speaker fallacy': Non-linguistic roots, non-pedagogical results. In G. Braine (ed.) *Non-native Educators in English Language Teaching* (pp. 77–92). Mahwah, NJ: Lawrence Erlbaum Associates.

Canagarajah, A.S. (2012) Teacher development in a global profession: An autoethnography. *TESOL Quarterly* 46 (2), 258–279. https://doi.org/10.1002/tesq.18

Daniels, J.R. and Varghese, M. (2020) Troubling practice: Exploring the relationship between whiteness and practice-based teacher education in considering a raciolinguicized teacher subjectivity. *Educational Researcher* 49 (1), 56–63. https://doi.org/10.3102/0013189X19879450

Flores, N. and Rosa, J. (2015) Undoing appropriateness: Raciolinguistic ideologies and language diversity in education. *Harvard Educational Review* 85 (2), 149–171. https://doi.org/10.17763/0017-8055.85.2.149

Haddix, M. (2015) *Cultivating Racial and Linguistic Diversity in Literacy Teacher Education: Teachers Like Me*. New York: Routledge.

Jain, R. (2021) (Re)Imagining myself as a transnational, a translingual, and a pracademic: A critical autoethnographic account. In B. Yazan, S. Canagarajah and R. Jain (eds) *Autoethnographies in ELT: Transnational Identities, Pedagogies, and Practices* (pp. 109–127). New York: Routledge.

Lu, M. and Horner, B. (2013) Translingual literacy, language difference, and matters of agency. *College English* 75 (6), 582–607.

Montecinos, C. (2004) Paradoxes in multicultural teacher education research: Students of color positioned as objects while ignored as subjects. *International Journal of Qualitative Studies in Education* 17 (2), 167–181. https://doi.org/10.1080/09518390310001653853.

Motha, S. (2006) Racializing ESOL teacher identities in U.S. K-2 Public schools. *TESOL Quarterly* 40 (3), 495–518.

Peercy, M.M., Sharkey, J., Baecher, L., Motha, S. and Varghese, M. (2019) Exploring TESOL teacher educators as learners and reflective scholars: A shared narrative inquiry. *TESOL Journal* 10 (4). https://doi.org/10.1002/tesj.482

Pham, J.H. (2018) New programmatic possibilities: (Re)positioning preservice teachers of color as experts in their own learning. *Teacher Education Quarterly* 45 (4), 51–71.

Rosa, J. and Flores, N. (2017) Unsettling race and language: Toward a raciolinguistic perspective. *Language in Society* 46 (5), 621–647.

Selod, S. (2015) Citizenship denied: The racialization of Muslim American men and women post-9/11. *Critical Sociology* 41 (1), 77–95. https://doi.org/10.1177/0896920513516022

Sensoy, O. and DiAngelo, R. (2017) *Is Everyone Really Equal?* New York, NY: Teachers College Press.

Solano-Campos, A. (2014) The making of an international educator: Transnationalism and nonnativeness in English teaching and learning. *TESOL Journal* 5 (3), 412–443. https://doi.org/10.1002/tesj.156

Solórzano, D.G. and Yosso, T.J. (2002) Critical race methodology: Counter-storytelling as an analytical framework for education research. *Qualitative Inquiry* 8 (1), 23–44.

Varghese, M., Morgan, B., Johnston, B. and Johnson, K. (2005) Theorizing language teacher identity: Three perspectives and beyond. *Journal of Language, Identity, and Education* 4 (1), 21–44. https://doi.org/10.1207/s15327701jlie0401_2

Yazan, B. (2019) An autoethnography of a language teacher educator: Wrestling with ideologies and identity positions. *Teacher Education Quarterly* 46 (3), 34–56.

4 Black Women's *Ibasho*: Creating a Space of Belonging in Japan

Kinsella Valies and Lisa M. Hunsberger

> 'I can't tell you how many times I've walked into a room and I'm the only Black person or woman or both, and it was always, for me at least, learning how to feel like I belong. And making my voice heard and my presence felt. And when I met Kinsella, it was like, oooh! Another Black person! It's really nice to see some melanin representing.' – Lisa

This chapter was born from a conversation between two Caribbean Black women in Japan who, at that time, knew nothing about each other but their countries of origin. Though our island nations – Curaçao and Jamaica – differed in language and culture, we shared a common diasporic heritage. In our talks, we discovered our shared eagerness to hear about our triumphs and challenges in Japan, in addition to those of other Black women. In this chapter, we explore Black women and non-binary individuals' journeys in Japan, and whether we have found a place of belonging, an *ibasho*. Our study is a dialogic, ethnographic, thematic, and linguistic analysis of Black women and non-binary individuals' experiences in Japan, and it is an affirmation of and testament to our resilience.

Dialogue, Cross-Cultural Adjustment and Identity

Our study uses an ethnographic and dialogic approach to gather and share the stories of Black women and non-binary individuals in Japan. Ethnographic research utilizes data about the self, its context and interrelatedness to gain an understanding of the connections between self and others in the same context (Chang, 2008; Denzin, 2006; Ellis, 2004; Ellis & Bochner, 2000). In collaborative autoethnography (CAE), researchers 'pool their lived experiences on selected sociocultural phenomena and collaboratively analyze and interpret them for commonalities and differences' (Hernandez *et al.*, 2017: 251). Eminent and seminal scholars in

CAE maintain that two of its distinguishing features are multivocality and multiplicity (Ngunjiri *et al.*, 2010). We extend our study to include multicultural and multinational volunteer participants, each with their own voices to add.

Dialogic approaches allow researchers to identify and embrace outcomes that are simultaneously competing and contradictory, unified and complementary, separate and unified (Kristensen, 2020). Through exploratory talk, researchers and participants reflect on their stories with each other, and their shared experiences give the researchers an insider status and the ability to create an environment that fosters trust (Morin, 2008; Chang, 2013; Guyotte & Sochacka, 2016; Haye-Matsui 2018; Kristensen, 2020). In our weekly research meetings and group discussions, we created safe spaces in which our individual and collective voices could be heard.

We led small, focused group discussions over a predetermined number of days due to our geographical locations and the COVID-19 pandemic. Peer-led focus groups have been found to promote exploratory talk and trigger collaborative thought (Djohari & Higham, 2020; Marková *et al.*, 2007; Mercer & Dawes, 2008), and the small size of our discussion groups allowed us to speak freely without feeling rushed. It also allowed us to prioritize our mental health and well-being.

In our discussions of our journeys in Japan as expatriates and immigrants ('transnationals'; Burkhard 2017), we explored the role cross-cultural adjustment played in our respective experiences. According to Huff *et al.* (2014) cross-cultural adjustment is the degree to which transnationals are psychologically comfortable and familiar with different aspects of a foreign culture within the context of transnational experiences. Researchers acknowledge the relationship between cultural adjustment and Behavioral Cultural Quotient (CQ), 'an individual's flexibility in demonstrating appropriate actions when interacting with people from different cultural backgrounds' (Huff *et al.*, 2014: 153). Behavioral CQ is related to interactional, interpersonal, and professional communication, and it is the capability to exhibit appropriate verbal and nonverbal actions in a cross-cultural setting (Huff *et al.*, 2014).

For many transnationals, this adaptation creates a double consciousness (Du Bois, 1903/1989) whereby we juggle both our individual identities and an interfacing identity. Additionally, while we are mostly aware of and able to adjust to our host country, our own challenges remain largely unknown. In Japan, expectations to conform and to put on a workplace persona can negatively impact Black transnationals' ability to fully express their individuality (Haye-Matsui, 2018, 2020). For our two non-binary participants, this impacted how openly they could self-identify in the workplace. During our correspondences, however, they came out to us as non-binary. We honor their trust and openness by including their gender identification throughout this paper.

Cross-cultural adjustment involves cultural flexibility on the part of the transnational as well as linguistic and cross-cultural sensitivity, emotional and psychological support, and social ties within the host country (Huff *et al.*, 2014; Peltokorpi & Froese, 2012). In Japan, where collectivism in group-oriented behavior, conformity to group norms, and displaying appropriate attitudes and behavioral patterns are key components of everyday interactions, understanding cultural norms is crucial. Parker and McEvoy (1993) propose that the degree of difficulty in cultural adjustment is proportionate to the degree of distance between the cultural norms and values of the transnationals' home country and those of the host country.

Jenifer and Raman (2015) identify five barriers that hinder cross-cultural communication: misunderstandings attributable to differing cultural backgrounds; norms and roles that determine acceptable and unacceptable behavior; culturally defined beliefs and values; stereotyping and value judgements, and ethnocentrism where a given culture or group behavior is regarded as the standard. In our conversations, several of these cross-cultural challenges take shape in our daily interactions, Japanese language learning, English language teaching, and English and Japanese language use in both social and professional contexts.

Analyzing Our Spoken Histories

Our chapter supports our exploration of ethnographic dialogue through the combination of corpus linguistics and thematic analysis. We follow the dialogic and ethnographic approaches of Hernandez *et al.* (2017) and Ashlee *et al.* (2017) and combine our stories with those of our volunteer participants.

The central questions to be answered are:

(1) What have our respective journeys in professional spaces in Japan been for us as Black women?
(2) How do we maintain our intersectional identities as Black women in spaces where we are the minority within the minority?
(3) How and where have we found support within social and professional communities in Japan as Black women?

We analyze our ethnographic dialogues for emerging themes related to our research questions. The thematic method, as proposed by Braun and Clarke (2012), is used to identify, organize, and analyze common topics and minority experiences. In the corpus analysis of our conversations, we focus on the use of collocations and attributive concordance lines in the node text. These approaches highlight how knowledge is constructed and how transnational Black women and non-binary individuals develop and maintain their identities in social and professional spaces in Japan.

Our Intersectional Identities

Due to our geographic distance, we – the authors – communicated regularly and coordinated our research meetings using Zoom, LINE and Google Workspace. We collaborated at all stages of the research process, shared our writings with each other, and reviewed and edited them per feedback. Both communication and relationship building were achieved through dialoguing and storytelling.

We began recruitment for added participants with a post in the Black Women in Japan (BWIJ) Facebook group (Figure 4.1) that included an overview of our study. We chose to post in BWIJ because membership is vetted by a team of administrators and moderators, and we believed that the group offered the highest probability that respondents would be Black women living and working in Japan.

We created a Google Form detailing our study, explaining the ethical guidelines and the background information we sought. Each participant chose a pseudonym for use in this chapter, and we added a request to participate in follow-up conversations on Zoom. The form was completed by 17 volunteer participants, two of whom were non-binary (Figure 4.2), and all of whom indicated an interest in participating in the follow-up conversations. Due to scheduling conflicts, fourteen of these individuals were able to dialogue with us about their journeys in Japan. We discussed topics related to our three research questions on identity, belonging and professional growth.

Figure 4.1 Image accompanying the Facebook call for participants

How do you identify?
17 responses

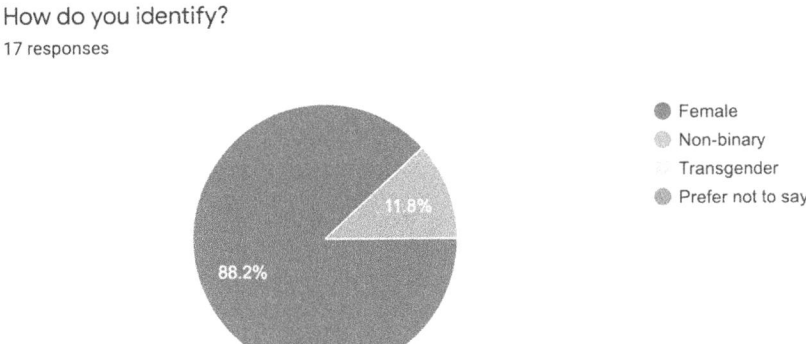

Figure 4.2 Responses to gender identity question on Google Forms

All 19 participants were multilingual transnationals from countries in the Caribbean, North America, Africa, the UK and Europe. Primary language proficiencies were English, French, Spanish, Jamaican Creole and Papiamentu. Additional language proficiencies were Japanese, Kikongo, Kikuyu, Kiswahili, Lingala, Luvale and Nyanja. Ages ranged from 20s to 40s, and among 14 different educational specializations, 17% were educators with linguistics-related backgrounds and 55% worked as English instructors. Only one individual worked within her field of expertise, namely human resources.

This study took a qualitative approach and initial analysis of the dialogues was done through the lens of corpus linguistics. We used the online transcription software Otter (Liang *et al.*, 2018) to transcribe the dialogues, and we consolidated the transcriptions into a node text. The node text was then analyzed using Antconc 3.5.9 software (Anthony, 2020). The focus of the analysis was a set of eight keywords identified by Otter. Finally, we studied the conversations from a thematic perspective, revealing a multitude of experiences and critical incidents tied to language learning, use, teaching, and their cultural and ethnic aspects.

Exploring Common Threads

In our dialogues, we were able to create a space in which we could open up, share our stories and find comfort in speaking with each other. During our conversations, a number of critical themes concerning identity, privacy, Japanese language learning, English language teaching and Japanese and English language use emerged.

> 'I just wanted to also say thank you to you guys because participating in this has been nice. And, obviously, feeling heard and also feeling like we're participating in something that's, as we say, bigger than ourselves feels nice.' – Renee

Black and Blackness

While speaking about how we found or crafted a space of belonging, many of us identified the BWIJ Facebook group as a space where we could feel heard and understood by fellow Black women and non-binary individuals.

> 'It helped that I could find other Black women in Japan to share things with … Just having other persons who I don't even know … comment on my posts, or having even the support of you all responding to our research and wanting to be a part of it to share your stories, has really helped a lot.' – Lisa

In our conversations, we opened up about our cultural backgrounds, and the adjective *black* had the highest frequency in the node text. Concordances with *black* highlight our wide range of nationalities, ethnicities, and cultures: *Caribbean, African, American, British* and *European*. Through the collocate *proud to be*, we shared our pride in our Blackness and our desire to widen our nets within professional communities in Japan as Black women and non-binary individuals.

Japanese language learning

We discovered a shared view of the importance of high Japanese language ability in social and professional spaces. *Speak* ranked high in frequency in the node text with the most notable concordances being *speak (fluent) English, don't speak any Japanese, speak perfect Japanese, didn't speak enough Japanese* and *speak to someone*. These referred to communication with Japanese nationals, and the struggles and successes we had mastering Japanese.

Unsurprisingly, we all concurred that learning Japanese and having a high Japanese language ability was integral to making strong social and professional connections in Japan. Persons with a high Japanese ability expressed being able to change careers and expand into a range of professional spheres. Meanwhile, those without this proficiency shared having had fewer career options.

Efforts to improve our Japanese ability also came with its fair share of challenges. Leya, who worked 16-hour days when she was in Japan, wanted to study Japanese but simply did not have the time. Another participant voiced that it would have been better if she had never improved her Japanese because now, she could understand the unsavory remarks that were being said about her in her presence. One participant shared the negative impact remarks about her body from students had had on her emotional health and well-being.

> 'I love wearing pants … And I remember having a class once and I passed some students, and this boy was staring at my butt. He's junior high

school, maybe first grade, and he was like, '*Dekai!*' ... He was saying 'That's so huge!'. And I broke down. I went home, and I cried.' – Kathy

Language and identity

'I think living in Japan, I've kind of had to, I guess, hide parts of myself, because I can be quite opinionated, and being opinionated here in Japan is not seen as a good thing at all.' – Antoinette

Whether in English or Japanese, some of us felt a loss of power in how we could express ourselves within a Japanese and a multinational context. Due to social or professional norms that dictate women's behavior, fears of being seen in a negative light (as intimidating, aggressive or opinionated) emerged. *Japanese* was another high-ranking keyword in the node text with a large variety of collocates. In our conversations on identity, the adjective *Japanese* was commonly preceded by the negative *not*. The combination phrase '*I am not Japanese*' or '*not a typical Japanese person*' was regularly said during discussions of identity and challenges faced in the professional sphere, indicating a frustration stemming from pressures to conform to Japanese gender norms.

The freedom we felt we had to express our identities varied. While many expressed feeling a pressure to tone down parts of their identities, collocates that appear with the words *my identity* indicate that for two participants *emphasizing* or *turning up* their identities was a way to remain true to themselves and keep their power. Three participants stated that they found their identities in Japan and that Japan had brought their Blackness to the foreground, while another three found that maintaining their identity was an active process, as if it were something that could indeed be questioned or lost.

'I gave up years ago on trying to fit in and be like a proper woman in Japan. Like now, I'm an American. You're gonna learn what it's like to talk to an American girl today.' – Chanté

Those of us who are natively bilingual or multilingual expressed how intricately linked our culture, language, and level of expressiveness are. For many of us, code-switching is a normal part of everyday life. However, in Japan we have found it challenging to express ourselves, as the conciseness that our native languages would afford is limited by the language we all share: English. Lisa, who is Jamaican, shares that her idiolect is a mixture of English and Jamaican Creole. Kinsella speaks Dutch, English and Papiamentu at home and is fluent in Spanish, and Japanese. All the flavor that we normally have when communicating in our native languages is gone when we speak only in English. As Lisa posits, 'How do I translate a concept, so that the receiver understands exactly what I mean when there's just one word or one phrase in my home language that gets it?'

Linguistic discrimination

In the English teaching sphere in Japan, linguistic discrimination presents as native-speakerism, and it is tied to dismissal of the multiplicity of Black women and non-binary individuals' racial and linguistic identities.

> 'No matter what job I've had, Japanese management wouldn't take me seriously unless I had the support/approval of one of my white male co-workers.' – Claudia

Leya hails from an African nation where English is the official language. Despite this, she was not regarded as a native speaker by her employer. A part of her identity critical to her eligibility for employment had been stripped. Leya reported that for many Africans in Japan, this was the case. It was difficult to find jobs, and it was common to learn that advertised pay would be reduced when they interviewed for a job. The reason given was they were 'not native English speakers'.

Leya's experiences in Japan were of two extremes. On the one hand, she had the kindness and support of Japanese friends, but on the other, she endured extreme bullying from her boss. On many occasions, her boss would enter her classes mid-lesson to yell at her or correct her pronunciation. Her boss criticized her accent as being 'too British' and 'not American enough', and she was often verbally abusive. The environment was so toxic that Leya reported having to take sleeping pills to get through the night. This experience was the reason she left Japan. Thanks, however, to the tremendous support system that she had while here, Leya is determined to return to Japan once again. Currently, she is studying Japanese in her home country, and she has found a job with a new company that wants their English assistant language teachers (ALTs) to learn Japanese.

Privacy and feeling understood

A lack of privacy in the workplace was another challenge that we faced. Lisa, Kathy and Suha reported feeling fearful of what they could share at work. Suha, who regularly experienced instances of sexual harassment from men on the street and coworkers at staff *enkai* (parties), shared a heartbreaking story of the detrimental impact this reality had on their ability to report an attempted sexual assault.

> 'I think like Kathy mentioned, when one person finds out about something that happened to you, everyone finds out. And my company is full of a bunch of expats and immigrants, so the community is pretty small. So, everyone knows, and I feel like that's been killing me. And I guess for context, the thing that happened was that my manager tried to rape me. And I was so alone. I didn't report it for four months because I was so scared that that would happen because I know people talk. And it is what

happened eventually when I reported it. So, things have just gotten worse, and a couple of people have blamed me for everything.' – Suha

An immediate outpouring of support for Suha followed, and Kinsella opened up about a similar experience in which she too felt unsupported after having reported a harrowing incident to her superiors. Feeling safe, being believed, and feeling heard are undeniably critical to one's ability to open up about trauma, and we made it our aim to craft a space in these discussions in which everyone could feel safe, believed, and heard.

Access to mental health care is another challenge that a number of us face in Japan. For one participant, a language and cultural barrier between her and her Japanese mental health provider impeded her ability to receive proper mental health care. She reported feeling anxiety and depression for the first time since coming to Japan, but because English was both her and the psychologist's second language, much was lost in translation. She identified not only language as being the challenge but their differing cultural, social, and economic backgrounds as well. Matters that were a problem for her were not regarded as a problem by the psychologist, and in one instance when she shared a personal story to seek comfort, the psychologist broke down crying instead. This reaction came as a shock, and she stopped seeing the psychologist as a result. Ultimately, her depression deepened. She found, however, that by diving into her creativity and using it as an outlet, she was able to find her way herself.

Lisa supportively responded, 'Depression is real. I know, for me, I had dysthymia. And it's very mild but pervasive depression ... and I do think that the "strong Black woman" trope really does us a disservice, because we are expected – regardless of what happens to us and regardless of our emotional, physical, mental well-being – we're supposed to just push through it and persevere'.

While dialoguing together, we opened up about the challenges we faced with microaggressions and racism in social and professional spaces in Japan. In a conversation between Lisa and Kinsella, Kinsella recounted a conversation she had had with a Japanese supervisor who, while responding to her struggles with racism in the workplace, told her that his experiences during a six-month stay in the US helped him fully understand racism, and that as a result of this, he believed that there was no racism there.

Finding an *Ibasho*

Question 1. 'What have our respective journeys in professional spaces in Japan been for us as Black women?'

Our findings illustrate the sometimes-conflicting aspects of *Black* and *Japanese*. The keyword *Japanese* for some of us correlated to a pressure to assimilate and be more Japanese. The prevalence of the combination of this word with *not* indicates a sense that being more like the Japanese was a major criterion for being accepted. Our dialogues support this conclusion with stories illustrating that despite assimilation efforts, we were not ever able to be seen as Japanese.

Efforts at cross-cultural adjustment helped in a number of situations, but while the same adjustment worked well in one instance, it did not in another, resulting in a feeling of being in limbo, professionally. A trifold pattern emerged. First, feeling a need to be accepted and wanting to grow within the wider professional community in Japan. Second, feeling limited and unable to advance within our fields. Third, being relegated to advancing mainly within the smaller transnational and Black communities in Japan.

Differences in communication styles also had a profound impact on our professional journeys. Communication styles in Japan tend to be largely indirect, and there is a general expectation that one will pick up on how things are done. For transnationals, this can be a major barrier to effective dialogue and knowledge acquisition, and by withholding or delaying communication, some of us were forced to learn things the hard way.

> 'I never had any training. Zero training. They just took me from the university, and they threw me in there. They gave me a title. And then everyone was expecting me to be perfect. And then I wasn't. And then I got all the *blacklash* of it ... I know the professional atmosphere of Congo, of France, of Belgium. In Japan, it was completely different. The hierarchy is different. The way you talk to people is different. The way you're supposed to dress as a woman is different ... I didn't get it. And I had no guidance. I was working nine to five, but I was expected to be overworking without being told to. So, when it's five, I pack my shit and go. But I'm looked at as a lazy person because I finish work at the exact time my contract is saying I should be finishing work. Oh! Mind blowing. No one is telling me all that and I'm just learning it after I actually finished my contract ... Then when I do introspection and asking friends ... they gave me a whole book of women behavior at work.' – Yllah

In Bri's case, she was able to find her way successfully around the differences in communication styles. Bri comes from a culture that is quite direct, and she explained this to her coworkers. She stressed that she would not be offended by directness, and she asked them to be direct but respectful with her. Her Japanese coworkers eventually came around, and Bri was able to cultivate meaningful professional relationships.

Question 2. 'How do we maintain our intersectional identities as Black women in spaces where we are the minority within the minority?'

Intersectional identity in this study starts with *Black*, *women*, and *non-binary individuals*. We shared stories of discovering and *turning up/*

down aspects of our Blackness and identities, of an otherness that cannot be ignored, of defying limitations. Bri and Chanté found their Black identity after coming to Japan. Leya discovered her Zimbabwean identity and shared it with Japanese friends and acquaintances through community cooking lessons and souvenirs. Kinsella rediscovered her Curaçaoan identity through Curaçaoan cuisine.

Expectations tied to views of Black women's identities, however, had detrimental effects on mental health.

> 'That's one of the burdens that we shoulder as Black women in Japan. I think most people … expect us to be iron born, and just force our way through everything. And originally, I was like … "Yes, I'm strong." And then I was like … "So, I gotta carry all of this and do that and do this and survive this? … Wait. No."' – Kinsella

A number of us shared how anxieties about self-presentation, body size, and hair lead to us limiting ourselves to palatable versions of our respective brands of Blackness and gender expressions. In effect, we had to drop parts of our identities to get along or face societal or professional repercussions.

> 'I'm non-binary and don't really tell anyone. I present as femme and I notice that I probably got a lot of positive responses because everything from my clothes and voice code as very feminine. Once during an interview, I attempted to come out as my true gender, but the term went over his head and that was that.' – Omnira

> '[A]s a female I have to be the super friendly ALT who smiles when a child is rude and wait for the male teacher to come to scold said child. Being firm displaces you from the title of friendly and approachable. It can also be tiring because I have to constantly be aware of my "resting bitch face" and replace it with a smile or be seen as a mean-looking person. In summary, because of my gender and the roles assigned to it here, I often times feel very suppressed.' – Kathy

Kinsella shared her struggles with getting her hair done in Japan and the challenges she subsequently faced in the workplace. Once, when she had moved cities and could no longer visit her usual Brazilian hairdresser, her natural hair had started to grow out. At work, she received negative comments about her natural hair looking 'rough' and that the head wraps she wore were unprofessional. She became nervous about the negative repercussions of changing her straightened hair and felt compelled to travel over two hours to another city to a more expensive hairdresser to get her hair straightened.

Some of us cited compartmentalizing different parts of our identities – and by extension personalities – with different groups: Japanese co-workers; transnationals in Japan; fellow Black people, and; a mix of the aforementioned. Exhaustion is one of the subsequent side effects stressed within the dialogues.

> 'I know that whenever I go to my workplace, whether it's Japanese people or non-Japanese people that I'm working with, I need to appeal to their sense of being like them. So, I cannot be too Black ... I really feel like the people who do know who I really am here in Japan is a very small close-knit group of Black women, and maybe some other non-Black people that are here. But I do feel like when I go out into the world, in Japan, even though I've lived here for 13 years, I still feel like I need to present some kind of palatable version of what they think I should be.' – JC

For Sana it was not difficult to maintain her identity as she does not try to assimilate. Though she has high Japanese proficiency, she shared that she always does morning greetings and farewells in English, so no one forgets she's not Japanese.

> 'I would say the biggest hindrance to my professional growth is probably the way I'm perceived, essentially, you know, as like, I'm tall, and I'm Black and I'm a woman, and I'm not a pushover. I'm very expressive about my opinions, and so I don't hide anything, but I think it definitely intimidates a lot of people, especially men. They really sometimes don't like it. But I'm not going to change myself for these people, because this is me ... And I think these qualities make me unique.' – Queen

Question 3. 'How and where have we found support within social and professional communities in Japan as Black women?'

Support is yet another high frequency word. Collocates that appear most frequently are *important, having* and *Japanese*. Concordances reveal that *support* resounded with each of us as we shared our own experiences in detail, and this support came primarily from family and friends near or abroad. Lexie and Leya received support from Japanese members of their local (religious) communities who 'went above and beyond'. Others received support from a mixed group of colleagues and student peers. For some, however, there was not much support, aside from their partners and maybe a few friends.

Despite our struggles and concerns around privacy, many of us were able to forge meaningful friendships. We found there was, however, a clear separation between Japanese and foreign friends. Bri stated that though she has Japanese friends, she wasn't getting emotional support from them, and Kathy's concerns about privacy kept these interactions generally task focused. Overall, we tended to have small core groups of friends consisting of non-Japanese persons, and the node text evokes the image of an inner and outer circle/core and non-core friends.

Notable exceptions were the experiences of Leya, Liza C., and WaNyeri. Leya hoped to make the move to Japan permanent thanks to her close relationships with her Japanese friends. Liza C., who described her Japanese friends as 'ride-or-die', recounted an incident when her bilingual sons were turned away on sight by a Japanese elementary school principal, and her Japanese friends came to the rescue. WaNyeri was close friends with a senior, married, Japanese couple who lived five minutes away. They were like parents to her, and the wife taught her Japanese.

The importance of a strong support system is undeniable, and we found that the lack of a good support system contributed to feelings of isolation. The majority of us who expressed having dealt with feelings of isolation attributed it to the language barrier and a minimal number of transnationals and Black people living in our areas. Making connections is important to making one feel at home in Japan, and this theme is repeated throughout the node text. The words *sharing* and *experiences* appear frequently, and the exact concordances found were *my friends, my closest friends, my core group of friends, my few Japanese friends, my foreign friends*.

Many of us found support among other transnationals and fellow Black women and non-binary individuals. Lexie has a close Black woman friend whom she reached out to during postpartum and who had been a tremendous support. For Renee, her Peace Corps experience gave her a good understanding of what minority transnationals need and where they can find it. She too cited the BWIJ Facebook group as an excellent resource and support system for transnational Black women and non-binary individuals in Japan. Additionally, by dialoguing together, we were able to create another safe space in which we could share our journeys, triumphs, and challenges, and receive support from each other.

Did We Find an *Ibasho*?

Yes and no. The answer is relative to our experiences. Our shared experiences have shown how essential feeling supported professionally, socially, and interpersonally is to our safety and sense of belonging in Japan. We found our greatest support by making meaningful connections and finding community. This support from family, friends, and fellow Black women and non-binary individuals within social and professional Black, transnational, and Japanese communities has been key to our psychological and emotional well-being. In places where we could not find community, we made our own. We turned to creative pursuits and reached out to others to start our own communities. Our perseverance in the face of challenges is a testament to our resilience.

Creating a space of belonging for transnational Black women and non-binary individuals in professional spaces involves taking actions and cultivating an environment in which we feel safe. Having a voice/say in the workplace, being believed, and feeling supported are vital components to achieving this. Most importantly, we need to feel accepted as we are with regards to the full range of our Blackness, gender and self-expression, and linguistic identities.

Identity and language use, language teaching, and language learning are varied within the multicultural, multi-ethnic, multilingual, and interlingual context of life as transnational Black women and non-binary individuals in Japan. We hope that reading the narratives of these amazing people will create a higher level of awareness as to what it means for us to navigate life here and will spur interest in and commitment to diversity, equity, and inclusion as a force for societal change. We are confident that this chapter will serve as impetus for the crafting and facilitation of more inclusive spaces for Black women and non-binary individuals in Japan.

Critical Discussion Questions

For further discussion of the themes and conclusions in this chapter, try answering the five questions below in groups.

(1) How can international communities create safe spaces that include the intersectional identities of transnational Black women and non-binary individuals?
(2) How does the view of what constitutes a (near) native English speaker affect transnational Black women's and non-binary individuals' professional prospects and power in Japanese work environments?
(3) What are good avenues in which transnational Black women and non-binary individuals can find and craft places where they belong?
(4) What do transnational Black women and non-binary individuals' professional challenges and experiences in Japan teach us about having a voice?
(5) To the Black community: how can we improve the way in which we as a community view mental health care?

References

Anthony, L. (2020) *AntConc* (Version 3.5.9) [Computer Software]. Tokyo, Japan: Waseda University. https://www.laurenceanthony.net/software
Ashlee, A., Zamora, B. and Karikari, S. (2017) We are woke: A collaborative critical autoethnography of three 'Womxn' of color graduate students in higher education. *International Journal of Multicultural Education* 19 (1), 89–104. https://doi.org/10.18251/ijme.v19i1.1259
Braun, V. and Clarke, V. (2012) Thematic analysis. In H. Cooper, P.M. Camic, D.L. Long, A.T. Panter, D. Rindskopf and K.J. Sher (eds) *APA Handbook of Research Methods in Psychology, Vol. 2: Research Designs: Quantitative, Qualitative, Neuropsychological, and Biological* (pp. 57–71). Washington, DC: American Psychological Association.
Burkhard, T.J. (2017) Horizons of Home and Hope: A Qualitative Exploration of the Educational Experiences and Identities of Black Transnational Women [Doctoral dissertation, The Ohio State University].

Chang, H. (2008) *Autoethnography as Method*. Walnut Creek, CA: Left Coast.
Chang, H. (2013) Individual and collaborative autoethnography as method. In S. Holman Jones, T. Adams and C. Ellis (eds) *Handbook of Autoethnography* (pp. 107–122). New York: Routledge.
Djohari, N. and Higham, R. (2020) Peer-led focus groups as 'dialogic spaces' for exploring young people's evolving values. *Cambridge Journal of Education* 50, 1–16. https://doi.org/10.1080/0305764X.2020.1754763.
Denzin, N.K. (2006) Analytic autoethnography, or déjà vu all over again. *Journal of Contemporary Ethnography* 35 (4), 419–428.
Du Bois, W.E.B. (1989) The souls of black folk. *WEB Du Bois: Writings* 357–547. (Original work published in 1903.)
Ellis, C. (2004) *The Ethnographic I: A Methodological Novel about Autoethnography*. Walnut Creek, CA: AltaMira Press.
Ellis, C. and Bochner, A. (2000) Autoethnography, personal narrative, reflexivity: Researcher as subject. *Handbook of Qualitative Research* (2nd edn, pp. 733–768). London: Sage Publications.
Guyotte, K.W. and Sochacka, N.W. (2016) 'Is this research? Productive tensions in living the (collaborative) autoethnographic process'. *International Journal of Qualitative Methods* 15 (1), 1–11. https://doi.org/10.1177/1609406916631758
Haye-Matsui, A. (2018) The narrative of a female Jamaican ALT in Japan: Status and identity. *Journal of the Faculty of Foreign Studies, Aichi Prefectural University: Language and Literature* (50), 237–255.
Haye-Matsui, A. (2020) Black, British and female in the Japanese university. In D.H. Nagamoto, K.A. Brown and M.L. Cook (eds) *Foreign Female English Teachers in Japanese Higher Education: Voices from Our Quarter*, 206–222. Candlin & Mynard epublishing.
Hernandez, K.A.C., Chang, H. and Ngunjiri, F.W. (2017) Collaborative autoethnography as multivocal, relational, and democratic research: Opportunities, challenges, and aspirations. *a/b: Auto/Biography Studies* 32 (2), 251–254. https://doi.org/10.1080/08989575.2017.1288892
Huff, K.C., Song, P. and Gresch, E.B. (2014) Cultural intelligence, personality, and cross-cultural adjustment: A study of expatriates in Japan. *International Journal of Intercultural Relations* 38, 151–157. https://doi.org/10.1016/j.ijintrel.2013.08.005
Jenifer, R.D. and Raman, G.P. (2015) Cross-cultural communication barriers in the workplace. *International Journal of Management* 6 (1), 348–351.
Kristensen, M. (2020) Introducing dialogic as a research methodology. *International Journal of Management Concepts and Philosophy* 13 (3), 196–216. https://doi.org/10.1504/IJMCP.2020.111024
Liang, S., Fu, Y., Apen, K., Ward, R. and Lau, S. (2018) *Otter* (Version 2.3.114 – 2b4b966e) [Computer Software]. Mountain view, USA. Available from www.otter.ai
Marková, I., Linell, P., Grossen, M. and Salazar Orvig, A. (2007) *Dialogue in Focus Groups: Exploring Socially Shared Knowledge*. London: Equinox Publishing.
Mercer, N. and Dawes, L. (2008) The value of exploratory talk. In N. Mercer and S. Hodgkinson (eds) *Exploring Talk in Schools* (pp. 55–72). London: SAGE.
Morin, E. (2008) *On Complexity*. Cresskill, NJ: Hampton Press.
Ngunjiri, F.W., Hernandez, K.A.C. and Chang, H. (2010) Living autoethnography: Connecting life and research. *Journal of Research Practice* 6 (1).
Parker, B. and McEvoy, G.M. (1993) Initial examination of a model of intercultural adjustment. *International Journal of Intercultural Relations* 17 (3), 355–379. https://doi.org/10.1016/0147-1767(93)90039-B
Peltokorpi, V. and Froese, F.J. (2012) The impact of expatriate personality traits on cross-cultural adjustment: A study with expatriates in Japan. *International Business Review* 21 (4), 734–746. https://doi.org/10.1016/j.ibusrev.2011.08.006.

5 Negotiating Identity, Language and Power: Dialogic Reflections on Non-Native English-Speaking Writing Instructors in the US Composition Classroom

Lan Wang-Hiles, Ekaterina Goodroad, Tong Zhang and Judith Szerdahelyi

Despite the widely-held belief that teaching English composition in the US should be the privilege of native English speakers, there is a growing number of non-native English-speaking writing instructors (NNESWIs) who occupy a vital space in the field of rhetoric and composition instruction. We, the authors of this chapter, are four female NNESWIs, two from China, one from Russia, and one from Hungary, affiliated with one of the Standing Groups for the Conference on College Composition and Communication (CCCC). As defined, NNESWIs are 'individuals whose first or native language is not English and who teach college-level credit-bearing writing courses in the US. This group believes that cultural, linguistic, and rhetorical diversity is an asset in composition instruction ...' (CCCC NNESWIs, 2019).

    This chapter is an extension of the many formal and informal dialogues about what kind of people we are as NNESWIs, how we look at ourselves, how we feel about ourselves, and how others perceive us both in and outside the classroom. While we differ in several ways (e.g. cultural background, age, color of skin, years of teaching experience, academic rank, etc.), our identities have been impacted by our familial, cultural, linguistic, and institutional backgrounds. The research question of this study has emerged naturally from our identities' positionality: 'How do our personal identities as foreign-born females shape our faculty identities of teaching English composition to native English-speaking students?'

The theoretical framework we applied to examine our identities is based on Gee's (2000) study of a person's identity in four perspectives: Nature-identity, Institution-identity, Discourse-identity and Affinity-identity. Gee's dynamic approach of analyzing one's identity goes beyond the more common race, class and gender intersectionality; it provides 'an analytic tool for studying important issues of theory and practice in education' (2000: 25). Through collaborative autoethnography (CAE) (Chang *et al.*, 2013), we conducted a multidimensional dialogic investigation, aiming at analyzing and understanding the impact of the sociocultural and educational system we grew up with, our value and belief systems as revealed in our educational practices, and our relationships with students and colleagues in our educational contexts.

Our dialogic exchanges shed light on the daily struggles and challenges we face in our teaching contexts and the strategies we use to overcome them. Our narratives indicated our frequent exposure to negative biases amidst questions regarding our legitimacy of teaching English composition despite our qualifications and teaching experiences. These encounters intensified our feelings of vulnerability and self-doubt while corroborating our underprivileged NNESWI status. Meanwhile, our shared experiences and similarities helped us recognize that we are not alone. Our dialogue provided us an opportunity to showcase our strengths while reinforcing the values of our work in composition instruction. Therefore, the purpose of this chapter goes beyond simply increasing NNESWIs' visibility and raising awareness of NNESWIs being assets to academia. By providing mutual support and finding a home in the community, NNESWIs should recognize power to 'reshape, reframe, and transform discourses of deficiency to those of empowerment and resilience' (Espino, 2008: 214).

Lenses for Interpreting Our Identities

Using Gee's (2000) four perspectives of identity as the theoretical framework, we explored our identities. The four perspectives pertaining to how people see themselves and how they are seen are (1) Nature-identity (N-identity), a state formed by nature; (2) Institution-identity (I-identity), a position authorized by institutions; (3) Discourse-identity (D-identity), an individual trait recognized in the discourse and dialogue of others; and (4) Affinity-identity (A-identity), experiences shared within affinity groups. Through these lenses, we reflected on our lived experiences, including exhilarations and challenges. We analyzed how we overcame linguistic and cultural barriers, power relationships and gender issues as we struggled to eliminate biases and negotiate for the equality and inclusivity of NNESWIs in US higher education.

Guided by Gee's identity framework, we conducted a thorough examination of our sociocultural experiences, initially emphasizing their impacts on our N-identity. Additionally, we analyzed our I-identity and D-identity as we noticed that they merged together, playing a pivotal role in our academic lives. We also reflected on the vital importance of our A-identity as NNESWIs.

Research on Non-Native English-Speaking Instructors

Academic challenges

The foci of the works concentrating on non-native English-speaking teaching professionals are the topics of linguistic bias, language ideology, and racial discrimination (Aneja, 2006; Guo, 2006; Kubota & Lin, 2006; Villarreal, 2013). The most discussed ideas in literature centered around the notion of native speakers being ideal English instructors (Chun, 2014), learners favoring native English-speaking instructors' accents (Lippi-Green, 2012), and challenges of non-native English-speaking instructors' language proficiency and teaching credibility (Constantinou et al., 2011).

In NNESWIs' educational settings, the presence of linguistic biases has been observed, indicating potential disparities in the treatment of NNESWIs by students, colleagues, and administrators. Since native speakers are usually perceived as English experts primarily because they do not have a perceived foreign accent, they are not considered to be responsible for miscommunication (Shuck, 2006). Consequently, when native speakers are confronted with a perceived accent, either unfamiliar or foreign to them, they can decide whether or not to continue the communication or even 'demand that a person with an accent carry the majority of the burden in the communication' (Lippi-Green, 2012: 72). Regretfully, failure in communication between native and non-native speakers is often blamed on non-native speakers, and rarely on native speakers' unwillingness or inability to understand (Kang et al., 2015). This lack of willingness to understand non-native speakers often impedes interaction (Lindemann, 2002). Even when native-speaking students understand their non-native instructors perfectly, some of them would still perceive the interaction as unpleasant. As Villarreal (2013) pointed out, the communication gap between native-speaking students and their international faculty caused by linguistic bias differs from misunderstanding.

As a result, non-native English-speaking instructors tend to receive lower course evaluations even though students learn just as much from them as they would from native English-speaking instructors (e.g. Finegan & Siegfried, 2000). Linguistic and racial biases against non-native English-speaking instructors damage their self-esteem and academic reputation. They even affect their retention, promotion, and tenure if students' evaluations are a key measurement for faculty evaluations of their institutions (Seldin, 1993). Furthermore, students' linguistic and racial biases can create an unhealthy teaching-learning environment, which, in turn, might negatively affect students' learning outcomes. Research also found that Asian females tend to receive more resistance from students, and even colleagues once they are hired (Hune, 2011; Subtirelu, 2015). Because of their 'otherness', they are sometimes labeled as 'strangers' of the academy (Li & Beckett, 2006).

Scholars (e.g. Holliday, 2005; Phillipson, 1992) noticed and criticized the discrimination against non-native English professionals, lamenting the native-speaker fallacy. Native speakership cannot be used to determine whether a teacher is qualified or not (Ates & Eslami, 2012). As Matsuda (2003: 15) claimed, 'the assumption that native is somewhat more positive than non-native needs to be challenged'. Canagarajah (1999: 80) also asserted that 'multilingual speakers' proficiency in more than one language system develops a deep metalinguistic knowledge and complex language awareness'. Non-native English-speaking instructors have repeatedly proved themselves to be better in some aspects of teaching than natives, including teaching methods, delivering linguistic and literacy knowledge, and addressing students' questions (Lipovsky & Mahboob, 2010; Tajeddin & Adeh, 2016).

'Otherness', power and identity

In addition to the challenges regarding their qualification and credibility, some students, faculty, and administrators might have misconceptions about non-native English-speaking instructors and their cultures. This deficit in awareness could lead to misunderstanding and prejudices, because students, faculty, and administrators sometimes do not recognize cultural differences (Mfum-Mensah, 2016), let alone value them. The pedagogical task of instructing in a foreign cultural context presents inherent challenges and complexities. It requires familiarity with the host culture, its standard pedagogical practices, and the norms of teacher-student relationships (Luxon & Peelo, 2009). Hence, non-native English-speaking instructors experience cultural barriers in US institutions due to the differences in their value systems. For example, US society is characterized by individualism (Sallee & Hart, 2015). Instructors apply rules and deadlines equally to everyone; they seem rarely flexible regardless of circumstances (Jaipal, 2006). Collectivist countries, on the other hand, are characterized by strong ties among people around, caring more about others, and sharing responsibilities (Sallee & Hart, 2015). Accordingly, instructors from collectivist cultures experience barriers when immersing in individualistic cultures. Such barriers occasionally cause mutual misunderstanding between foreign-born faculty and their students in the classroom, which could otherwise be resolved by mutual understanding and compromise.

Collegiality, characterized by a sense of community, provides both social and intellectual support (Thomas & Johnson, 2004). However, many non-native English-speaking instructors experience a lack of collegiality and feel alone. Collins's (2008: 183) study indicated that 63% of non-native English-speaking instructors were 'not coping well with loneliness'. Female faculty of color reported a lack of support or a sense of belonging, even feelings of being marginalized (Skachkova, 2007; Stanley, 2006). Marginalization of non-native English-speaking instructors could manifest itself in refusing to consider them for employment positions, refusing to acknowledge their international work experience, and excluding them from networking events (Odhiambo, 2012). They are often perceived as guests in the US (Hutchison, 2016). Studies also found negative gender stereotypes toward female non-native English-speaking instructors (Vargas, 2002); Asian female instructors seemed to receive the least respect (Li & Beckett, 2006).

Variations in power relationships are also noticeable in teaching contexts. In the US, power distance aims at distributing power equally between professors and students. However, in cultures associated with a large power distance where non-native faculty come from and where individuals follow a certain hierarchy, instructors are respected and looked up to (Hofstede, 1984). As a result, perceptions of power relationships may vary between students and their non-native English-speaking instructors (Achankeng, 2016). Non-native English-speaking instructors' teaching practices and interaction with students may appear unfamiliar to students.

Shaping identities of non-native English-speaking instructors' involves cultural identity blending of both American culture and their home culture. The process of blending two cultures can be challenging as it determines how successful these instructors will be in the host culture; thus, regardless of their subject matter expertise, non-native English-speaking instructors need to seek acceptance by the host culture and create a new identity to fit in (Hutchison, 2016). This new hybrid identity formation requires non-native English-speaking instructors' substantial effort and sacrifice; yet, it can also be rewarding as they could develop a deeper understanding of who they are, gain insights into how others perceive them, and cultivate a positive sense of self-esteem (Rice & Dolgin, 2005). Their new transformed identity can even be used as teaching pedagogy to benefit students (Zheng, 2017).

Research on NNESWIs

Composition instruction witnesses a rapidly increasing number of NNESWIs in the US classroom. Yet, challenges that NNESWIs face (Tseptsura & Ruecker, 2023) are substantial. Kumar (2002), an Indian American female, revealed her writing students' apprehensions and preconceived notions about her ethnicity after seeing her and hearing her accent. As she described, although students' attitudes toward her changed by the end of the semester after taking her class, they still commented on her accent. Similarly, reflecting on her journey of becoming a NNESWI, Shehi (2017) shared her difficulties facing linguistically privileged native-speakership, and advocated for linguistic diversity. Ruecker *et al.* (2018) introduced the intertwined bias NNESWIs often encounter, endorsing NNESWIs' needs for linguistic diversity and pedagogy support.

Collaborative Autoethnography via Dialogues

To answer our research question, we chose collaborative autoethnography (CAE), a qualitative method in which researchers collect their autobiographical materials to analyze and interpret their data collectively to gain a meaningful understanding of sociocultural phenomena reflected in their autobiographical data (Chang *et al.*, 2013). CAE also addresses researchers' contribution while advancing their understanding of a social phenomenon through collaboration. During virtual meetings and email exchanges aimed at exploring our respective identities and posing questions to recognize commonalities and distinctions, we employed dialogue as a means to maintain engagement and enhance our understanding of each other's lived experiences.

One advantage of CAE is that researchers are participants who gain a meaningful understanding of their identities as reflected in data. Moreover, the research process of CAE is interactive; each individual's voice is closely examined within the group. In our study, CAE could yield many advantages, including fostering collaboration, enhancing efficiency, enriching the research process, and facilitating deeper self-exploration and understanding of our community. Hence, our study was strengthened by employing CAE through dialogues.

Data collection was conducted through writing about our identities while self-reflecting on our lived experiences; the process of data analysis involved engaging in self-analysis. According to Chang *et al.* (2013: 78), 'self-reflective and self-analytical data capture researchers' present thoughts and perspectives as well as their past'. Within a three-month time frame, we conducted virtual meetings and communicated via email weekly, sharing and analyzing our identities via dialogue in both written and verbal forms. During our conversations, we took notes when identifying similarities and differences. Then we performed focused writing about our identities respectively and analyzed how our personal identities impacted our faculty identities regarding the issues of language and power. This was followed by exchanging, reading, commenting and responding to one another's writing via email and dialogic discussion during virtual conferences. During both verbal and written dialogues, we analyzed and interpreted our identities.

Finding: Our Dialogic Reflections

Dialogue served as the primary instrument employed at every stage throughout our writing process. To answer the research question, we actively engaged in nuanced dialogue drawing from our lived experiences, critical incidents and shared reflections as sources of insights and understanding. Then we wrote our personal identity narratives respectively, and compiled them into a single document to share our insights and comments. We also added to and modified the document based on what we had discussed during our dialogues when having virtual conferences. For example, after we wrote the first draft of our narratives, we all read and commented on each other's texts to find commonalities and differences in our identities; we exchanged ideas and asked questions virtually and in written form. Dialogues afforded us opportunities to continue reflecting on and discovering our identities.

As introduced earlier, we are four foreign-born female NNESWIs coming from different cultural and family backgrounds; we were nurtured in different societies (collectivism vs. individualism), and have different physical characteristics, age, years of teaching experience and academic ranks. Yet, we believe our personal and cultural backgrounds play a major role in shaping our faculty identities, they demonstrated in our value and belief systems and classroom practices. Based on our dialogic analyses, we summarized our identities below.

Authentic selves (N-identity)

Despite seemingly different backgrounds, we discovered during our dialogues that our N-identities prepared us well for competitive faculty life, but they also created barriers for us to participate in the academic community. Ekaterina's formative years were shaped by a period of transformation in her home country, as it underwent significant changes in politics, economics and social dynamics following a historic era. This cultural transformation required willingness to embrace adaptability and acquire new proficiencies. Aside from the broader societal influence, her parents, who are well educated and belong to the middle class, believed that education played a pivotal role in determining an individual's future success. Consequently, Ekaterina obtained graduate degrees both in the US and her home country, culminating in the attainment of a doctoral degree in the field of education.

For Lan, her family and home culture have had a great impact on her education. With both parents being university professors and her being influenced by Chinese culture that values education, Lan completed her undergraduate degree in China and graduate degrees in the US and followed her parents' legacy, becoming a teacher. As Lan said, 'Chinese culture and my family help shape my N-identity and I-identity. They influence my transnational trajectory and professional growth.'

Tong, who is also from China, saw similarities in her life to what Lan and Ekaterina shared. Born in the 1980s, Tong identified herself as a Chinese female taking advantage of the fast economic development in China, such as seizing the opportunity to study abroad. As the only child in her family, Tong's parents dedicated everything they could to support her in pursuing her dreams, including coming to the US and acquiring a doctorate.

Similarly, Judith's mother devoted her life to Judith's socioeconomic advancement in Communist Hungary. As a business professional, her mother had a chance to travel to Western countries where she brought Judith English-language books to study and later to teach from. Judith saw herself as ambitious, hard-working, driven and committed, which she considered essential qualities to get ahead in life in addition to an opportunity for education.

Lan and Tong's appearances betray them as they are more readily identified as foreign when coupled with their accented English. In contrast, based on their appearances, Ekaterina and Judith would blend in more as native speakers because of their light skin complexion and blond hair. We even joked together that Ekaterina and Judith's NNESWIs' status is not obvious as long as they do not start talking. While differing in several ways, we have a major commonality that we were all well nurtured by our parents who considered education a high priority and had high expectations for us. Our historical and cultural environments also played a significant role in facilitating us to value and pursue an education. Our personal and cultural backgrounds as driving forces shaped each of our N-identities. We admitted that education had changed our life trajectories significantly in a positive way. Our N-identity prepared us for more opportunities but also challenges in academia.

Challenges and strategies as NNESWIs (I-identity and D-identity)

Through dialogues, we agreed that NNESWI is our I-identity because we all teach main-stream composition courses as part of our teaching responsibilities at different US institutions. Such common I-identity also has brought us together as a driving force. Judith established the NNESWIs group at the CCCC in 2015, and all of us have held leadership positions in this professional community. This group provides an opportunity for NNESWIs' voices to be heard. The four of us met at CCCC and have done research projects together, organized professional events for NNESWIs, and facilitated training opportunities for all members. We felt NNESWI status was noteworthy in shaping our I-identity because we fostered a nationwide community of individuals who shared similar experiences and beliefs, coming together through ongoing dialogues to provide mutual support in navigating the challenges we NNESWIs collectively encountered.

In the context of our D-identity, our dialogue centered around the perceptions and perspectives of how we were viewed by our students and colleagues. Our dialogue commenced with the sharing of several incidents that resonated with all of us as NNESWIs. These examples could be interpreted as a display of ignorance by students and colleagues. However, as the dialogue continued, we started interrupting each other with 'that happened to me, too' statements. Our examples became more progressively intense and turned from examples of ignorance to discrimination. We agreed that we were challenged due to our NNESWI status. Facing challenges, we experienced self-doubt, self-reflection and adjustment stages.

In her first semester teaching at the current institution, Lan received racially-based discriminatory 'outlier' comments in students' evaluations, such as 'too bad, she is Chinese', verifying a finding that some students resist Asian female faculty. Even though Lan is an experienced instructor and understood that non-natives' linguistic proficiency and teaching credibility are constantly questioned by native English-speakers, she still felt hurt and restless when reading such comments. Instead of being discouraged, Lan engaged to (1) uncover the reasons why some students held a negative attitude by communicating with students, and (2) reflect on her teaching methods for improvement. By doing so, she realized that she might be the first NNESWI to her students as most of them were first-generation college students. Finding out that being a NNESWI teaching English writing caused students' skeptical attitude toward her, Lan continued demonstrating her qualifications as a knowledge informant and reinforcing to students that she is a subject-matter expert in English. Simultaneously, she kept improving her teaching effectiveness and proactively communicating with students. Using herself as an example, Lan encouraged her students to be more aware that we live in a linguistically, racially, and culturally diverse world.

Gradually, Lan felt her students' attitudes changing toward her; a mutual understanding formed through negotiating with students for power and justice as a NNESWI. Previous biased evaluations tapered off and were replaced by positive comments. 'She is a very caring professor. Her true intentions are to educate us in the best possible way and to give us infinite support and help along the way' was one among many. 'With mutual efforts from students and I, I believe a better teacher-student rapport was established, and gradually my students see me, a NNESWI positively,' Lan reflected.

It is noticeable that teachers' cultural background and beliefs shape their standards of teaching. Influenced by Chinese culture, Tong frequently reflected on her day-to-day teaching practice and interactions with students. Being an international teaching assistant, she perceived her status to be vulnerable as she was not a faculty member. Tong said that her peer colleagues who are also teaching assistants used the word 'introspective' to describe her discursive identity, saying that Tong placed too much emphasis on teaching and reflecting on her teaching. Being a novice NNESWI, Tong felt that she had to work harder than her native-speaking peers. 'Since my cultural and linguistic backgrounds differ from most of my native English-speaking peers, I pay extra attention to communicating with my students, and found that this has been helping me in teaching effectively,' Tong said. Tong considers her being introspective as legitimate. 'Being introspective and learning to be a reflective practitioner is my approach to be relevant to students and to forming my identity as a teacher.' Tong's home culture of valuing opportunities for learning and advancement as well as her high self-esteem pushed her to work harder and focused on communicating with her students in order to build a positive image of NNESWI in the classroom.

As for Judith, the popularity and respect she enjoyed in her prestigious teaching position in Budapest quickly evaporated with her teaching composition to native speakers in the US. Unexpected teaching challenges resulted in conflicting identities. Personality traits associated with her N-identity, such as being driven, disciplined and thorough, may have served her well during her studies in an elitist Hungarian system, but these did not always characterize American students who were paying for their education at an 'open-admission' regional university. The realization that her students were not like her when she was a student and that they were sometimes also less open to learning, especially in mandatory General Education courses, left her confused.

High course standards and rigorous requirements, the essential components of her idea of teaching excellence, were perceived as 'unreasonable' or 'ridiculous' by some students. Their resentment over unattainably high expectations coupled with negative bias and prejudice due to Judith's foreign accent contributed to course evaluations below departmental averages. The 'good teacher' self-image that was vital for her identity became shattered, which led to an identity crisis. After lowering course requirements, she asked one of her colleagues for advice on additional strategies to improve her course evaluation scores. He responded honestly: 'There is nothing wrong with your teaching. You are a woman with an accent, and you are in the South.' The problem seemed to be unrelated to her teaching performance.

According to Ekaterina, her NNESWI identity helped her build rapport with her students, especially with those who required additional support in navigating college, such as students with disabilities, low income and first-generation students. Ekaterina recounted her journey of successes, challenges, and strategies for overcoming obstacles during her classes. She shared how she initially felt overwhelmed by the differences between the systems of education when transitioning to a graduate student in the US, particularly in adapting to egalitarian discussion-style classrooms, and it took her some time to learn effective participation in classroom discussions. However, her personal experiences served as a motivating factor for her students, inspiring them in their own educational pursuits.

However, as a Russian-born faculty teaching English to native speakers, Ekaterina occasionally experienced the power dynamics related to her national origin. This was particularly prominent at the beginning of her teaching career at a US college. Her colleagues laughed the first time they heard she was from Russia and was teaching English. As Ekaterina shared, an administrator once stated jokingly, 'Don't we have enough English teachers here? Do we need to bring them all the way from Russia?' Such remarks caused Ekaterina to feel that being a Russian-born English teacher was viewed as an anomaly, even among her educated colleagues.

To summarize our dialogues, we discovered that we encountered occasional mistreatment and even discrimination from colleagues and students alike. However, we recognized the importance of our presence in US institutions and the vital role we played in educating the academic community about the complexities of working and living in a multilingual and multicultural world.

Seeking and building professional support (A-identity)

In our dialogues, both written and verbal, we actively discussed that being NNESWIs, we sometimes felt alone, even isolated because our experiences were unique or different from those of native English-speaking instructors. We longed to share with other instructors of similar experiences so that our feelings could be understood. We also came to the realization that as NNESWIs, we require a community of our own. We were fortunate to have the support of the NNESWI community affiliated to CCCC where backgrounds, experiences, and challenges we faced were similar among members of this group, and mutual support and solidarity were found within this community. This group has brought to many NNESWIs a strong sense of belonging. Tong's reflection represented our common perception of our A-identity: 'before becoming a member of the NNESWIs community, my affinity identity had not been formed. Being a NNESWI was not one of my identities until I found the NNESWIs group.' Truly, through communicating with group members, we realized that there are many NNESWIs we can relate to emotionally and rationally. This A-identity offers us an opportunity to view our career paths from a different perspective and build a better image of NNESWIs.

In our dialogues, we agreed that NNESWIs have played an important role in shaping our faculty identities. We are proud that we made our contributions to the creation and development of the NNESWI community, especially Judith, the founder of the NNESWIs Special Interest Group and first Chair of the Standing Group of CCCC after years of hard work. In turn, we benefit from being members of this group. It provides us with the opportunity to connect with individuals who share similar perspectives and work collaboratively and purposefully towards common goals. Being part of such a community empowers us in US higher education. We actively engage in dialogues and practices that hold deep meaning, advocating for the rights of NNESWIs and negotiating for linguistic, racial, and cultural justice throughout professional activities.

Conclusion and Discussion

Our identities are shaped by various factors, such as familial, historical, societal, and cultural circumstances, as well as our teaching experiences. Through reflective dialogues and analyses, we gained a deeper understanding of how these identities inform our teaching beliefs and practices. By answering the research question, we explored various aspects of our underprivileged status as NNESWIs in the classroom, highlighted our struggles against linguistic, racial, gender and cultural biases, while striving to empower ourselves in the field of composition instruction dominated by native English-speaking faculty. We further shared our strategies of how we accepted those challenges as a driving power to negotiate for justice and inclusion along with establishing a more positive professional image for NNESWIs.

Being NNESWIs, we hope our first-hand personal and professional experiences could offer some tips to those who share similar situations. Our first strategy is learning to become a better educator. As we reflected on our lived experiences, we recognized our personal and professional growth and the development of our NNESWI identities. We realized the importance of reflecting on feedback we received and making necessary adjustments to improve and grow. Doing so benefits our students too. Willingness to make adjustments enables us to navigate an ever-changing world and face new challenges. For example, the flexibility and adaptability we developed as NNESWIs allow us to be able to adjust to various circumstances and mutually empower ourselves and our students. We acknowledge that keeping our original identities and transforming to shape a new identity to fit in US institutions are equally important. Therefore, our second strategy is providing a learning opportunity for cross-cultural communication in a professional setting. We take pride in, and reinforce, our foreignness, multilingualism and cultural awareness and experiences. Even though we received some comments that are not always culturally sensitive, we understand that for some students and colleagues, this might be their first experience and cross-cultural communication with NNESWIs in a professional setting. Finally, we advocate for NNESWIs by sharing our vulnerability and positionality, yet we also acknowledge the joint efforts many of our students, colleagues, and administrators are willing to make to support us, such as creating training opportunities, affinity groups and an inclusive work environment in daily interactions. Many students and colleagues seem to be genuinely interested in our backgrounds; we hope they are willing to learn from us and about us just as much as we learn from them and about them.

We believe that joining our efforts to eliminate biases about NNESWIs and promoting equality and plurality in US institutions is critical, which requires collaborative efforts of both native and non-native instructors, departments, and administrators to ensure an inclusive, positive, and productive teaching and learning environment.

Critical Discussion Questions

With the purpose of NNESWIs being understood and seen not only as equal to native English-speaking writing instructors, but also as unique assets in the field of composition instruction, and by empowering ourselves in US academia, we propose the following questions, attempting to engage more international faculty from various disciplines to join our dialogic discussion:

(1) How do our identities based on individual, cultural, and institutional backgrounds shape our teaching pedagogy?
(2) What unique qualities do international faculty bring to our current program/department/institute?
(3) How do we maintain our original identity as we develop our new identity?
(4) How do we form and negotiate our faculty identity in order to connect, succeed, and belong to our current program/department/institute?
(5) What actions can we take to empower international faculty in US higher education?

References

Achankeng, F. (2016) From essential and central to constructivist trenches: Navigating the transnational contexts of the instructional practice of a foreign-born professor. In C.B. Hutchison (ed.) *Experiences of Immigrant Professors: Cross-cultural Differences, Challenges, and Lessons for Success* (pp. 155–165). New York: Routledge.

Aneja, G. (2006) (Non)native speaker: Rethinking (non)nativeness and teacher identity in TESOL teacher education. *TESOL Quarterly* 50 (3), 572–96.

Ates, B. and Eslami, Z. (2012) An analysis of non-native English-speaking graduate teaching assistants' online journal entries. *Language and Education* 26 (6), 537–552.

Canagarajah, S. (1999) *Interrogating the 'Native Speaker Fallacy': Non-linguistic Roots, Non-pedagogical Results*. In G. Braine (ed.) *Non-native Educators in English Language Teaching* (pp. 77–92). Mahwah, NJ: Erlbaum.

Chun, S.-Y. (2014) EFL learners' beliefs about native and nonnative English-speaking teachers: Perceived strengths, weaknesses, and preferences. *Journal of Multilingual and Multicultural Development* 35 (6), 536–579.

Chang, H., Ngunjiri, F.W. and Hernandez, K.C. (2013) *Collaborative Autoethnography*. Walnut Creek, CA: Left Coast Press.

Collins, J.M. (2008) Coming to America: Challenges for faculty coming to United States' universities. *Journal of Geography in Higher Education* 32 (2), 179–188.

Constantinou, P., Bajracharya, S. and Baldwin, S. (2011) Perceptions of international faculty in the United States. *International Journal of Science in Society* 2 (3), 253–271.
Espino, M.M. (2008) Master Narratives and Counter-narratives: An Analysis of Mexican American Life Stories of Oppression and Resistance Along the Journeys to the Doctorate. [Doctoral dissertation, University of Arizona] University of Arizona Thesis and Dissertation Archive.
Finegan, A. and Siegfried, J. (2000) Are students rating of teaching effectiveness influenced by instructors' English language proficiency? *American Economist* 44 (2), 17–29.
Gee, J.P. (2000) Identity as an analytic lens for research in education. *Review of Research in Education* 25, 99–125.
Guo, Y. (2006) Between the worlds: Searching for a competent voice. In G. Li and G.H. Beckett (eds) *'Strangers' of the Academy: Asian Women Scholars in Higher Education* (pp. 211–232). Sterling, VA: Stylus.
Hofstede, G. (1984) Cultural dimensions in management and planning. *Asia Pacific Journal of Management* 1 (2), 81–99.
Holliday. A. (2005) *The Struggle to Teach English as an International Language*. Oxford: Oxford University Press.
Hune, S. (2011) Asian American women faculty and the contested space of the classroom: Navigating student resistance and (re)claiming authority and their rightful place. In G. Jean-Marie and B. Lloyd-Jones (eds) *Women of Color in Higher Education: Turbulent Past, Promising Future* (pp. 307–336). Bingley: Emerald.
Hutchison, C.B. (2016) *Experiences of Immigrant Professors: Cross-cultural Differences, Challenges, and Lessons for Success*. New York: Routledge.
Jaipal, R. (2006) Anatomy of 'difference': The meaning of diversity and the diversity of meaning. In C.A. Stanley (ed.) *Faculty of Color: Teaching in Predominantly white Colleges and Universities* (pp. 182–195). Boston: Anker.
Kang, O., Rubin, D. and Lindeman, S. (2015) Mitigating U.S. undergraduates' attitudes toward international teaching assistants. *TESOL Quarterly* 49 (4), 681–706.
Kubota, R. and Lin, A. (2006) Race and TESOL: Introduction to concepts and theories. *TESOL Quarterly* 40 (3), 471–493.
Kumar, P. (2002) Yellow lotus in white lily pond: An Asian American woman teaching in Utah. In L. Vargas (ed.) *Women Faculty of Color in the White Classroom* (pp. 277–291). New York: Peter Lang.
Li, G. and Beckett, G.H. (eds) (2006) *Stranger' of the Academy: Asian Women Scholars in Higher Education*. Sterling, VA: Stylus.
Lindemann, S. (2002) Listening with an attitude: A model of native-speaker comprehension of non-native speakers in the United States. *Language and Society* 31, 419–441.
Lipovsky, C. and Mahboob, A. (2010) Students' appraisal of their native and nonnative English-speaking teachers. *WA TESOL NNEST Caucus Annual Review* 1, 119–54.
Lippi-Green, R. (2012) *English With an Accent: Language, Ideology, and Discrimination in the United States* (2nd edn). New York: Routledge.
Luxon, T. and Peelo, M. (2009) Academic sojourners, teaching and internationalisation: The experience of non-UK staff in a British university. *Teaching in Higher Education* 14 (6), 649–659.
Matsuda, P.K. (2003) Proud to be nonnative English speaker. *TESOL Matters* 13 (4), 15.
Mfum-Mensah, O. (2016) Negotiating the trilogy of blackness, 'Africanness', and 'accentness': A 'native-alien' professor's tale. In C.B. Hutchison (ed.) *Experiences of Immigrant Professors: Cross-cultural Differences, Challenges, and Lessons for Success* (pp. 144–154). New York: Routledge.
Odhiambo, E. (2012) Marginalization: A continuing problem in higher education. In A. Hidalgo-de Jesus and V. Yenika-Agbaw (eds) *Race, Women of Color, and the State University System*. Lanham, MD: University Press of America.
Phillipson, R. (1992) *Linguistic Imperialism*. Oxford: Oxford University Press.

Rice, F.P. and Dolgin, K.G. (2005) *The Adolescent: Development, Relationships, and Culture* (11th edn). Boston: Allyn & Bacon.

Ruecker, T., Frazier, S. and Tseptsura, M. (2018) Language difference can be an asset: Exploring the experiences of nonnative English-speaking teachers of writing. *College Composition & Communication* 69 (4), 612–641.

Sallee, M. and Hart, J. (2015) Cultural navigators: International faculty fathers in the U.S. research university. *Journal of Diversity in Higher Education* 8 (3), 192–211.

Seldin, P. (1993) The use and abuse of student ratings of professors. *The Chronicle of Higher Education* 39, 40.

Shehi, M. (2017) Why is my English teacher a foreigner? Re-authoring the story of international composition teachers. *TETYC* 44 (3), 260–275.

Shuck, G. (2006) Racializing the native English speaker. *Journal of Language, Identity, and Education* 5 (4), 259–276.

Skachkova, P. (2007) Academic careers of immigrant women professors in the U.S. *Higher Education* 53, 697–738.

Stanley, C.A. (2006) Walking between two cultures: The often misunderstood Jamaican woman. In C.A. Stanley (ed.) *Faculty of Color: Teaching in Predominantly white Colleges and Universities* (pp. 328–343). Boston: Anker Publishing Company.

Subtirelu, N.C. (2015) 'She does have an accent but …': Race and language ideology in students' evaluations of mathematics instructors on RateMyProfessors.com. *Language in Society* 44, 35–62.

Tajeddin, Z. and Adeh, A. (2016) Native and nonnative English teachers' perceptions of their professional identity: Convergent or divergent? *Iranian Journal of Language Teaching Research* 43 (3), 37–54.

Thomas, J.M. and Johnson, B.J. (2004) Perspectives of international faculty members: Their experiences and stories. *Education and Society* 22 (3), 47–64.

Tseptsura, M. and Recuker, R. (eds) (forthcoming 2023) *Nonnative English Speaking Teachers of Writing*. WAC Clearinghouse.

Vargas, L. (2002) My classroom in its context: The struggle for multiculturalism. In L. Vargas (ed.) *Women Faculty of Color in the White Classroom: Narratives on the Pedagogical Implications of Teacher Diversity* (pp. 35–52). New York: Peter Lang.

Villarreal, D. (2013) Closing the communication gap between undergraduates and international faculty. *The CATESOL Journal* 24 (1), 8–28.

Zheng, X. (2017) Translingual identity as pedagogy: International teaching assistants of English in college composition classrooms. *The Modern Language Journal* 101 (S1), 29–44.

Part 2

Digitally-Mediated Public Scholarship

6 Twitter/X as Thinking Communities: Responding, Reacting and Acting on Linguistic Discrimination

Clara Vaz Bauler and Vanja Karanović

Social media is a fertile ground for vociferous parents, language enthusiasts and educational practitioners to disseminate and sell ideas about language learning. Claims that dictate or prescribe how parents should raise their bi-multilingual children are widespread on the web. While the majority of linguists have reached a consensus that there is no hierarchy of languages and that using more than one language is a fundamental part of one's identity, with personal, professional and social consequences (Crystal, 2010), monolingual ideologies are widespread on social media. And, with most controversial issues, misinformation is often shared with little criticism if not by communities of linguists and researchers that come together in public forums to challenge common sense views and myths. Twitter/X is one of these public platforms.

Twitter/X is a social media microblogging service that allows users to post and comment on messages called 'tweets.' Twitter/X conversations are rapid and short given its threaded format where users can 'like, tweet or retweet' 140-character-long messages. Some people find the word limitation and the restrictive nature of tweets a real constraint for engaging in dialogue. However, participation in Twitter/X conversations are often driven by common interest and shared purpose or values. As such, Twitter/X can be considered an 'affinity space' (Gee & Hayes, 2011) where people join by shared endeavor, not by credentials. This is a crucial aspect of Twitter/X conversations as, in theory, everyone can produce and distribute knowledge in a somewhat open forum.

This chapter will focus on particular Twitter/X communities and conversations around linguistic discrimination, especially focusing on immigrant multilingual parenting, schooling, and government practices. Linguistic discrimination, based on perceived accent, use of language or monolingual and standard language ideologies, is rarely contested outside of circles of linguists (Lippi-Green, 2012). Particularly when connected to ideas about immigration and immigrants, what one sounds like and what one looks like are intimately connected and are frequently used to index laziness, ignorance and inferiority (Flores & Rosa, 2015; Piller, 2017). When it comes to bi/multilingualism, there seems to be a misguided insistence on the exclusive use of the majority language or variety at home and in school to benefit minoritized children (García & Alonso, 2019).

As linguists, multilingual individuals and language educators, we sought conversations and joined #linguistics, #EAL, #TESOL and #L2 communities on Twitter/X to find a forum to share and voice ideas against linguistic discrimination. Clara became active on Twitter/X after the COVID-19 pandemic started. She was particularly drawn to threads on multilingualism, linguistic diversity, and linguistic discrimination. On Twitter/X, she discovered the power of just 'saying it' with the backing of her newly found peers. Vanja joined Twitter/X a few years ago in order to go back to her linguistic roots and reconnect with the linguistic community, not only for personal interest, but also to inform her teaching of A-Level English Language. She has found the Twitter/X experience inspiring and enriching, as she is able to express her love of language and passion for multilingualism.

Through an autoethnographic perspective, we will analyze how we each and together responded and reacted to tweets and threads generated from linguistic discrimination cases disseminated through social media. We will also reflect on ways Twitter/X community members engaged with what we posted or shared. The questions below will guide our accounts:

- What made us join the conversation? What points and topics draw our attention?
- What do we think we (this community we formed) are?
- How do we act on linguistic discrimination through this community?
- What makes us react differently to posts or comments: like, comment, retweet? What makes us tag someone?

Our Stances and Experiences

Our participation in Twitter/X communities is framed by our beliefs and attitudes towards multilingualism and linguistic discrimination. As multilingual teachers, scholars, family members, and citizens we have adopted views that are shaped and directly informed by our experiences and knowledge. Because there are many myths associated with multilingualism, especially when it comes to parenting and home language practices (García & Alonso, 2019), Twitter/X can be a site for confronting deficit-based discourses regarding children's multilingualism.

Clara Vaz Bauler is a mother of two young children (5 and 8) whose home language practices involve Portuguese, English and playing with other languages such as Hebrew, Spanish, Italian, Chinese Mandarin,

Latin and more. At home, Clara and her family engage in fluid, dynamic and flexible language practices that leverage her children's full linguistic repertoires. This view and enactment of language learning better aligns with a translanguaging stance and theory. Translanguaging is about transgressing artificial language borders and naturalizing multilingual ways of being, knowing, doing. The prefix 'trans' indicates the idea of transcending artificial language borders, going beyond colonial understandings of separate and national languages (Otheguy *et al.*, 2015). The verb 'languaging' signals the deployment of multilinguals' full linguistic and semiotic unitary repertoire of meaning in a process of knowledge construction (García & Li, 2014). Instead of seeing (and policing) her multilingual children's translanguaging practices as deficient attempts at sounding like an ideal 'native speaker,' Clara believes that we should shift our listening practices to hear resistance, maintenance and creativity.

Vanja Karanović is a Bosnian-English bilingual, who, in 1992, came to the UK from Bosnia as a war refugee with her parents and sister. The family's main linguistic focus is the maintenance of Bosnian as the home language in a very powerful monolingual host community context. Families who are determined to maintain their heritage language in such a context will always face an uphill struggle, as the support from the wider community isn't there. Vanja passionately believes that all the languages a person speaks are part of who they are and that any linguicism must always be challenged.

In addition to challenging and resisting myths about bi/multilingualism, we have also both been united in our fight against linguistic discrimination, unveiling language ideologies of purism, standard language, monolingualism and raciolinguistic ideologies of nativism and colonialism. The standard language ideology conceives of language as an idealized, homogeneous, rational, logic variety which is perpetuated through traditional schooling practices (Piller, 2015; Lippi-Green, 2012). The standard language variety is believed to be superior to all other varieties, embodying the values, sounds, and abilities of upper, middle-class, White mainstream speakers in English-speaking imaginations (Baker-Bell, 2020; Flores & Rosa, 2015). The ideology of purism is a direct consequence of the standard language ideology, claiming what features of language are 'good,' 'proper' or 'appropriate,' demoralizing and inferiorizing perceived less prestiged varieties of language and accents (Horner & Weber, 2018). As linguists, multilingual individuals and educators, we see our role in dismantling these harmful ideas whenever they show in public discourse on Twitter/X.

Twitter/X as Cultural Artifacts

In this study, we adopt an autoethnography methodological approach to selecting, recording and interpreting our data (Ellis *et al.*, 2011). We examine Twitter/X threads and our participation in these threads as cultural artifacts. In this process, we acknowledge our subjectivities, identities, opinions, emotions and attachment to the topics being discussed. We purposely selected two Twitter/X threads that led us to retrospectively and selectively write about moments of revelation or epiphanies that stemmed from being part of a specific Twitter/X culture and possessing a particular cultural identity (Ellis *et al.*, 2011). We both joined these specific communities, which could be identified through the hashtags #linguistics, #EAL, #TESOL and #L2, to find a forum to share and voice ideas against linguistic discrimination. We followed each other as part of the same communities, sharing common interests that included language development, multilingualism, sociolinguistics, and education (Gee & Hayes, 2011).

We engaged in co-constructed narratives illustrating the meanings of our posts, comments, likes and retweets, cultural practices enacted by members of the Twitter/X community. We met regularly to write together and used speech-to-text or voice tools on Google documents to better record our ideas and memories as we talked about our participation in the conversations we selected. We considered the narrative as jointly-authored, incomplete, and historically situated (Ellis *et al.*, 2011; Lave & Wenger, 1991). We discussed what Twitter/X conversations were salient and significant to unveil the growth of our intellectual affinity, friendship, allyship and thinking. This relational dimension of our research was crucial for our understanding of the meanings we were making as we participated in the selected Twitter/X threads. Figure 6.1 illustrates our iterative analysis and narrative process.

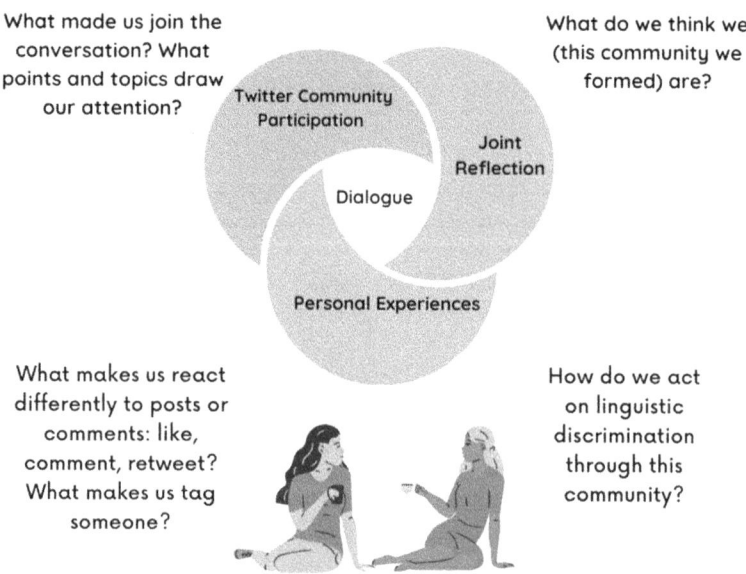

Figure 6.1 Joint autoethnography analysis process

Responding, Reacting and Acting on Linguistic Discrimination

We selected two threads to illustrate our participation in Twitter/X communities. Thread 1 in Figure 6.2 was initiated by Clara Vaz Bauler (CVB) on July 23, 2020. Thread 1 is about bilingualism myths. Thread 2 in Figure 6.3 was initiated by Vanja Karanović (VK) on the lack of cultural and linguistic sensitivity and responsiveness in the UK census questionnaires. We selected two different threads we initiated to provide a sense on how we each are drawn to post, comment and engage in Twitter/X conversations. In particular, the two threads are a vivid example of how we feel a part of a community that shares the common goal of fighting against linguistic discrimination. By clicking on Figure 6.2 and Figure 6.3, the readers have access to the flow of comments and reactions to Thread 1 and Thread 2. Examples of comments to Thread 1 and Thread 2 are also illustrated in Appendix 6.1 for readers of a print version of this chapter. In this session, we discuss our participation in detail via a back-and-forth dialogue. Our conversation purposefully reflects a dialogical style, keeping a non-standard usage while resisting and recreating typical norms for academic writing in standardized English.

What made us join the conversation? What points/topics draw our attention?

VK: In Thread 1 (Figure 6.2) we discussed an Instagram post that Clara posted which stated some inaccuracies about how bilingual people

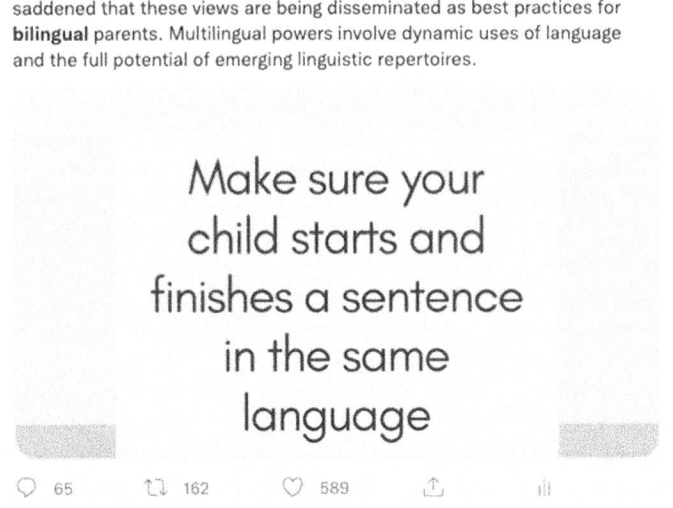

Figure 6.2 Twitter/X Thread 1: 'Make sure your child starts and finishes a sentence in the same language'

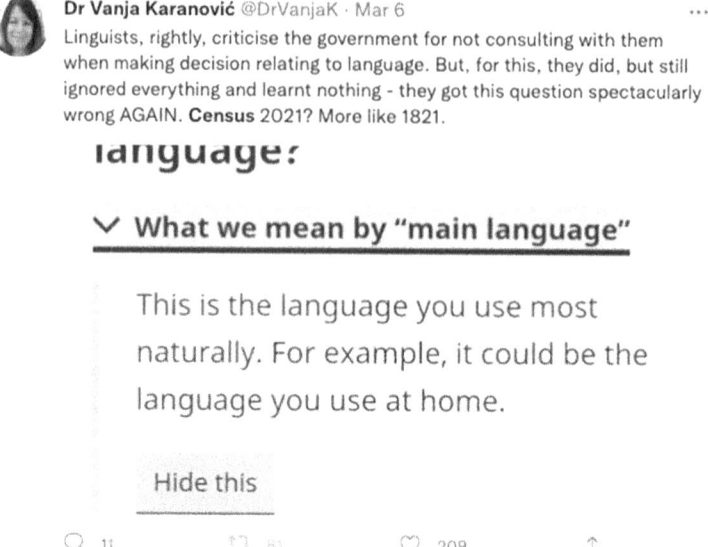

Figure 6.3 Thread 2: UK Census 2021 'What do we mean by 'main language'?

use language and how bilingual children should use language. This was posted about a year and a half ago and I was already on Twitter/X. I was really enjoying being part of #linguistictwitter, because my passion is to fight against the myths that exist around how bilingual and multilingual people use language and the monolingual ideologies that are imposed on such usage, especially when bilingual speakers are compared to monolingual speakers. The initial post in Thread 1 (Figure 6.2) claimed that bilingual children should only produce sentences in one language, and start and finish one sentence in one language, which is completely inaccurate as we know that all bilingual or multilingual speakers draw on all the languages in their repertoire depending on the context, and so it is absolutely normal and common place for bilingual children to use translanguaging or code switching within a sentence, and there is nothing wrong with that as can be seen in examples provided in the comments to Thread 1 (Figure 6.2). It is, actually, creative and sophisticated language use. This is what attracted me to join the discussion and raise my voice against such ideologies that exist and are, unfortunately, very popular as we can see from the views that the post attracted.

In Thread 2 (Figure 6.3), I decided to start the second thread that we are analyzing, as I had been following Dr Thomas Bak's work on the 'Healthy Linguistic Diet' blog, which discussed the 2021 Census in the UK and how narrow and unfair it was in terms of its language question. I was very aware of this when I, myself, had the chance to answer that question in the Census in March 2021. I felt that awareness needed to be raised about how multilingual speakers, including speakers of British Sign Language, were misrepresented in official government material, which clearly reflected monolingual bias.

CVB: I remember at the time of Thread 1 (Figure 6.2), I was new to Twitter/X. I joined it when the pandemic started around the end of March or beginning of April 2020. I had Twitter/X before but I never used it. I started using it because of the social isolation I felt during lockdowns. I was also experimenting with Instagram which I ended up not engaging with as much as Twitter/X because, to me, Twitter/X is more text-based and tends to focus more on ideas and opinions. When I received this post telling parents to make sure their child started and finished a sentence in the same language on Instagram, I was outraged because it is something that I oppose so strongly. I decided to share it on Twitter/X. I was very surprised when people started responding. That was when I started building a community. Before that post, I did not have many followers. I did not have any sense of community on Twitter/X but because of that specific thread I have gained a lot of Twitter/X friends including Vanja. That is visible by all the supportive comments that tweet received in Thread 1 (Figure 6.2).

There are some Twitter/X peers that joined that specific conversation and we have continued supporting each other since then, especially, Malwina Gudowska (@MalwinaGudowska), Constanze Ackermann-Boström (@ConstanzeAB) and Ruth Kircher (@ruth_kircher). When I look at it now, I feel such a sense of community because we all joined together to fight against that false claim about multilingualism. We created a sense of fighting for justice. We wanted multilingualism to be highlighted, especially multilingual parenting and bilingual education. Some of us even tried to contact the person that posted that message on Instagram without success. There were so many threads that came out of that.

One of the most popular threads was exactly the one we banded together to challenge the language of the UK Census (Figure 6.3). At this point of our community engagement in these conversations, we were already almost one year in the pandemic and we had already built a steady flow of conversations about linguistic discrimination. When Vanja posted the initial thread, we all jumped in and we saw it as an opportunity to voice our discontent and our strong feelings about how monolingualism was portrayed as natural and multilingualism was seen as abnormal in a Census questionnaire. Many of those comments can be seen in Thread 2 (Figure 6.3). That ideology became official because it's an official document where you have to fill out information about yourself, about your family practices. It's a time when people feel excluded officially, so I feel that this was a crucial conversation that led to many people sharing their experiences about linguistic discrimination that were enacted in public spaces or in public documents like the Census.

What do we think we (this community we formed) are?

VK: The community that we have created has resulted from discussions relating to issues raised in the two threads (Figure 6.2 and Figure 6.3): multilingual language use, monolingual language ideology, heritage language maintenance and translanguaging. The community consists of like-minded, passionate practitioners, educators and linguists who have experience of those issues in their private and professional lives. The sense of community is created through seeing others who share your concerns, but also share your values about language and want to raise awareness of what is actually true and what isn't. The community is also very powerful in that it addresses hugely important issues such as linguistic discrimination which can have huge repercussions on individuals, families, and society.

As far as Thread 2 (Figure 6.3) is concerned, I feel that we built a slightly different community from the first thread, as it drew more linguistic experts into the discussion as can be seen in the comments. I think the reason for that is that challenging an official government document requires not only a certain level of confidence, but also a willingness to engage with and criticize government policy that maybe some people did not wish to participate in. The community that we formed and eventually the hashtags that were born out of it (e.g. #AllMyLanguagesCount) challenged the government's monolingual ideology and, as a whole, the arguments became more impassioned and critical in highlighting the obvious overt discrimination that is unacceptable in a public official document such as the Census. Many of the comments in Thread 2 (Figure 6.3) make those arguments visible.

CVB: Building off of what Vanja said, we still have bonds with many of those that commented on the threads until today. This is interesting because it shows that it is a bond that connects us. It also makes us question who still is involved in this discussion and in this fight and who left the community or conversation. Vanja and I often talk about who is still there, commenting, liking, reacting and who is not anymore. We wonder why. That is something that also makes us think about our evolving ideas about translanguaging, bilingual parenting, multilingual families, linguistic discrimination that we care about. It makes us think about how our ideas have evolved in dialogue with the other members of the community and with each other. We have noticed that sometimes the discourse tends to be polarized which might make some members of the community leave these circles or form different circles. The core remains, but other people join and people leave. I always wonder about what makes someone join and what makes someone leave. I think it has to do with the core beliefs that we have together.

One Twitter/X strategy that helped keep the community together was the use of hashtags. One of them was #MultilingualismIsNormal created by Cate Hamilton which we always used whenever an issue about linguistic discrimination in multilingual parenting would come up. When the UK Census discussion started, it was such a great contrast between the ways we were using the hashtag #MultilingualismIsNormal which we mainly used for discussions about children being able to use all of their languages to then being able to shift the conversations to a political act. The UK Census conversation looked more like a movement. From there, there was a concerted effort to make the public aware of the linguistic discrimination in the language items of Census questionnaires. We united to make it more official. Led by Thomas Bak, we created a new hashtag #AllMyLanguagesCount which attracted a lot of attention and support.

How do we act on linguistic discrimination through this community?

VK: My main motivation in joining Twitter/X initially was to try and raise awareness of linguistic discrimination relating to accents and dialects, so non-standard varieties in the UK, and to multilingual language use and the myths that exist around the discrimination that bilingual children and their families experience. There are two ways in which we can act on linguistic discrimination through our Twitter/X community and this is highlighted in the interactions in both threads in Figure 6.2 and Figure 6.3: we can share both our opinions and our practice. Obviously, the community, as Clara said earlier, will grow and then will shrink, but what is most important is that we get people to start thinking about issues surrounding discrimination and even if they don't agree fully at least they have been made to consider aspects that they might not have thought of before. However, the issue sometimes is how to reach beyond the community, i.e. how to reach those whose opinions are based on linguicism. Twitter/X allows followers of other people to see posts, which has enabled us to reach people beyond our community as well and hopefully change some opinions and raise awareness around linguistic discrimination.

CVB: Twitter/X provides us with a platform to voice our ideas about linguistic discrimination within a space to share examples and personal experiences. This helps with raising awareness. I remember really feeling attracted to posts sharing stories about people's own experiences with children translanguaging and not following the advice that was given in the Instagram post. Hopefully, like Vanja said, we also reached out outside of the community with examples of how these ideas are flawed and can cause harmful practices towards bilingual children. I remember that following Thread 1 (Figure 6.2), we started sharing other examples of actual linguistic discrimination; for example, children in school not being allowed to use their languages. After the initial stir caused by this Instagram post and the UK Census language in Thread 2 (Figure 6.3), people started to use each other to draw attention to news articles and personal stories. The community started to grow after that. So, I think that the fight against linguistic discrimination intensified because we formed a community around that shared goal of trying to dismantle bilingualism myths and language ideologies. Over the years, though, I feel that some members took different paths. I have increasingly become more aware of issues of racism in language teaching and learning contexts. This, I feel, can be taken as radicalized by some Twitter/X communities. So, I feel I started disconnecting from some while connecting or intensifying my bonds with others. It's interesting to observe these movements.

What makes us react differently to posts or comments: like, comment, retweet? What makes us tag someone?

VK: This is a really interesting question that has made me reflect on how and why I use Twitter/X, how I see myself as part of the Twitter/X community and the role I play. In general, I 'like' posts that I find interesting and agree with, but might not feel that I know enough about the issue in the post to comment on it. In the case of Thread 1 (Figure 6.2), I felt that I wanted to comment on and retweet it because it exemplified the falsehoods that exist about how bilinguals use language and I just couldn't let it remain unchallenged. I commented on it because I wanted to express my opinion both as a linguistic expert and also somebody who is bilingual and to lend my support to others who were also disagreeing with that particular post, which, in turn, created a community of like-minded professionals. I tend to comment on posts I feel passionate about, like the example of the Census language question in Thread 2 (Figure 6.3), and when I want to support somebody who has posted something that I very much agree with, and that needs highlighting and needs other people to see it, such as Thomas Bak's extensive research on monolingual ideologies on a national level. In terms of engaging with others, I tend not to engage with people who are confrontational and deliberately want to challenge in a rude rather than constructive way. It's a form of self-care to avoid a backlash and not have to deal with that. I think that's also part of being on Twitter/X in general. However, this wasn't the case with either post and I would have felt very comfortable if someone had showed support for the falsehood that was posted, as I know a lot about the subject.

CVB: It's interesting to think about these specific practices of Twitter/X now that I feel I am more proficient as I have been part of these communities for one year and a half engaging daily in these conversations. Going back to Thread 1 (Figure 6.2), I was not really aware of the tools of 'liking,' 'commenting' and what difference they would make, especially the nuances. For example, quoting, subtweeting, tagging are very specific practices on Twitter/X. It is really about becoming more knowledgeable of how to participate and how to use these tools effectively. By the time I made my first popular post, I remember that I started tagging Vanja and others in our group whose posts and comments became really tight around these issues. We would tag each other to say, 'Look at this!' It was fun doing that because we knew we were connected. Tagging is an interesting community-building bonding activity and I use it a lot to invite others to join me in a conversation. Concerning retweeting and quote tweeting, I feel it is about highlighting something because when you comment or like something, it is not as visible. When you retweet or quote tweet that gets more attention. We tend to endorse people's ideas by retweeting. You can also quote tweet to say something against the original post. In the case of the Thread 1 (Figure 6.2), although I was not very proficient in doing that yet, 162 people quote tweeted while 81 people quote tweeted Thread 2 (Figure 6.3). These are both high numbers and neither Vanja or I had many followers at that time.

Belonging in Twitter/X as Thinking Communities

Our dialogue has led us to reflect about ways our participation in Twitter/X community conversations on linguistic discrimination affected us as professionals and people. Instead of writing a traditional conclusion, we decided to keep the dialogical nature of our thinking as we assessed and processed our learning and growth.

VK: I continue to enjoy and revel in being part of our community on Twitter/X and eagerly anticipate taking part in our discussions of the issues mentioned earlier. Some people have left and others have stayed, but the core group is still strong, vocal and passionate. Sometimes we have time to immerse ourselves in discussions and other times we are busy, but knowing that there is a community with which you can share your experiences, your passions and your fight is to me, as a professional, extremely empowering and inspiring and you feel that you're making a difference because you have the support of your colleagues. On a personal note, the members of the group have become friends. You become a better person when you can engage with people who you can discuss things openly with, possibly disagree with, but learn from and share important experiences. Having this community has made me a better professional, in terms of being a linguist and a teacher but also a better person overall.

CVB: Thread 1 (Figure 6.2) helped us start and build a community. I think since then it gave me strength to continue on Twitter/X because I feel that there is a community there. I also feel that I have a space to voice ideas that I care about with other people that I know care about it too. So, this sense of community allows us to have a forum to say things that might not be very easy to say in other spaces, such as in academic settings that can be more stifling or a professional context where one might not feel very comfortable sharing these ideas. I feel that Twitter/X has provided me since then with that space where I can say something controversial because I know other people will be in sync with me and support me. If I felt that I would post something and I would only receive opposing opinions or be in a hostile environment, then I would not post anything. However, because I know I have this community, I can say it. This feeling and thinking have helped me so much as a person and as a professional. As a person, I feel more vocal. It has helped me with speaking up about what I believe in. In addition, on the personal level, I have gained friends who are really amazing, like Vanja, with whom I am writing and thinking. We even have virtual coffee! As a professional, I really am grateful because I was able to gain so much insight and resources this year. Twitter/X conversations have helped me rethink a lot of what I am doing in my classes and in my writing. For example, we are writing this chapter as a direct result of participation in this community. Also, due to conversations and thinking being done on Twitter/X, I have changed frameworks and directions in my teaching, impacting the conversations I have with my students. It has been very productive in a very positive way to be part of these communities.

Critical Questions

(1) In what ways have your experiences with linguistic discrimination impacted your identities, language practices, and your relationships with the broader communities to which you belong?
(2) To what extent does the current use of social media illuminate, produce or challenge linguistic discrimination?
(3) Are you a part of any social media online communities? If yes, which ones? What made you join? If not, why not?
(4) How does social media redefine communities and friendships?
(5) In what ways have your online communities helped you grow as a person?

References

Crystal, D. (2010) *The Cambridge Encyclopedia of Language* (Vol. 2). Cambridge: Cambridge University Press.
Ellis, C., Adams, T.E. and Bochner, A.P. (2011) Autoethnography: An overview. *Historical Social Research/Historische Sozialforschung*, 273–290.
Flores, N. and Rosa, J. (2015) Undoing appropriateness: Raciolinguistic ideologies and language diversity in education. *Harvard Educational Review* 85 (2), 149–171.
García, O. and Alonso, L. (2019) 8 The glotopolítica of English teaching to Latinx students in the US. *Worldwide English Language Education Today: Ideologies, Policies and Practices*.
García, O. and Li, W. (2014) *Translanguaging: Language, Bilingualism and Education*. Cham: Springer.
Gee, J.P. and Hayes, E.R. (2011) *Language and Learning in the Digital Age*. New York: Routledge.

Lippi-Green, R. (2012) *English with an Accent: Language, Ideology and Discrimination in the United States*. New York: Routledge.
Otheguy, R., García, O. and Reid, W. (2015) Clarifying translanguaging and deconstructing named languages: A perspective from linguistics. *Applied Linguistics Review* 6 (3), 281–307.
Piller, I. (2017) *Explorations in Language Shaming*. https://www.languageonthemove.com/explorations-in-language-shaming/

Appendix 6.1

Comments to Thread 1 (Figure 6.2)

Comments to Thread 2 (Figure 6.3)

Tweet

60 Retweets 14 Quotes 196 Likes 4 Bookmarks

Gabriele Paleari @PaleariGabriele · Mar 8, 2021
How about people who have been using 4 or 5 languages since childhood, which is far from being unusual?

Dr Vanja Karanović @DrVanjaK · Mar 8, 2021
Well, seems they are being denied a voice.

Show replies

Weronika Ozpolat @MulticultureMum · Mar 7, 2021
So how is everyone filling out this part of the survey? Which language do you choose? Or do you just tick other?!

Dr Vanja Karanović @DrVanjaK · Mar 7, 2021
Good question. I still haven't decided, because neither option is true for me. So I have to lie. How absurd is that???

Weronika Ozpolat @MulticultureMum · Mar 7, 2021
Yes! I will probably tick English coz it's my dominant language but for my husband I have really no idea! He speaks 3 languages in a daily basis.

Dr Vanja Karanović @DrVanjaK · Mar 7, 2021
It's absolutely ridiculous, asking people to ignore a part of them. It's like asking 'Who is your main child?' – your first born, the one you see most often, the one you speak to or play with the most, the youngest, as they are the neediest...?

7 Forming Performative Space through Legitimate Peripheral Participation: Digitally-Mediated Dialogic Inquiry of Four BIPOC TESOL Professionals

Ching-Ching Lin, Derek Baylor, Yasmeen Coaxum and Shuzhan Li

What does it mean to become a BIPOC (Black, Indigenous and People of Color) TESOL professional? To be positioned or to position oneself as a BIPOC TESOL teacher has different implications according to how one is racialized and classified and, consequently, calls for resistance, reinterpretation, agentive investment and strategic action. Challenging and interrogating TESOL teacher identity as an unacknowledged and unexamined norm or position of privilege, which structures our identity and language teaching and learning practices, involves ways of being, a sense of place and belonging, meaning-making, narrative construction, and agentive investment.

In this chapter, we adopt a dialogic approach to examine our identity development, and explore how we navigate our complex, multiple and dynamic identities in the context of a wide range of societal structures and opportunities and how our multidimensional identities impact our personal and professional lives.

Drawing on theories of intersectionality from the lens of Critical Race Theory (Bradbury, 2014; Taylor *et al.*, 2009), this chapter presents a collaborative narrative inquiry of four BIPOC TESOL professionals. Through a process of dialogue, collaborative learning, mutual engagement and support, Ching-Ching, a non-Native English Speaking Taiwanese female, Derek, a Native English Speaking African American male, Yasmeen, a Native English Speaking African American female and

Shuzhan, a non-Native English Speaking Chinese male, engaged in reimagining TESOL practices by reflecting on their journeys from an apprentice in the field of TESOL to a self-identified TESOL professional, and how their journeys have shaped their teaching philosophy, research interests and professional identities. Digitally mediated or recorded dialogue is used to operationalize an intersectional analysis of our identities as embodied and lived experience in an ever-shifting language and professional landscape. Our narratives, understood as performance acts of individual and collective reflection and critical action, are built around our identities as meaning-making and strategy-making embedded at the intersection of language learning, culture, schools, socioeconomic status and power.

Theoretical Frameworks: Identity Negotiation and Performance beyond Intersectionality

Since identities and language practices can only take place within the interlock of mutual recognition and interaction in a space marked by tension, power, strategic mobilization and identity construction (Klein *et al.*, 2007), we have been exploring an intersectional analysis of our identities and framing our professional identity development as performance acts in agentive investment through dialogic interaction. Although there has been a growing body of literature on intersectionality, there are few studies that address how intersectionality can be used in a dialogic context. Therefore, we have also been bringing together different theories in critical tradition to shed light on our professional practices and the greater social implications that underpin them. We focus particularly on how our lived experiences as BIPOC and our journey in TESOL can be analyzed through meaning-making and strategy-making processes informed by spatial, social, and historical power relationships in dialogic interaction.

Intersectionality

Since its emergence in Black Feminist Theory several decades ago (Crenshaw, 2017), intersectionality has become a critical concept and analytical tool for understanding how aspects of a person's social and political identities combine to create different modes in the sociocultural domains (Anthias, 2008; Brah & Phoenix, 2004; Levine-Rasky, 2011; McCall, 2005). As a social construct, intersectionality signals belonging, interconnectedness, systematic oppression and trauma, and accounts for how we perceive and experience the social world may influence the way we think, feel and behave (Yep & Lescure, 2019a). From an intersectional perspective, identities can be characterized as political, historical, dynamic, and form a fluid continuum (Brah & Phoenix, 2004; Levine-Rasky, 2011; Yep, & Lescure, 2019a).

While intersectionality can be useful to investigate how identity, belonging and oppressions are collectively intertwined for minoritized groups, authors like Yep and Lescure (2019a) argue that intersectionality theories may also serve to homogenize people inhabiting similar intersections. For example, in the American educational system, multilingual learners, despite the diversity among them, are often lumped into the same social groups based on seemingly identical identity categories, irrespective of their own life experiences, personal trajectories, individual beliefs and shared memories. Such homogenization contributes to the erasure of their subjectivities and nuanced experiences.

In addition, an essentialized notion of intersectionality tends to oscillate between marked (e.g. poor people, people of color, and in particular those who are non-Native English speakers) and unmarked identities (e.g. White, middle- to upper-class, heterosexually identified, able-bodied, who are mostly Native English speakers), at least, in English-speaking countries. In the process of assimilation, certain characteristics like Whiteness, middle- to upper-classness, heterosexuality, ability, and being native speakers of English are reinforced as the norm. This invisible standard is then used to measure 'other' identities and declare them deviant from the norm (Yep & Lescure, 2019a).

In the context of today's ever-changing language reality, the essentialist approach that is so often seen in mainstream educational discourse fails to capture the complexity and nuances of BIPOC's experience in our current complex world. Reflecting on the interconnectedness between identity, language, and culture for Latinxs and other racialized communities in the United States, authors such as Nelson Flores and Jonathan Rosa (2015) and Yep and Lescure (2019a) brought our attention not only to the need to understand the complex implications of normalized English language teaching and learning for minoritized communities, but also how multiple identities intersect, and strategic social constructions are created through social interaction in shared public spaces. In other words, although intersectionality was conceived as a perspective to focus on the experiences of minoritized individuals and the structures of inequality, when framed as a contained entity, it may fail to authorize the complex, diverse and nuanced experience of the minoritized individuals as embedded in sociopolitical contexts.

Tackling thick(er) intersectionalities

Given the diverse and complex experiences of BIPOC professionals in the field of TESOL, there is a need to understand and capture the complexity of intersectionality dynamics in their public engagement to reauthorize their voices and perspectives through innovative research approaches. We leverage Yep and Lescure's concept of 'thick intersectionalities' (henceforth TI) to highlight more complex and embodied ways of thinking about intersectionality (Yep & Lescure, 2019a).

Inspired by the work of Clifford Geertz (1973) relating to understanding and interpreting cultures, TI highlights the importance of understanding human social action not just as physical behaviors, but as meaning and strategy making processes driven by active agents, in order for us to convey its contextual and cultural specificities in a fuller sense. TI acknowledges that our experiences are always part of social relationships and helps us to develop a deeper understanding of the interplay between individual subjectivity, personal agency, affective investment and structural forces in live interactions.

Building on the concept of TI as developed by Yep and Lescure (2019a), we identify three defining characteristics associated with multidimensional identities of BIPOC TESOL professionals through the lens of TI: first, our identities as a work-in-progress, an ever-evolving process that resists essentialism and 'premature closure of identity' (Yep & Lescure, 2019b); second, our identities as the affective and agentive investments that we make in our identity development; and third, our identities as embodied and lived by us within specific sociopolitical and historical contexts.

Struggling against essentialism and premature identity closure

TI emphasizes that identity is an ongoing and ever-evolving process, one that is more about 'becoming' than 'being' (Yep & Lescure, 2019a). Given the fluid, dynamic and context sensitive nature of becoming, identity (in its thick intersectionality) is a complex process that is always incomplete, open-ended and anchored in future possibilities. Acknowledging the incompleteness and openness of identity development, we will demonstrate these possibilities by elucidating how both the micro-contexts (such as communication settings and interpersonal dynamics) and macro-contexts (such as larger social and structural forces) impact our identity development and how we enact and pursue our agency as we navigate through our professional trajectory in the field of TESOL.

Focusing on the affective and agentive investments of identity performances

TI sees identity development as acts of performance that carry affective and agentive investments that encompass many forms. As such, TI calls attention to the following three affective and agentive aspects of identity development: processes of identification, counter-identification, and disidentification (Muñoz, 1999). Identification is the process of conforming to dominant cultural ideologies, which produces 'good' citizens who accept those ideologies. Counter-identification is the resistance to dominant cultural ideologies, resulting in 'bad' citizens who oppose them. Disidentification is a strategy adopted by individuals that allows them to neither completely conform to nor reject those ideologies: instead, they seek to transform the culture while still engaging in everyday struggles against it (Muñoz, 1999).

These three modes of identity development together represent a nuanced spectrum of individuals' performance repertoire and strategies, that they can employ in seeking to rework and transform dominant cultural and language ideologies as active agents in their own change process.

Understanding identities as embodied within particular sociopolitical and historical contexts

TI hence can help us understand identities as embodied and lived by people within spatial, social and historical relations of power. In this light, we urge for a deeper understanding of the power dynamics in real-time, interpersonal encounters, such as those that occur during structured, critical dialogues. Drawing on Bakhtin (2010) and Feldman (2000) we advocate for dialogue's significance in helping individuals understand each other better, to identify themselves in another while acknowledging their autonomy or difference from the self. Being aware of how power works in conversations and interactions can help individuals comprehend their own privileges. Moreover, it can assist them in recognizing how the intersection of identity, language and power functions on multiple levels, showing them the way to join forces with others to examine, counteract and transform oppressive systems.

Digitally-mediated dialogue

In line with TI, we aim to interweave several frameworks of dialogue into an intersectional analysis of our individual and professional identities. Matsuo (2014) argued that participating in dialogue was a form of political power, as it allowed individuals an opportunity to negotiate social values, options and courses of action. Furthermore, it could create connections between people from varying backgrounds and increase understanding between them.

However, Parsons and Lavery (2012) claimed that the greatest power of dialogue lies not in creating dialogue, but using it to foster further meaning-making and elevate real-world understanding. They studied how filmed dialogues could be used as generators for this outcome. The effects of dialogue didn't come to an end when completed – instead, it had an 'ongoing multiplier effect' as more audiences engaged with it and furthered the discourse (Parsons & Lavery, 2012: 4). Moreover, the dialogue processes can build important relationships among people who did not previously know, trust or empathize with each other, and thus, increase the mutual understanding or abilities to interact with people of different backgrounds.

In this chapter, we define digitally mediated dialogue as a form of critical dialogue that involves using a recorded dialogue to help participants reflect on their perspectives and experiences in a safe and respectful space. This setup allows participants to develop strategies for expressing their identity in a way that is authentic and aligned with their values.

Theorists like Erving Goffman (1959) have proposed that group dynamic relationships can be explored through the way people perform in front of an audience. We further suggested that watching ourselves in a recorded video can help us identify the different identities we take on in our everyday lives. Kapchan (1995) noted that performing could mean carrying out a number of things – such as a story, an identity, an artwork, a remembrance, or an ethnography – into effect. Through this lens, definitions of race, ethnicity, gender, class, age, or ability are all formulated and known by oneself and others via performances which both comply with and challenge social norms (Goffman, 1959; Kapchan, 1995).

Digitally mediated dialogue hence can be used as a method for capturing a strategic making and performance-like nature of self-discovery and identity exploration. Trede *et al.* (2009) describes dialogue as a process of mutual recognition, the ability to see, and possibly share, the 'horizons' of others. Seeing the faces of others is important for recognizing our common humanity and for fostering obligations to listen and respond to other persons respectfully. To allow participants to interact with and contemplate on the thoughts of others, as well as articulating their own views attentively and respectfully, digitally mediated dialogue employs a participant-driven 'co-editing' process, which enables participants in the dialogue to negotiate ways to represent themselves in diverse and real settings.

Based on the preceding literature review, this chapter seeks to use the digitally mediated approach, as outlined above, in a coordinated effort to understand the spectrum of lived experiences of BIPOC TESOL professionals surrounding their identity formation, language experience and power dynamic in the context they navigate.

Intersectionality in Action: Why and How?

Adopting TI as a theoretical framework for our study and digitally mediated dialogue as our primary research method, we formulate our research question as follows:

(1) How do we resist the flat, formulaic, superficial, 'roster-like' approach to intersectionality that contributes to the reification and erasure of our identities and experience as BIPOC TESOL professionals?
(2) How do we account for affective and agentic investments that we make in our identity performances?
(3) How do we understand the intersection of identity, language and power as embodied and lived by people within specific socio-political and historical contexts?

Research method

As discussed previously in the literature review section, we leverage 'digitally mediated dialogue' (through a combined use of various digital platforms such as recorded Zoom meetings, WhatsApp and Google Docs), as a participatory research action tool to explore the interplay of identity, language and power in historical, political and social specificities. Our current study is based on the idea that recorded dialogue can be used to generate and collect data as well as analyze it. By using video recordings of dialogue, we hope to create a space in which new knowledge and opportunities for reflection can emerge. Being aware that our conversations are being recorded makes us feel vulnerable and human. This makes it possible for us to engage in meaningful interactions with one another. As we reflect on our recorded dialogue, we open ourselves up to new interpretations and understandings. Our goal is to remain committed to authenticity, lived reality, multivocality, and accountability throughout this process.

Data

We drew our data from the following three sources:

(1) A brief account of our career paths and how we had grown as TESOL professionals. Our reflections on the information surrounding our individual practices led to further conversations and personal revelations.
(2) Narratives of critical incidents that happened while learning, teaching or using language that highlighted elements of identity, language, and power.
(3) A series of dialogues which were recorded and reflected on as part of a participatory action research project.

Instead of carrying out a traditional coding process in an automated fashion, we used a collaborative dialogue approach for our research. We began by sharing our narratives and each discussion was recorded for us to refer back to and extract themes from for the next round of reflection. As guided by our research questions, we asked each other to review the previous video recordings and explore topics until we felt our conversation had been thoroughly discussed. Our accountability to one another acted as a form of checks and balances.

Data collection and analysis

For six weeks starting in April 2021, we held meetings at two-week intervals, with the occasional disruption from unexpected scheduling conflicts.

We began by discussing key experiences that related to the tensions between identity, language and power within our careers as TESOL professionals. Data collection and analysis go hand in hand as a continuing process: exploring and analyzing data by listening to recordings and reading transcripts to search for patterns among themes and concepts, that could build further conversation topics when compared. An ongoing dialogic approach is taken for each stage, where subthemes are collected and contrasted, then examined to identify points of convergence and divergence in relation to the research questions. We acknowledge there may be various interpretations to any outcome.

Every participant (contributing author) was invited to review their own words in the transcripts of each recorded video, making sure that: (a) the narrative accurately reflected their perspectives; (b) there was a balance between the general narrative and their specific perspectives; and (c) they were comfortable with sharing the words with the public. After creating edited versions of each transcript, every participant reviewed each other's texts individually, considering their meanings and implications, then formed questions, comments and responses to present at our next meeting. This analytical session was also captured on video, analyzed, and reviewed with input from all participants until everyone felt confident enough to share it with the public. Lastly, subsequent analysis meetings included exchanging opinions on how best to present our shared conversations based on the available data.

Intersecting Voices: A Dialogue on Intersectionality

Using recorded dialogue to help us communicate and reflect on our thoughts, analysis of theories related to being educators of color, our critical incidents, and our individual and shared reflection, we (Ching-Ching, Derek, Yasmeen and Shuzhan) have come together to share our experiences as professionals in varied contexts to bring each other out of our respective silo and into a shared space of transparency. All of the above acts play an important role in shaping the discourse of our individual and professional identities and connecting us in ways that empower us as people as well as educators.

Research Question 1

How do we resist the flat, formulaic, superficial, 'roster-like' approach to intersectionality that contributes to the reification and erasure of our identities and experience as BIPOC TESOL professionals?

In the current study, we positioned ourselves as BIPOC as a strategic and intentional stance to resist and transform the interlocking nature of structural oppression that consistently creates a system of hierarchy and othering that benefits some while discriminating against others. We intentionally use the label, BIPOC, not to comply with the norm that we have learned and what is expected of us, but rather to launch a narrative of resistance as well as to further dialogue with people surrounding us. More importantly, we want to participate in collective work to reconstruct, reimagine and, hopefully, alter the cultural and historical practices of the communities that we associate ourselves with.

Here are snapshots of how we grapple with representing ourselves through an array of identity expressions and performances:

Yasmeen's story. As an African American woman, Yasmeen was often told, 'You sound like a White girl.' This statement, usually said in jest, was thrown at her by Latinx strangers in the Bronx, at summer work programs where most of her colleagues were also African American, and by her own cousins from Birmingham, Alabama. In response to these experiences, she consciously pursued a cosmopolitan lifestyle through her career as a TESOL professional. After college, she went right into corporate America and then decided to live abroad. She wanted to be as far away from home as possible but still find support for getting settled in; this led her to Tokyo, Japan and other places before she eventually returned to New York a few years ago. Teaching in the field of TESOL became symbolic of the freedom and adventure Yasmeen cherishes within her – the exploration of new possibilities and experiences.

Derek's story. Derek's story is similar to Yasmeen's in the respect that his career in TESOL gave him the opportunity to journey around the world. As a Hip Hop enthusiast, connoisseur, and practitioner, Derek never expected his travels would influence his efforts to advocate for pedagogical legitimacy, cultural sustainability, and linguistic equity for those in Hip Hop communities of practice. However, when he returned to the United States and attempted to pursue this interest in his graduate studies, one of his advisors informed him bluntly that Hip Hop pedagogies had no place in academia and advised him to choose another research topic. Experiences such as this motivated him to learn more about the unique challenges facing BIPOC scholars and search for different ways to express himself artistically.

Ching-Ching's Story. In contrast with Yasmeen's and Derek's experience, Ching-Ching broadened her world by studying English, and this made her value the internationalizing scope of TESOL as a field. As she embraced the new culture of her adopted society, she also gained a deeper understanding of coloniality in her education. During one pivotal interview for doctoral studies in her earlier years, a White professor suggested that she should pursue research on something taking place in Taiwan so that no one would be able to challenge her authority. Little did he know, his remark had sparked within Ching-Ching a process of questioning and defiance against simply being confined by a particular social label.

Shuzhan's story. Like Ching-Ching, Shuzhan came to the US as an international student in search of a better life and broader perspectives. He recounted his personal transformation from teaching wealthy students in elite academies to dedicating himself to working with immigrant students. It was through witnessing other English language learners that he found his calling – he began to recognize the struggles they faced every day as taking on more of a systematic nature. His journeys down Nolensville Pike, Tennessee, for student teaching gave him insight into the experiences of these immigrant families. He met a mother from Egypt who needed to score a 90 on the TOEFL (Test of English as a Foreign Language) exam to get her pharmacist license recognized in Tennessee. This powerful experience helped shape his identity as a BIPOC professional.

By recognizing each other's experiences – however complex and nuanced – we can see our shared identity as BIPOC emerges in conversations about both similarities and differences in our lives. We also acknowledge the systemic oppression we have endured and continue to endure.

Resisting categorization and the difference fixation

What can be a better way to illustrate the experience of BIPOC than through an 'everyday' experience? In one of our conversations, Derek shared a story where he went into a barber shop in the neighborhood of Columbia University in New York City and was denied the service he wanted, because the barber claimed he did not do his 'kind' of hair. In response, Yasmeen and Ching-Ching suggested that the barber's act of refusal might be due to his lack of the 'specialized' skill in question, that the barber only knows how to treat certain types of hair. However, Derek refused to overlook the underlying theme of exclusion from mainstream society. This incident was not merely due to differences. He further elaborated:

> [B]ecause it's like structural selfishness, because if you were to say that: I only want to do this kind of hair, you wouldn't be able to have the platform to be in that space. If you want to put forth an image that you are inclusive and that you are able to do all of these things, but then, in reality, not do it. That's the issue that I have.

Yet, Derek is reluctant to interpret his barbershop experience as an act of racism/discrimination only. He wrote:

> Additionally, I feel that, very often, when we talk about these things, sometimes people mention the word racism. I very often don't mention the word racism, because it has so many nuances that people don't really address.

Derek explained that when public policies, social practices, cultural representations, and other norms work in various – often reinforcing – ways to perpetuate racial status quo, it allowed privileges to be associated with 'the status quo,' and disadvantages associated with people who don't have the power to contribute to making changes in the system.

Through reflecting on our recorded dialogue together, we examined the intersection of language and identity when it comes to talking about race. Derek shared a cartoon he created depicting a lion out of its element in water trying to explain why it couldn't swim. At the next meeting, Derek proposed the term 'trans-identity' – similar to translanguaging – as a way of describing how people's identities can be hybrid and ever-changing, as Derek remarked: 'there are just different sides of the diamond, and this is part of me and my dialogue with education and identity performativity. They're all different parts of myself that I'm trying to tap into as I try to articulate these things in a different world.'

Yasmeen noticed that, after watching herself on video, she didn't recognize herself in her own words. Watching our dialogue made clear that the languages we choose to identify ourselves with are context sensitive and allow for strategic making. We discussed how racialized language shapes our understanding of identity and how it has affected the way we chose to represent ourselves.

Research Question 2

How do we account for affective and agentic investments that we make in our identity performances?

Elevating the narrative of resistance to a metaphorical level seems to have helped further discourses of our experience as BIPOC and gives us opportunities to examine our life as a conscious effort taken to present ourselves in social interactions.

Through this elevated perspective, we come to see 'identity' as a project or work-in-progress, or an ongoing process of self-invention through a plethora of strategies such as acculturation, resistance, or neither, etc. We draw our inspiration from Erving Goffman's theatrical metaphor theory where, in social situations, we put on a social persona and perform a role in front of the audience, which we perform to move or impress (Goffman, 1959). In discussing Ching-Ching's experience of being characterized as unprofessional when she expressed her discontent about the department's student assessment policies, which she regarded as unfair, Shuzhan wrote:

> That reminded me of the model minority myth. I guess it's sometimes the expectations of a larger society and these expectations, if we think critically of them, they come from problematic roots sometimes. And pushing us into a persona of teacher educator, especially in this field. Unconsciously, maybe, sometimes consciously to speak in a certain way.

To this, Yasmeen Coaxum interjected:

> This should be looked at whether or not you're really morphing into a different persona when you decide to code-switch, or it's just part of the

> multiple layers of who you are. Just because everyone has different kinds of complexities to themselves, to their personalities – so you may choose to speak a certain way within a certain group and a different way within another group – does that mean that you're necessarily morphing into this different persona or just that you're able to be context-appropriate?

Through the virtual space created by digitally mediated dialogue, we reflect on how we have created our alternate identities. The theatrical metaphor of our identity performance, hence, is particularly heightened in the digitally mediated nature of dialogue, since it compels us to become audience conscious, and to work to best represent ourselves.

This is not to say that our identities are manufactured. Rather, the point is that we can deliberately choose to represent ourselves in accordance with different contexts. This is further illustrated in an episode of our dialogue, after we had viewed a recording of our previous dialogue. As an exploration into our various identities, we all shared several pictures of ourselves. Shuzhan shared a picture of him and his little girl at Yellowstone National Park. 'I think this represents me well because I want to try to be a cool father for her,' he said. Ching-Ching interpreted his image as that of somebody who 'invites trust,' always thinking about teaching and his students: 'You take it home, you take it to sleep.'

This activity led us to understand the notion that identity can be fluid, context-dependent and multifaceted rather than fixed. It also prompted us to open a line of inquiry as to the interconnectedness of identity, discourse and power. One important focus in our following conversations is to explore the concept of 'agentic investment', or the idea that we each take responsibilities for how we shape and then engage our identities in both professional and personal settings, and that as educators of color who are from diverse backgrounds, our personal identities cannot be separate from what we bring to the table professionally.

Beyond conformity and resistance

What emerged from our series of dialogue was a plethora of ideas on how we can express ourselves as agents in the way we shape and provoke discussions around our identities. We discussed the possibility of publishing our recorded dialogue as podcast episodes, though have not yet done so. As BIPOC in a world filled with structural racism, we understand that resistance is sometimes the only way forward. Our career paths are focused on eschewing categorization and typical forms of expression such as two-dimensional writing and, instead, replacing them with more inclusive and holistic ways of expressing ourselves. Our lives don't always fit neatly into one category; they contain elements of ambivalence, messiness, openness and complexity that cannot be captured by standard typologies.

Research Question 3

How do we understand the intersection of identity, language and power as embodied and lived by people within specific geopolitical and historical contexts?

We have talked about the mediated role of dialogue that creates a space to allow for alternate portrayals of ourselves, and the agentic roles we enact through social interaction. Disruption and struggle have been a recurrent theme in our conversation. We carry out our struggle by drawing on the repertoires that we have at our disposal, be it emotional, cognitive, linguistic or social. For BIPOC professionals, struggles are constant and ongoing. Yasmeen said,

> I want to mention various ways that people have decided to put us into boxes in terms of language. You know, because each of us have expressed some kind of, I guess, some of these terms, you know there's always some kind of term that someone is trying to impose in our space.

In discussing our experiences as BIPOC, we have often felt caught between a rock and hard place; perpetually trying to be noticed and heard in the face of the dominant narrative. We can find ourselves trapped in conversations that simply perpetuate Whiteness without taking into account the variety of experiences within different minoritized populations. The underlying reality is so much more complex than one might imagine: racism at work, language discrimination, othering, tokenization, essentializing, stereotyping – all our obstacles to overcome in pursuit of recognition and change.

TESOL is a field where race, language, and power are scrutinized. The unmarked status of Whiteness and 'standard' English remains the most important code and any deviation from this norm is seen as imperfect and stigmatized. Ching-Ching reflected on her experience with her dissertation committee: despite being able to communicate effectively, she was criticized for not being 'good' enough based on difference from the norm. Through their collaborative dialogue, she realized that her choice to engage with standard language was an act of identity performance meant to make herself visible or heard depending on how it would be received.

Similarly, reflecting on the idea of going beyond conformity and resistance, Derek proposed that Critical Race Theory can take us further. He wrote:

> It is not surprising that many BIPOC professionals were drawn to Critical Race Theory, because it frames the issues that we share. I feel like there's a space to go after the idea of critical race theory, especially given how many people are muddying the narratives around these terms but, besides that, there are other places that Critical Race Theory can go. And I sometimes struggle with helping to define or trying to define the Critical Race Theory and then also thinking about what else it could do and how to balance that.

We all agree with his sentiment, there's so much we can achieve if we engage in constructive dialogue. Our conversations open up a world of possibilities, allowing us to respond thoughtfully and creatively to unavoidable social constraints while exercising our own individual agency. We can fuse different perspectives together, creating an ever-expanding horizon of understanding.

To sum up, through recorded conversations, we were willing to confront our fragility and humanity. We were made aware that BIPOC are not immune from prejudice and stereotyping by one another. In this chapter, digitally mediated dialogue was engaged as a method of reflection to foster our critical stance. Through collaborative reflection, we formed strong bonds that emboldened us to examine our own accountability within the system. The dialogue demonstrated how our identities are shaped by how we appear to onlookers, or how their view of us provides a reflection of ourselves.

Conclusion

Through six months' constructive dialogue, we, four self-identified BIPOC professionals, shared how we negotiated our identities through our career journeys as TESOL professionals. In our collaborative study into our identity development, digitally mediated dialogue was used as a looking glass for us to explore our intersecting identities more in depth. Dialogue requires a theatrical exchange between speakers and their implied audiences, whose gazes and presence demand our awareness of the others and our active engagement in the process accordingly.

Given the diversity within our group, we were given the opportunities to explore the complexity and nuances within our shared experience and how our identities intersect with other social factors, such as race, linguistic identities, genders, and our own unique life trajectories. However, it also brought to light the dilemmas we are facing in participating in a broader social discourse, when our differences were obscured under the umbrella label, BIPOC. Our dialogue has not only added insight into the complex negotiation process in our claims of self as identity performance but also drawn attention to the complex reflexivity that can be involved in identity performance. We believe that there is much to be gained through the opening of a shared dialogic space where we can construct mutual understanding.

Critical Discussion Questions

(1) Thinking about 'identity' as fundamentally intersectional, we invite the readers to explore what it means to position oneself as a TESOL professional in the field of TESOL. How does the term 'TESOL' capture the multitude of aspects of identities of TESOL professionals, for example, TESOL professionals who are BIPOC, who do not identify

as native speakers of English, who identify as a member of the LGBTQIA community, and who come from other marginalized backgrounds? In other words, what is considered the norm of the TESOL professional workforce? How does exploring the relationship between identity and language in TESOL empower or further marginalize diverse TESOL professionals?
(2) As a field situated in the interconnections of global cultures, languages, and people, the field of TESOL is inherently diverse. However, the TESOL workforce is still predominantly White and the notion of native-speakerism is still privileged in many educational contexts. How do you think the field of TESOL could recruit and retain more diverse TESOL professionals? In what ways can learners in TESOL classrooms benefit from having diverse TESOL educators?
(3) Language sometimes categorizes us and informs our self-concept. What languages do you find confining? What languages do you find liberating and empowering? How did those languages reflect your relationship with others in your communities or society in general?
(4) How can we mobilize our identity and language as resources for learning, in such a way to challenge, to provoke, to inspire and to create dialogue in such a way to give room to others to speak, and for us to listen?
(5) Why is it important to understand identity as a lived experience reflecting our life trajectories embedded in today's complex social reality? How does exploring the intersection of identity, language and power relate to the school and the world? How does it relate to the way we learn and teach?

References

Anthias, F. (2008) Thinking through the lens of translocational positionality: An intersectionality frame for understanding identity and belonging. *Translocations: Migration and Social Change* 4 (1), 5–20.

Bakhtin, M.M. (2010) *The Dialogic Imagination: Four Essays*. Austin: University of Texas Press.

Bradbury, A. (2014) Identity performance and race: The use of critical race theory in understanding institutional racism and discrimination in schools. In R. Race and V. Lander (eds) *Advancing Race and Ethnicity in Education* (pp. 17–31). London: Palgrave Macmillan.

Brah, A. and Phoenix, A. (2004) Ain't I a woman? Revisiting intersectionality. *Journal of International Women's Studies* 5 (3), 75–86.

Crenshaw, K.W. (2017) *On Intersectionality: Essential Writings*. New York: The New Press.

Feldman, R.M. (2000) Encountering the trauma of the holocaust: Dialogue and its discontents in the broszat-friedlander exchanges of letters. *Ethos* 28 (4), 551–574.

Flores, N. and Rosa, J. (2015) Undoing appropriateness: Raciolinguistic ideologies and language diversity in education. *Harvard Educational Review* 85 (2), 149–171.

Geertz, C. (1973) Thick description: Toward an interpretive theory of culture 1973. In C. Geertz (ed.) *The Interpretation of Cultures: Selected Essays*. New York: Basic Books.

Goffman, E. (1959) *Presentation of Self in Everyday Life*. New York: Anchor Books.

Kapchan, D.A. (1995) Hybrid genres, performed subjectivities: The revoicing of public oratory in the Moroccan marketplace. *Women & Performance: A Journal of Feminist Theory* 7 (2), 53–85.

Klein, O., Spears, R. and Reicher, S. (2007) Social identity performance: Extending the strategic side of SIDE. *Personality and Social Psychology Review* 11 (1), 28–45.

Levine-Rasky, C. (2011) Intersectionality theory applied to whiteness and middle-classness. *Social Identities* 17 (2), 239–253.

Matsuo, C. (2014) A dialogic critique of Michael Byram's intercultural communicative competence model: Proposal for a dialogic pedagogy. Comprehensive study on language education methods and cross-linguistic proficiency evaluation methods for Asian languages: Final report, 3–22.

McCall, L. (2005) The complexity of intersectionality. *Signs: Journal of Women in Culture and Society* 30 (3), 1771–1800.

Muñoz, J.E. (1999) *Disidentifications: Queers of Color and the Performance of Politics* (Vol. 2). Minneapolis: University of Minnesota Press.

Parsons, J.A. and Lavery, J.V. (2012) Brokered dialogue: A new research method for controversial health and social issues. *BMC Medical Research Methodology* 12 (1), 1–9.

Taylor, E., Gillborn, D. and Ladson-Billings, G. (eds) (2009) *Foundations of Critical Race Theory in Education*. New York: Routledge.

Trede, F., Higgs, J. and Rothwell, R. (2009) Critical transformative dialogues: A research method beyond the fusion of horizons. In *Forum Qualitative Sozialforschung* (Vol. 10, No. 1, pp. 1–17). Institut fur Klinische Sychologie and Gemeindesychologie.

Yep, G. A. and Lescure, R. (2019a) A thick intersectional approach to microaggressions. *Southern Communication Journal* 84 (2), 113–126.

Yep, G.A. and Lescure, L. (2019b) Development of ethnic identity. In M. Leary and J. Tangney (eds) *Handbook of Self and Identity* (3rd edn, pp. 360–386). New York: Guilford Press.

8 Professional Communities in the Making: Critical Dialogues in the ELT Field

A.R. Shearer and Clara Vaz Bauler

Communities of practice (CoP) are a group of people who come together to engage in collective learning around a shared goal or endeavor (Lave & Wenger, 1991). Establishing and sustaining a CoP is challenging for any educational organization, institution or endeavor. For CoPs to succeed, it is crucial that opportunities for dialogue are created so that old and new members can actively participate in socially-situated ways of constructing and renegotiating knowledge, identity, power and meaning (Lave & Wenger, 1991). Often, as new leadership and interests shift, passion and commitment from members wane. Online environments, especially social media, can be a way to tackle these challenges, moving the dialogue beyond the limitations of a specific time frame and physical space (Schlager *et al.*, 2002).

In order for a group of individuals to be considered a CoP it must satisfy these three criteria: the domain, the community, and the practice (Wenger-Trayner & Wenger-Trayner, 2015). The *domain* may be easily understood as the issue, topic, or interest that brings individuals together. The second criteria is the *community*, which is the actual act of interacting together within the domain. The third and final criteria is *practice*, which comprises the collective knowledge, resources, and repertoires developed by the members located and constructed within socio-historical moments and interactions. One way to gauge the success of CoPs can be through the creation of materials used for educational purposes or as guiding frameworks for those within the community (Yarris *et al.*, 2019).

As members of the English Language Teaching (ELT) field, we were particularly interested in promoting conversations around current race and identity issues surrounding the teaching of English, especially in bi/multilingual contexts. This was not an easy feat, as mainstream conversations in the ELT field have traditionally been marked by disembodied language practices in which linguistic content or teaching strategies are often disassociated from the bodies or humans that enact them (Gerald,

2020; Flores & Rosa, 2015). Notable still is the lack of representation and voice of linguistically and racially diverse ELT professionals in leading workshops, especially keynote speakers in international conferences (Kiczkowiak & Lowe, 2021). There is a pressing need to act towards these inequities by designing, inviting, and promoting more inclusive conversations that are not only led by diverse scholars and professionals, but also focused on centering the concerns and knowledge of marginalized and racialized multilingual students and educators. With this concern in mind, we decided to create a series of webinars via Zoom and conversations on Twitter/X that aimed to be more inclusive and critical of inequities in the ELT field. We did this within the already established CoP – B-MEIS, the Bi/multilingual interest section of the Teachers of English to Speakers of Other Languages (TESOL) International Association.

As the chair of B-MEIS, Clara Vaz Bauler was charged with planning, selecting, promoting, and organizing the webinars and Twitter/X conversations. As a multilingual, minoritized scholar, Clara has experienced the direct effects of marginalization and discrimination towards linguistically diverse teachers and racialized students in ELT. She was determined to use her role to impact concrete change. A.R. Shearer stumbled into the company of Clara Vaz Bauler through the TESOL B-MEIS Twitter/X account. A.R. Shearer joined the B-MEIS community in hopes to get a better understanding of bilingual/multilingual education, the direction the field was heading into, and to increase exposure in this field. A.R. Shearer's role in the online conversations was to help Clara by promoting the events and participating in them.

This chapter will explore how each opportunity for online dialogue unfolded, especially examining our own experiences as participants and organizers. We will look at demographics and characteristics of the participants, what is said or not said, and the differences in participation among the diverse synchronous and asynchronous spaces for dialogue. Through a back-and-forth dialogue and autoethnographic analysis, we inquired into the impact of the opportunities for critical dialogue we designed via webinars and Twitter/X conversations to understand how to promote and sustain a vibrant and inclusive CoP. Particularly, we inquired into the ways participation unfolded and looked, the kinds of online platforms, the identity, cultural, racial, gender, and linguistic differences of the presenters and participants between spaces, types of accessibility, and the outcomes of shifting and centering critical topics such as multilingualism, anti-Black racism, and linguistic discrimination.

Our Observed Community of Practice

The main drive of our work in this chapter is to determine whether we were successful in creating and sustaining our CoP. Concerning the domain, we wanted to move from a variety of issues in bi/multilingual education to center concerns in the intersection of the co-construction of race and language (Flores & Rosa, 2015); that is, the process that renders nouns as verbs in the fluidity of the more dynamic actions of racialization and languaging (García et al., 2021). The community then needed to concentrate efforts in including individual and collective representation of racial and linguistic diversity in leadership as well as membership. The CoP practices needed to expand to involve dialogical spaces that would resist typical traditional lecture styles where most of the participants are listeners of an authority or experts and not participants in the conversation. The work of our CoP focused on dismantling some of these structures.

The goal of an organization's interest session/group is to become an authentic CoP where members share a common goal, concern and/or passion, and work towards improvement or action by interacting and learning together. We chose to look at the already established professional CoP in the TESOL International Interest Section – B-MEIS. The B-MEIS interest group aims to support and promote all multilingual learners' linguistic repertoires and multiliteracy skills as fundamental to the acquisition of a second or additional language. The CoP comprises a hierarchical structure which is composed of a chair, chair-elect, past chair, editors, community managers, historians, and a member-at-large. At the time this chapter was written, the chair was Clara Vaz Bauler, the past chair was Ching-Ching Lin, and the chair-elect was Zhongfeng Tian. The CoP was composed of 796 community members, discussion boards, libraries, and events.

In 2021–2022, we aimed at creating spaces to promote dialogue that would be at the same time critical and celebratory of bi/multilingualism. We built on the work previously started under the leadership of Ching-Ching Lin to counteract dominant discourses, providing alternative spaces for questioning, affirming and decentering monolingualism and Whiteness. Through our Twitter/X account *@TESOLBiMulti* we promoted a series of Twitter/X chats to encourage dialogue on the intersections of race, racism, Whiteness, language(ing), and identity. From April 2021 to December 2021, we offered four Twitter/X chats and five one-hour webinars. The webinars were World Englishes: Diversity, Contexts and Cultures, Learn, Act and Advocate with the CUNY-Initiative on Immigration and Education, TESOL B-MEIS Multilingual Education Chat, Simply Talking: Bringing the World Together Through Discord and Family Language Policies among Quebec-Based Parents Raising Multilingual Infants and Toddlers. The Twitter/X chats were named after their hashtags *#WorldEnglishes, #ELTAfterWhiteness1, #LanguageIsAVerb,* and *#CriticalConversations*. The chats were all-day, 'slow chats,' except for *#LanguageIsAVerb* which lasted seven days. See Table 1 in Appendix 8.1 for a detailed description of each event.

With the leaders, topics, and formats chosen, we intentionally targeted representation of both linguistic and racial diversity and a variety of perspectives. Among the presenters and hosts, we aimed at validating Black, Indian, South Asian, Latinx and other often minoritized and racialized voices and perspectives in ELT. The event leaders and organizers included: Kirti Kapur for *World Englishes*; JPB Gerald for *ELT After Whiteness*; Cynthia Carvajal and Tatyana Klein for *CUNY-IIE*; Vanja Karanović, Eowyn Crisfeld, Cate Hamilton for *Multilingual Education Chat*; Linh Phung for *Simply Talking*; Tasha Austin for *Critical Conversations*; Ruth Kircher, Krista Byers-Heinlein, Susan Ballinger, Linda Polka, Alexa Ahooja and Melanie Brouillard for *Family Language Policies*; and Clara Vaz Bauler, Vanja Karanović, Constanze Ackermann-Böstrom, Malwina Gudowska, Alia Amir as Twitter/X Chat hosts and Ching-Ching Lin, Ruth Kircher, A.R. Shearer, Tasha Austin, María Rosa Brea, JPB Gerald, John Rihalf, Anna Belew, Warda Farah and Madalena Xanthopoulou as organizers and supporters for *#LanguageIsAVerb*. For a detailed list of events, presenter and topic diversity, see Table 1 in the Appendix 8.1.

The format of the events was also intentional to include accessibility both of mode of delivery and of time flexibility to accommodate for different time zones. We also emphasized critical topics, particularly centering conversations that challenged and resisted standardized English, anti-Black racism, Whiteness, monolingualism, language ideologies and linguistic discrimination. These dialogic events culminated with the publication of the Winter 2022 issue of the *Bilingual Basic* TESOL B-MEIS newsletter where we featured four articles written by four webinar and Twitter/X chat leaders – Kirti Kapur, Cynthia Carvajal, Tasha Austin and Lin Phung – and a summary of the *#LanguageIsAVerb* Twitter/X event.

Our Dialogical Methodological Lenses

We chose to observe the Twitter/X account that exists for TESOL B-MEIS – *@TESOLBiMulti*. We used an autoethnography approach so we could include and bring ourselves as individuals into the conversation allowing for intersectional perspectives not generally found in academic literature (Masta, 2018). Autoethnography, from Ellis *et al.* (2010), is the use of our own personal experiences to synthesize or analyze the community being observed. By using this ethnographic approach we are able to better understand our own positionality within the community and how that affects the community and those within the community.

We examined dialogues put on by the TESOL B-MEIS community via their social media presence on Twitter/X under *@TESOLBiMulti* from April 2021 to December 2021. These dialogues took place on a few social media platforms (Zoom, Padlet and Twitter/X) outside the general message board and online platforms hosted by the interest section of TESOL International – B-MEIS. Many of these online platforms afforded participants to freely express emotions through expressive codes via writing, emojis and visuals

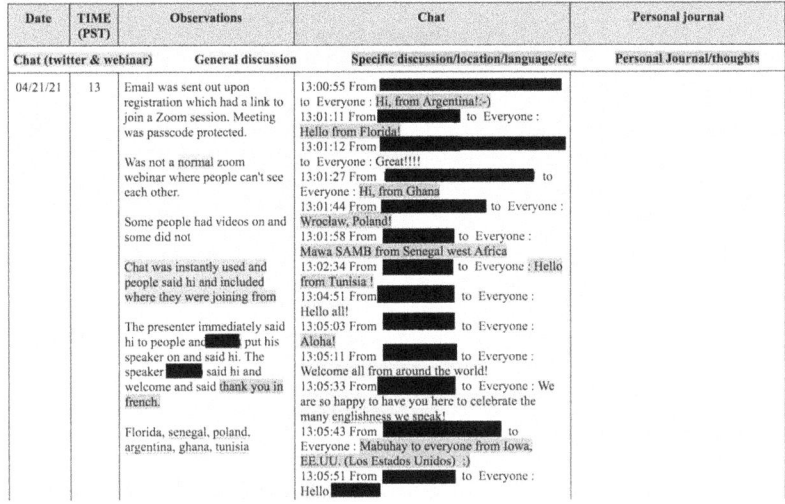

Figure 8.1 Coding for participation

Note. Blue = Chat (Twitter/X & webinar), Yellow = General discussion, Red = Specific discussion/location/ language, and Purple = Personal journal/ thoughts.

(Sade-Beck, 2004). We were interested in examining these platforms in terms of flexibility, engagement and criticality. As a community of practice, we wondered whether the type of digital platform would influence participation and belonging.

How we experienced and interpreted the data was informed by our own positionalities and goals as part of our CoP. Our ethnographic analysis included personal accounts of our experiences and observations that stemmed from epiphanies, notes, and memories (Ellis *et al.*, 2010). We met several times via Zoom and recorded our conversations, which we used as the basis for the arguments we made in the analysis and findings section. Our dialogues on Zoom provided a rich and dynamic autoethnographic record. We also utilized email exchange and comments in Google Documents to share ideas and make meaning of the data and our experiences in the events. Figure 8.1 displays the initial process of ethnographic coding for the events.

Out of the nine events held by B-MEIS we chose one webinar and two Twitter/X chats: B-MEIS Webinar: TESOL B-MEIS Multilingual Education Chat, *#LanguageIsAVerb,* and *#CriticalConversations.* After an initial analysis, we chose these specific events because we felt they generated the most dialogue due to their non-typical structures and their ability to foster engagement from both presenters and participants. These events were also selected because of their ability to facilitate discussions on topics not generally openly discussed among ELT practitioners. Figure 8.2 demonstrates our recursive process of analysis, selection and dialogic inquiry.

Figure 8.2 Analysis, selection and dialogic inquiry sequence chart

Analyzing Our Dialogical Spaces

Multilingual Education Chat

The Webinar: TESOL B-MEIS Multilingual Education Chat had three female presenters, each from a different location and who spoke different languages, with English as the common language of use. Two of the presenters identified as Canadian and British and one as Bosnian. They were all female. The four spectating participants were all female, as well. There were eight participants total in the event, including presenters.

For A.R. Shearer (AR), this webinar was the most engaging, fulfilling, and easiest to attend and participate in, compared with the other webinars. This webinar felt interactive where the other webinars felt stagnant.

Though AR is fully aware that her gender and skin color aligned with that of the three presenters, she did not feel this was the reason for her feelings of ease regarding the webinar. She attributes this to the additional platform (Padlet) used with this webinar and its relaxed nature. AR felt the webinar was intimate, not necessarily because of the small participation turnout, but because presenters and participants spoke freely with each other. This lent itself to a more meaningful and deeper discussion. AR also felt she learned the most in this webinar because it seemed like presenters could take their time discussing the points and ideas brought up by participants' questions.

Clara Vaz Bauler (CVB) was intrigued and grateful for AR's feedback as an active participant. Indeed, she wanted the webinar to be structured differently from the beginning. Together with the presenters, CVB decided for the 'unwebinar' format where participants could post their ideas prior instead of during the event. Presenters could then use the questions posed to guide the conversations. This flexible format afforded participants the chance to be more active in the conversations. We made the digital board in the form of a Padlet available on Twitter/X via @*TESOLBiMulti* for possible participants to ask questions. Figure 8.3 shows the digital board made with Padlet which supported the alternative format of the 'unwebinar' with questions on the left and presenter bios on the right.

As a participant, AR feels the webinar also was enlightening in that it had monolingualism come up in different ways throughout the discussion. Cate, one of the presenters, was empathetic toward monolingual learners and touched on providing these learners with skills that allowed them to see value in their language and that of others. Presenter Vanja also brought up monolingualism, but rather in the matter of policy practices in education, such as the monolingual model and how this model hinders

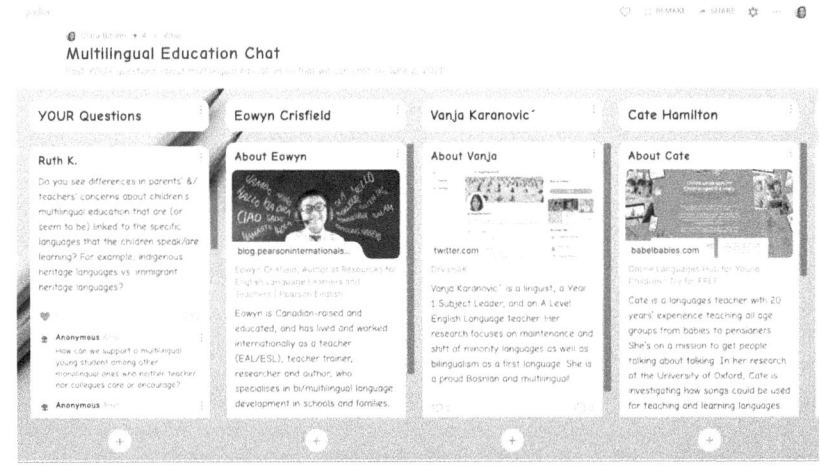

Figure 8.3 Multilingual Education Chat Padlet digital board

bilingual and translanguaging practices. The focus on a concern about monolingual ideologies can be seen in the questions posed by participants which involved critical issues of language maintenance and promotion among marginalized indigenous communities, immigrant children and university students in higher education. The topic did not seem to get pressed further, which means there may have been missed opportunities to see how these two comments are connected. This was something AR immediately noticed during the presentation, but, given her position as an early career ELT participant who lacks confidence in these settings where you do not know anyone personally and you're unable to read body language and facial language, was unable to bring awareness to this missed opportunity. As an organizer, CVB wondered about the impact of AR's sentiments on event participation and promotion. CVB feels the topics and questions could have reached a wider variety of perspectives given a broader and more diverse audience.

#LanguageIsAVerb

The slow Twitter/X chat *#LanguageIsAVerb* consisted of seven days of discussions. Each day was met with a unique question for that day which participants could interact with and discuss further. This Twitter/X event was particularly unique in that, in its creation, an Affinity Group (AG) was formed. Fifteen individuals were invited to join based on our aim for the event. These 15 individuals varied in location, cultural, racial and linguistic backgrounds, with English being the primary source of communication. Additional considerations were made due to their involvement with anti-racism, anti-colonialism, and other social justice issues in the field of ELT and bi/multilingual education. The formation of this group also included a Google Document that outlined the event and was a place where ideas and thoughts could be noted. This event was the first in the series to garner large participation and this may be due to the collaboration with the 15 individuals in the group chat, as well as participation from those more prominent in the field of ELT or Linguistics.

For AR this involvement in the small group chat allowed her to learn more about other scholars in the field in a natural, more holistic, manner as well as create a place where she didn't feel isolated within the bigger B-MIES online community. Being close to other prominent scholars in the field helped expand her thinking on what could be possible in the classroom, in the community, and academically. It made it easier to participate without self-doubt. The creation of this AG, and the impact it had on the authors, alludes to the importance of such practices. Figure 8.4 below displays the schedule of daily prompts for the event.

Participation in this seven-day event attracted individuals from all over the world, at various stages in their life journey and careers, from various cultural, racial and linguistic backgrounds, and increased gender

Professional Communities in the Making: Critical Dialogues in the ELT Field 115

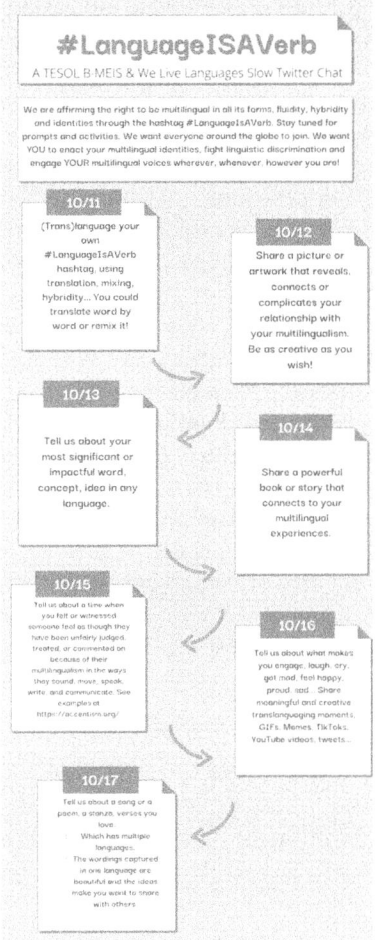

Figure 8.4 #LanguageIsAVerb prompts

diversity. According to Twitter/X Analytics, the 7-day average of impressions (i.e. number of times users saw the tweets) ranged from 30,000 to 40,000, with engagement (i.e. retweets, replies, follows and likes) ranging from 576 on the first day, 447 on the second day, 490 on the third day, 284 on the fourth day, to the peak of 1,217 on the fifth day, and then 377 and 371 on the sixth and seventh day, respectively.

As an organizer, CVB felt the large participation shed hope on the possibility of events that are at the same time celebratory and critical of the many experiences surrounding multilingualism. CVB was concerned in making the event a space for multilingualism to be expressed via multimodalities as a way to naturalize multilingualism in ways of being, knowing and doing. CVB and AR both felt that by allowing participants to share video, images, drawings, poems, etc., participants were able to use various modalities to express themselves outside of the 280 character limit on Twitter/X. However, one flaw in this was accessibility, specifically for those who utilize screen readers, since none of the images posted had alternative text written.

In particular, the fifth day stood out in our analysis for the huge participation with 110,972 impressions, 1,217 engagements, and the nature of its topic which asked participants to share experiences of linguistic discrimination, biases and racism they faced and witnessed. Figure 8.5 shows examples of posts on Day 5.

AR feels *#LanguageIsAVerb* was the heaviest regarding the subject and filled with the most self-reflection. She was able to read the experiences of people regarding their heritage languages or their bi/multilingualism and see how they embraced these identities despite the prejudice and discrimination. She saw the laughter, joy, and artwork that came out of these various bi/mutlilingual identities. It was wonderful to see so many individuals embrace their bi/multilingualism, but for her, and potentially others, it is still really difficult because of who raised us, how we were raised, and the state of the world currently to embrace these bi/multilingual identities. It creates another type of self-doubt and isolation, especially if we as teachers are supposed to lead by example and give to our

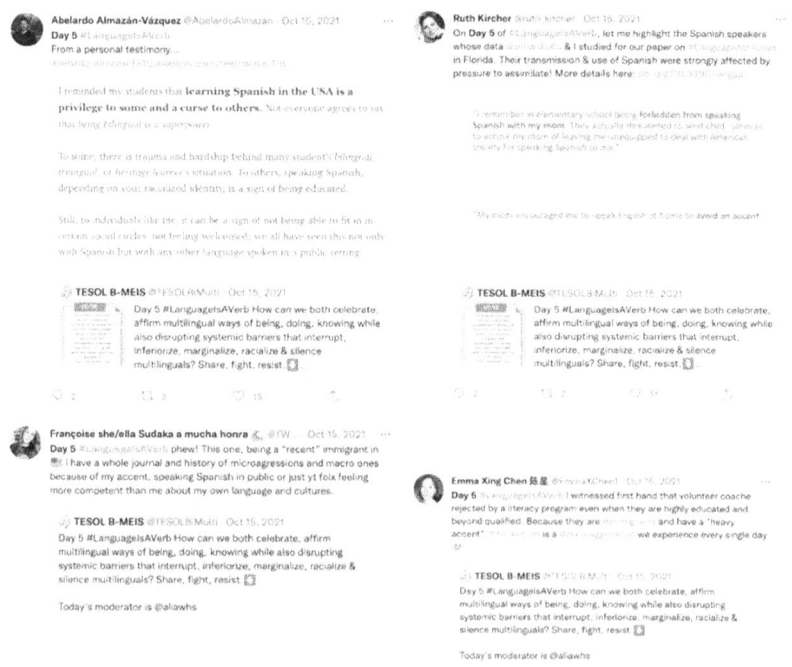

Figure 8.5 Linguistic discrimination experiences on Day 5 of #LanguageIsAVerb

students what we are asking them to do. It can make one feel fraudulent in their identity. For AR, there is still a lot of pain from generational trauma and ongoing trauma that makes embracing this identity difficult. Something like *#LanguageIsAVerb* allowed individuals, like herself, the ability to explore identity and what it means and what it looks like. It, in turn, allowed others to observe and learn and start to gather what it means, feels, and looks like for them. The event was successful at naming linguistic racism and discrimination and empowering others to keep sharing and keep posting.

#CriticalConversations

#CriticalConversations was facilitated by Dr Tasha Austin, who was very present throughout the conversation and actively commented on everyone's postings. Dr Tasha Austin's research uses Critical Race Theory and Black Feminist epistemologies to qualitatively examine language, identity and power. The focus of *#CriticalConversations* was intentional on countering anti-Blackness in language education. We made it a 24-hour slow chat to expand participation and accessibility. The participants for this conversation were from various locations, though it seemed most were currently located in the US and from various cultural backgrounds. It was an extremely successful event in terms of participation with an average of 20,000 impressions and 200 likes or retweets for each of the six questions posed. Figure 8.6 displays the Twitter/X call with the six prompts.

Countering anti-Blackness is rarely done overtly and directly in ELT. CVB thinks that the leadership provided by Dr Tasha Austin was crucial,

Figure 8.6 #CriticalConversations Twitter/X invitation

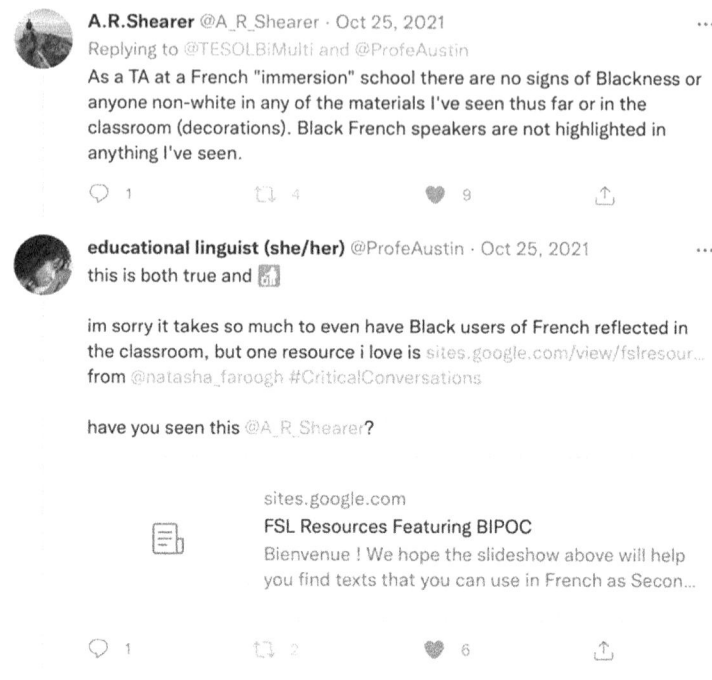

Figure 8.7 AR and Tasha Austin share in #CriticalConversations

given her experience as a podcast host (Austin, 2021) activist, language educator and scholar. There was a fundamental sense of community where Black joy, liberation and brilliance were centered. This was made evident in the many resources shared at the culmination of the event. AR feels that participants appeared to be very open and honest with the responses toward the prompted questions. AR noticed there were some participants who mentioned the lack of support for Black learners in ELT and other multilingual educational fields of practice. Due to the small group chat formed and the success of #LanguageIsAVerb, AR felt more comfortable being present and posting her own experiences in the classroom. AR is glad she felt confident enough to interact with this event as it provided her with invaluable resources for her next classroom experience. Figure 8.7 shows AR's interaction with Dr Tasha Austin in addressing question #2 about examples of anti-Blackness in participants' experiences.

Dismantling Traditional Structures Via Our CoP

In this section, we reflect on what we learned from our analysis in moving forward with initiatives that center concerns in the intersection of racialization and languaging. At the beginning of our journey, we determined that we needed to be intentional about including individual and collective representation of racial and linguistic diversity in leadership as well as membership. We also identified the need to create dialogical spaces that would resist typical traditional lecture styles. Our guiding questions during our observation and discussion, which still guide us today are as follows: Were we successful? Were we able to dismantle some of the existing structures that could hinder our aims? If so, in what ways?

Examining further why the webinar Webinar: TESOL B-MEIS Multilingual Education Chat was successful at providing an atmosphere of sharing and learning, the use of the additional online platform Padlet was essential for promoting a dialogic space. With the use of Padlet, users were able to participate when they felt comfortable doing so and on their own time, which is not common in traditional webinars, presentations, or how knowledge is shared and presented. Padlet afforded participants anonymity, time, and accessibility to write their questions prior to the event. However, the webinar was unable to delve deeper into monolingualism and its role in translanguaging and bi/multilingual education; this may mean that this medium – Zoom – was not conducive for this type of deconstruction of thought. It was good at bringing these ideas to the surface, but not the best at being able to dissect them further. This may be where a platform like Twitter/X or Padlet comes in. Perhaps Padlet could be used further as the vehicle webinars need to help facilitate deeper exploration of thought by replacing the use of the chat feature on Zoom with Padlet. This way, participants all have anonymity, which may curb the feelings of insecurity attached to students and early career participants in these dialogic spaces. This also allows participants the ability to engage at their pace by allowing the Padlet to exist pre- and post-webinar/presentation.

Looking further at *#LanguageIsAVerb*, we saw the creation of a potential AG in the form of a 15-member Twitter/X group chat. This group of individuals may be one of the main reasons why this particular Twitter/X chat saw the most participation among all the events; there were more individuals personally invested and involved in leading the organization, promotion, and engagement in the dialogue. The highly multimodal aspect of the prompts might also have encouraged participation. Day 5 of the event presented participants with the most intimate question asked of them. Given the popularity and delicate nature of this topic, we learned that future events could develop a survey to ask everyone who participated about the ways the prompts were designed as well as the emotions triggered/activated in sharing personal and possibly traumatic experiences. Survey results might better tell us if people are in need of spaces to share their painful experiences. We could also follow up by providing participants with tools for fighting back against linguist discrimination.

With #*CriticalConversations* we were able to see the CoP come to life and one way was through the creation of a resource-sharing document for anyone with access to the *@TESOLBiMulti* community on Twitter/X. This was one way we could measure the success of the CoP through the knowledge gained and shared amongst community members (Wenger-Trayner & Wenger-Trayner, 2015). CoPs are understood to provide to those in the community the ability to have a deeper or better understanding of the topics discussed in the group. We saw this unfolding through participant responses and interactions with each other and the presenter. Participants seemed more aware of themselves in relation to anti-Blackness in ELT and global anti-Blackness. More participants cited self-reflection as a way to counter anti-Blackness in language. CB and AR also saw this unfold in our own lives and participation within the community. AR was provided tools, resources, and encouragement to keep pushing for the inclusion of Black lives and voices in the French language classroom.

In reflecting back on our dialogic journey as participants, organizers, and researchers, we feel the *@TESOLBiMulti* events allowed for learning and sharing, and, in this respect, we were successful. However, we feel that the high engagement of some of the events, especially #*CriticalConversations* and #*LanguageIsAVerb* did not extend to sustaining the CoP as a whole. There is much work to be done to establish the entirety of the CoP as a space where there is consistent participation and action from diverse individuals and perspectives. It is only when we are able to have that consistency that we will be able to truly dismantle some of the existing structures that frequently hinder critical efforts in the ELT field. Future studies can look at how CoPs and AGs can become vehicles for systemic change outside of the more established institutions, challenging organizations.

Critical Questions

(1) Do you belong in a community of practice? If so, how active are you? If not, why not?
(2) What is your experience regarding attending events with diverse (e.g. linguistic, cultural, racial, gender, etc.) presenters, participation, and topics? Do you feel represented? Do others also feel represented? In what ways?
(3) In what ways does event organization impact participation and dialogue? What is your experience with different face-to-face and online platforms?
(4) Have you ever organized an event or led a community of practice? If so, what was your experience? If not, would you like to? Why?
(5) What could be done to help sustain and promote communities of practice?

References

Austin, T. (Host) (2021–2022) *Critical Conversations with NJTESOL-NJBE*. Video podcast. YouTube.

Ellis, C., Adams, T.E. and Bochner, A.P. (2010) Autoethnography: An Overview. *Forum Qualitative Sozialforschung/Forum: Qualitative Social Research* 12 (1). https://doi.org/10.17169/fqs-12.1.1589

Flores, N. and Rosa, J. (2015) Undoing appropriateness: Raciolinguistic ideologies and language diversity in education. *Harvard Educational Review* 85 (2), 149–171.

García, O., Flores, N., Seltzer, K., Li, W., Otheguy, R. and Rosa, J. (2021) Rejecting abyssal thinking in the language and education of racialized bilinguals: A manifesto. *Critical Inquiry in Language Studies* 18 (3), 203–228.

Gerald, J.P.B. (2020) Worth the risk: Towards decentering whiteness in English language teaching. *BC TEAL Journal* 5 (1), 44–54.

Kiczkowiak, M. and Lowe, R.J. (2021) Native-speakerism in English language teaching:'native speakers' more likely to be invited as conference plenary speakers. *Journal of Multilingual and Multicultural Development* https://doi.org/10.1080/01434632.2021.1974464

Lave, J. and Wenger, E. (1991) *Situated Learning: Legitimate Peripheral Participation*. Cambridge: Cambridge University Press.

Masta, S. (2018) What the grandfathers taught me: Lessons for an Indian Country Researcher. *The Qualitative Report* 23 (4), 841–852. https://doi.org/10.46743/2160-3715/2018.3254

Sade-Beck, L. (2004) Internet ethnography: Online and offline. *International Journal of Qualitative Methods* 3 (2), 45–51.

Schlager, M., Fusco, J. and Schank, P. (2002) Evolution of an online education community of practice. *Building Virtual Communities: Learning and Change in Cyberspace* 129, 158.

Wenger-Trayner, E. and Wenger-Trayner, B. (2015, April 15) Communities of practice: A brief introduction. *Introduction to Communities of Practice*. https://wenger-trayner.com/introduction-to-communities-of-practice/

Yarris, L.M., Chan, T.M., Gottlieb, M. and Juve, A.M. (2019) Finding your people in the digital age: Virtual Communities of Practice to promote education scholarship. *Journal of Graduate Medical Education* 11 (1), 1–5.

Appendix 8.1

Table 1 *Dates, Topics and Lead Presenters for TESOL B-MEIS April–December 2021 Events*

Date	Topics/Themes	Modality	Lead Presenter(s)/ Host(s)	Bios
April 21, 2021	World Englishes	Zoom Webinar & Twitter/X Chat	Kirti Kapur	Professor **Kirti Kapur**, a Fulbright Fellow, is an ELT expert and teacher trainer who has 33 years of experience in English language teaching. With over 100 papers (presented and published) to her credit, she has contributed to national and international studies on cultural contexts and TESOL.
May 18, 2021	CUNY-IIE	Zoom Webinar	Tatyana Kleyn Cynthia Carvajal	**Tatyana Kleyn** is Associate Professor and Director of the Bilingual Education and TESOL Programs at The City College of New York. She is the Principal Investigator for CUNY-IIE, served as president of the New York State Association for Bilingual Education, and was a Fulbright Scholar in Oaxaca, Mexico. **Cynthia Nayeli Carvajal, PhD.** is the Project Director for CUNY-IIE. Originally from Guadalajara, Mexico, she immigrated to East Los Angeles, CA at five years old. Her personal and professional goals are grounded in her experience as a formerly undocumented immigrant for twelve years of her life.
June 2, 2021	Multilingual Education Chat	Zoom (Un)Webinar	Vanja Karanovic, Eowyn Crisfeld, Cate Hamilton	**Vanja Karanović** is a proud Bosnian and multilingual linguist, a Year 1 Subject Leader, and an A-Level English Language teacher. Her research focuses on maintenance and shift of minority languages as well as bilingualism as a first language. **Eowyn** is Canadian-raised and educated, and has lived and worked internationally as a teacher (EAL/ESL), teacher trainer, researcher and author, who specializes in bi/multilingual language development in schools and families. **Cate** is the founder of Babel Babies and a languages teacher with 20 years' experience teaching all age groups from babies to pensioners. In her research at the University of Oxford, Cate is investigating how songs could be used for teaching and learning languages.
June 10-11, 2021	#ELTAfterWhiteness1	Twitter/X Chat	JPB Gerald	**JPB Gerald** is an EdD candidate at CUNY – Hunter College in Instructional Leadership, and a theorist seeking justice for the racially, linguistically, and neurologically minoritized. He identifies as Black and neurodivergent. His scholarship focuses on the harm caused by the centering of Whiteness in language education.

October 11–17, 2021	#LanguageIsAverb	Twitter/X Chat	Clara Vaz Bauler, Vanja Karanović, Constanze Ackermann-Böstrom, Malwina Gudowska, Alia Amir	**Clara Vaz Bauler** has a PhD. in Education with emphasis in Applied Linguistics and Cultural Perspectives and Comparative Education from the University of California, Santa Barbara. She advocates for the naturalization of multimodality in language teaching and learning spaces via digital media technology. **Vanja Karanović** is a proud Bosnian and multilingual linguist, a Year 1 Subject Leader, and an A-Level English Language teacher. Her research focuses on maintenance and shift of minority languages as well as bilingualism as a first language. **Constanze Ackermann-Böstrom** is a sociocultural linguist with an interest in multilingualism, minoritized languages and language revitalization. Her current research focuses on young Tornedalians, (Swedish) Kvens and Lantalaiset, their linguistic practices and attitudes towards Meänkieli. **Alia Amir** is a social interaction researcher. Her research and teaching interests lie at the intersections of applied linguistics, sociolinguistics and language policy. **Malwina Gudowska** is a Polish-Canadian writer, editor and linguist based in London, UK. She is a linguist currently working on her PhD in Applied Linguistics with a focus on multilingualism and motherhood.
October 18, 2021	#CriticalConversations	Twitter/X Chat	Tasha Austin	**Tasha Austin** is a PhD candidate in Language Education at Rutgers University. She is the Teacher Education Special Interest Group Representative for NJTESOL-NJBE and co-created and hosts their "Critical Conversations" podcast. Her research uses Critical Race Theory and Black Feminist epistemologies to qualitatively examine language, identity and power.
October 19, 2021	Simply Talking	Zoom Webinar	Linh Phung	**Dr. Linh Phung** has been teaching English to EFL students and international students in the US for over 15 years and is currently the Director of Eduling International Academy, which offers online English courses to students from any location. Her research interests include L2 language pedagogy, task-based language teaching, and international education.

(continued)

Table 1 (continued)

Date	Topics/Themes	Modality	Lead Presenter(s)/Host(s)	Bios
	Family Language Policies	Zoom Webinar	Ruth Kircher, Krista Byers-Heinlein, Susan Ballinger, Linda Polka, Alexa Ahooja, Melanie Brouillard	**Ruth Kircher** is a researcher at the Mercator European Research Centre on Multilingualism and Language Learning, which is part of the Fryske Akademy in Leeuwarden (Netherlands). Her research focuses on societal multilingualism, with a particular interest in language attitudes and ideologies, language practices, and language policy and planning – especially in relation to minority language communities. **Krista Byers-Heinlein** is a Professor in the Department of Psychology at Concordia University, where she holds the Concordia University Research Chair in Bilingualism and Open Science, and directs the Concordia Infant Research Lab. Her research focuses on language acquisition and cognitive development, with a focus on bilingual infants and toddlers. **Susan Ballinger** is an Associate Professor of Second Language Education at McGill University. Her research focuses on bilingual education contexts. **Linda Polka** is a Professor and Graduate Program Director in the School of Communication Sciences & Disorders at McGill University, where she trains clinical and research students. Her research focuses on development of speech perception and production during infancy, with a special interest in infants growing up in bilingual families. **Alexa Ahooja** is a Ph.D. candidate in the Language Acquisition Program at McGill University. Her research interests include the inclusion and experiences of bi/multilingual students in Québec schools. **Melanie Brouillard** is a doctoral student in Clinical Psychology at Concordia University, in Montreal. Her research investigates how to best support the language development of bilinguals. **Nicola Phillips** is a Ph.D. student in Communication Sciences and Disorders at McGill University. She is interested in the qualitative aspects of adult-infant interactions in multilingual families. **Erin Quirk** received her Ph.D. in Linguistics from the Graduate Center of the City University of New York and is currently a postdoctoral fellow at the Concordia Infant Research Laboratory. Her research investigates multilingual children's language use and exposure in relation to their language development.

9 Escaping the H-Index: On the Value and Voice of Public Engagement for Racialized Scholars

JPB Gerald and Clara Vaz Bauler

Language education, in all its forms, is tied to various axes of oppression and social hierarchies, and unfortunately, academia is complicit in reifying the ideologies upholding these discrepancies. Indeed, it is in fact, a primary source of the epistemology that justifies their perpetuation. One of the ways that academia holds these hierarchies in place is through the system of academic publishing and its connection to power, prestige, and promotion. The H-Index is a system where the value of a researcher's work is calculated based on a specific quantitative metric that combines the number of publications and citations a study receives. A paper considered high on the H-index is highly cited and highly achieving in academic circles (Hirsch & Buela-Casal, 2014).

As a racialized scholar and language educator, I (Gerald) have learned through both my professional experience and my studies that following the prescribed path and chasing the vagaries of the H-Index was not only unlikely to provide me with a better chance of the type of potential academic career I might have wanted, but also was certain to silence the authorial voice I have attempted to cultivate. Instead of aping the style of prestigious journals, I instead opted to position myself as a more public scholar, developing a podcast and a social media presence that focus on my research interests of language education, racism, Whiteness, and ability, and, though I do have a handful of traditional journal articles – including one on decentering Whiteness (Gerald, 2020) that informs my contributions to this essay – I have made considerably more progress (e.g. keynote speeches, book contract) in establishing myself in this way than I would have had I followed the path set out before junior academics.

I (Bauler) have also been frustrated and disappointed in the academic publication process of what is considered 'more prestigious' journals. As a minoritized, racialized, foreign, multilingual writer, I often feel my writing is more judged by what it 'should' look like than what it actually says. Because of that, I have been engaging in alternative ways of publishing and sharing my ideas. Social media, especially, has allowed me to not only speak to a wider audience, but also expose my ideas more, having people directly critique or align with what I voice without feeling silenced by the overt and underexamined 'authority' of highly cited journals and peer review practices.

In this chapter, we adopt a critical lens to ask the potentially unanswerable question of the relative value of public engagement as an alternative publication path for racialized scholars. Through dialogue, we examine our own stances and frameworks, assessing the impact of our ideas and experiences in shaping our academic publication journeys. Through Critical Discourse Analysis, we investigate the effect of using satirical graphics as an alternative to sharing and communicating our work in academic circles and beyond. We discuss and attempt to determine, to the extent that it is possible, whether the decision to mostly eschew the beaten path is viable and advisable for all racialized scholars, to the point that we might overpower the H-Index through our collective action, or if our own good fortune is just good fortune indeed.

Our Stances and Guiding Frameworks

We come into this point of our academic journey marked by a series of traumatic experiences that have shaped and informed how we feel about the H-Index measures and associated academic practices. The following section is excerpted from an analytic discussion about our experiences and attempts to break from the H-Index, and then moves into how we decided we would benefit from challenging these ideals together, a progression from disillusionment to productive collaboration. We use a non-standard, fluid, and hybrid discourse to reflect our individualities, positionalities, and the proximity of our friendship and collegiality (Baker-Bell, 2020). This intentional choice of language(ing) also works to counteract the typical academic genres and standardizing currents that have often oppressed and nullified our uniqueness, ideas and ideals (Canagarajah, 2021). Below we share our dialogical process, making visible our framework through a reflective conversation about our frustrations, our individual efforts, and our move towards collaboration.

Initial frustrations

Clara Vaz Bauler (CVB): I feel that every time I write, I have to be vigilant not to be too much who I am, standardizing my whole self, playing a hurtful guessing game to adhere to political, ideological hidden norms. Everywhere there are marks of my multilingualism that are often seen as defects, errors that need to be purged so that my work fits the academic 'style' of selected publications. Because of that, I haven't had much luck with writing in typical traditional journals. I often feel I get a lot of rejections, and when I get comments on my work, they usually don't match the intention of the work. It's difficult to distinguish whether it's political or if it's something about what my text looks like. For example, I'm never sure if the reviewer comments are about a critical methodology I am using which might not be in line with a journal's political direction, or if the reviewers feel there are so many errors that I don't have the ability to write 'well' in English. Most of the time, I really hesitate before I submit something.

JPB Gerald (JPBG): One of the things that is interesting to me is that I didn't know that the H-Index existed until I was already a doctoral student. Obviously, I knew that journals existed, but I didn't realize that there was a hierarchy of journals at all. I didn't know anything about the different levels of prestige - in fact, I thought it was *all* prestigious, and if you got into any journal, you should be commended. In my program, they told me that these are the gold standard. The more I learned about critical methodologies and different axes of oppression and exploitation and the fact that, of course, nobody gets paid except for the companies ... I realized that it was all nonsense. That doesn't mean there isn't really good work in journals, but the more I've learned, the more disillusioned I have become. Like you, I hesitate now to submit, and I'm not even nearly as far into my career as you are, so I got jaded very quickly. I don't at this point expect to randomly submit to any journals, because, like you, my style and my aims tend not to fit what other scholars are looking for and when I get comments back, they're much more about the way that I'm writing, and they are not about the actual argument I'm making. I would much prefer people engage with my argument and tell me how to make it stronger than to have a problem with the words that I'm using – as if I did not make these choices deliberately – so I think that the journal system prioritizes a certain type of thought but that they use a certain type of languaging as a proxy for that type of narrow ideology.

CVB: Yes, there is this idea that is widespread if you don't publish in those journals, and if you don't publish a lot as a single author, your scholarship does not count. Then, you realize, as someone trying to resist a lot of these ideas that are mainstream in academia, that you don't align with most of what is said in those journals. Especially, if you are someone that does not speak standardized[1] English, you are always behind in their expectations. Plus, the typical style and discourse found in academic journals are much more aligned with quantitative research, which has its own language. If you were not part of that group, reviewers and editors try to mold your language. Even if they want to accept your paper and your ideas, they will try to mold it to fit right in the language of that journal. That has happened to me so many times before. I had to change so much of what I wanted to say to fit in and be published.

JPBG: Early in my program, they told us to look at certain journals within our subject matter and their style, which has come up a few times in comments I've received. Now for certain things this makes sense - if you're in a Canadian journal, they would prefer you spell 'labour' with a 'u,' that sort of thing, not a big deal. But far too many journals use what seem to be innocuous comments about protocol as a way to keep out innovative ideas and action. This is a particular challenge for language scholars because there are a lot of people in the language world who are really emotionally tied to standardized language ideologies, and they'll think that what they're doing is revolutionary, but because they're so tied to the standardized languaging, they won't allow truly groundbreaking work to emerge. Now, it sometimes does anyway, or else translanguaging, that is, the idea that bi/multilinguals' use of language transposes and transgresses linguistic borders (García & Li, 2014), would never have emerged as a concept, but even that is frequently dismissed by a certain subset of scholars preferring to be obtuse. In other words, the way that people comment on languaging as a way to dismiss ideas without having to take the risk of actually commenting on the ideas is something that we need to bring forth in this work.

Individual efforts and social media

CVB: I have been trying to break free from these constraints in publishing in 'highly cited' journals via publicizing and sharing ideas using different media. For example, I have been using social media just to put ideas out there. When I'm thinking and reflecting about something in my daily life, I use social media to test it, to see what people will say and how they react to it. In contrast, what happens in traditional journal writing is that we have to follow a certain format. We have first to introduce the topic, then we have to connect to existing literature and share our analysis, findings, and results. All of that takes a lot of time and energy. Before you even get to the part where you put your ideas out, you have already taken a step back. Although I believe ideas are always in dialogue with each other (Bakhtin, 2010), having to back up our claims with previous research every time we say something is a form of standardization of our ideas as well. Social media is a very different genre that allows my thinking to go more freely. I also feel that people are less vigilant about how I say things. I often make many grammatical mistakes and typos, and people don't care. Social media, Twitter/X specifically, has allowed me to be more free to put my ideas out there.
JPBG: In my first semester of my doctoral program, my dean suggested that I use Twitter/X to connect with people. I did not believe him, but he turned out to be right. So not only is it true that you don't have to be as polished, but on the plus side, once I started to get out and gain a following in the language and race space, I think about it with the critical

scholars that I engage with in mind. For new ideas, I test them through the scholars that I engage with and trust. I basically put out brand new things that aren't yet a fully-formed thought, and I'm just sort of workshopping it like a comedian. If I see that something gets a big response on Twitter/X sometimes, I realize that I should write about it in more detail, and if it doesn't get any response from people who are right in my wheelhouse, then the general public probably isn't going to like it either. I'm much more compelled by what the people who pay attention to me on Twitter/X believe than the anonymous journal reviewers. Additionally, you know I started my podcast two and a half years ago, and the intent was not originally scholarly; I just wanted to have some conversations, and I thought maybe 40 people would listen. Over time when I started talking to different people, the podcast became more radical, and eventually, I started to realize that people don't necessarily pay attention to conference presentations or articles as much as they do to other modalities.

Moving towards collaboration

CVB: Our collaboration started immediately as we found that we were both trying to resist raciolinguistic ideologies that co-construct harmful ideas about language, race, and ability in language teaching (Flores & Rosa, 2015). We began by engaging in a back-and-forth dialogue via direct messaging. We shared posts and comments to which we had a very negative reaction. I vividly remember sending you public posts or flyers with simplistic lists of language teaching strategies or claims about language learning framed by harmful raciolinguistic ideologies. When we saw posts of such nature, we would have a discussion trying to unveil what was happening. It was super fun to work together this way, but we started to realize that this work was too important to keep it to ourselves. We needed to not just challenge harmful ideas out there, but also make them count in a certain way. We, as all academics do, chatted about publishing these ideas, and that is how this chapter came about. However, we both felt that academic publications might not reach the wider audience we were aiming at. That was when we started creating satirical graphics that would use humor to draw attention to the ways anti-Black racism, Whiteness, and raciolinguistic ideologies directly shape ideas about language, learners, and ability (Gerald, 2020; Rosa & Flores, 2017).

JPBG: The graphics came about because we saw a group of language teachers having a discussion about so-called 'equity strategies' with this big bright graphic, which included translanguaging as a strategy to learn standardized English. I jumped into that discussion to question the ideologies at play, one of the people argued with me, and I realized the standard approach was not getting through to them. I wrote a book that'll be out by the time this chapter is released, and we're writing this chapter that's going to be released about a year-and-a-half after this discussion we are now having. The thing about academic books and writing is although my book is going to be fairly cheap most of the books are $90, and they come out a year-and-a-half after the work that goes into them. I'm not dismissing the value of these books, or else I wouldn't have written one myself, but sometimes we need to do something immediate, and we need to put it in the same place that their harmful graphics are being disseminated (i.e. social media). I asked you if you could put a graphic together since I've seen you make graphics before, and I wrote down some jokes, and that was how we created that first one which is still the most popular.

Using Humor as a Path to Justice and Public Engagement

To counteract typical traditional research discourses, we decided to create an alternative space to voice and enact our ideas. This alternative space took the shape of what we are calling a 'satirical misinfographic'. We manipulated, reinvented, and toyed with an existing genre – infographics being used to illustrate lists of teaching strategies or to report research findings – to establish a provocative ethos (Maingueneau, 2004; Ramírez, 2013). We actively used humor to contest hegemonic ideologies, especially educational practices that seemed to downplay or let racial injustice and linguistic discrimination go unquestioned (Rossing, 2016), tying back to Gerald's call to action (2020) for the language education field to move away from White epistemologies. The fact that our dialogic collaboration included pointed racial humor is no accident and an approach that has been documented and used as a disarming pedagogical strategy:

> Emancipatory racial humor functions as a vital participant in this struggle over knowledge, identity, power relationships, and agency ... Humor proves 'emancipatory' because it brings to the forefront perspectives and knowledge that challenge dominant realities, and therefore it bears potential for promoting critical questioning and reflection about racial oppression. (Rossing, 2016: 2)

We tried to unpack the way that checklists and self-congratulations in language education are sort of condensed into how they look and feel to teachers. They use bright colors, fun-looking symbols, and comforting language while revealing a lack of self-examination and cultural responsiveness. We needed to do something immediately and show people that there was emancipatory value in often satirizing well-meaning language educators' intentions. Our satirical graphics became a tool to stimulate and promote critical consciousness or *conscientização*, refusing, questioning, and resisting dogmatic and unexamined positions and ideologies in language education (Freire, 1996).

Methodological Lenses

To illustrate the impact of our dialogic collaboration in our efforts to escape the H-Index and create alternatives to public engagement, we selected one of our graphics as a pivotal moment in our academic journey. We wanted to use the process of creation, publication, and our ongoing imagination to demonstrate ways we, as racialized scholars, have charted another possible path to sharing our ideas and work with others, both inside and outside academia. We began by adopting a critical and ethnographic lens in co-constructing our recollections and dialogue, which has directly impacted our choices on ways to record, select and interpret our data (Ellis *et al.*, 2011). In the context of our work, auto- and duoethnographic approaches helped us ground the dialogic nature and context of our inquiry, granting us a principled guide into co-documenting the insights we had about our graphics as cultural artifacts to generate meaning (Sawyer & Norris, 2012).

To examine the discourse of our satirical graphics, we utilized two critical discourse analysis methodological lenses: Critical Discourse Analysis (Fairclough, 2003) and traditions in Argumentative French Discourse Analysis (Maingueneau, 2004). These lenses provided us with a mode of inquiry to challenge our own discourses and the discourses we engaged with during the creation and publication of our graphics. As Critical Discourse Analysis questions the role of texts in perpetuating or changing ideas, it helped us examine the implicit, assumed, or explicit choices we made when employing specific linguistic and semiotic resources when creating our graphics (Fairclough, 2003). Traditions in Argumentative French Discourse Analysis helped illuminate the roles of ethos and scenography in the recreation and repurposing of the existing genre 'educational infographics' through the use of humor. We also employed this lens to assess the reception of the graphics so that we could better judge the impact of our unconventional publications. Table 9.1 shows the critical questions we asked during our analysis of our satirical graphics as an alternative publication platform:

We documented our ongoing dialogue, both verbal and written, via direct messaging on Twitter/X, Google Documents, Zoom and email to provide an encompassing picture of the process of creation, public engagement and reception, and future directions. We adopted a translingual orientation as we creatively transformed and resisted traditional standardized academic writing norms in the ways we transcended artificial linguistic borders with our own languaging practices (Canagarajah, 2021). We selected our first graphic entitled 'How to be the World's Most Not Racist English Teacher' (Figure 9.1) to make visible the alternative path we created to the traditional academic publication process. We end by discussing how the first and subsequent satirical graphics led to the creation of @Graphics4Chaos, a Twitter/X account we developed with the purpose of officializing the work we did and do with our satirical graphics.

Table 9.1 Critical Discourse Analysis of our satirical graphic publication process

Satirical Graphic Publication Process	Critical Questions
The Creative Process	• How does dialogue impact our purpose, decisions, creative process and sustain our work? • What implicit or explicit linguistic and semiotic choices do we make? Why? • What platforms have we selected for publication? Why?
Public Engagement	• To what ethos and scenography have we appealed to? What effect were we expecting? How has it legitimized our work? • In what ways has the public on social media received and reacted to our work? • What are social and political implications?

Analyzing the Creative Process

Dialogue

Since we are, respectively, parents of a toddler (Gerald) and elementary-age children (Bauler), we had to be creative on how to communicate and think together. Asynchronous modes of communication worked best for us. We have used direct messaging (DM) on Twitter/X and Google Documents as thinking and designing spaces. The asynchronous nature of our conversations has helped us fight the usual barriers imposed on racialized and minoritized scholars, including full support and devoted time for research. The DM platform has allowed us to work on our ideas on our own time, without the need to schedule a formal meeting at a specific time. In Figure 9.2, we demonstrate how we organize our launching of new 'misinfographics' and the list of priorities that we keep changing depending on what we find is the most relevant. As Google Documents affords both authors to write, delete and add to existing texts in real time, it becomes a crucial tool for ongoing collaboration.

Linguistic-Semiotic choices

We adopt a multimodal and translingual orientation towards the design of our 'misinfographics'. In doing so, we actively resist typical standardizing norms for academic writing, which are repurposed and redefined in our alternative path to publication. The translingual orientation helps us go beyond artificially created borders between formal and informal, appropriate and non-appropriate, expanding the idea of academic writing to include our variable repertoires and embodied voices as racialized and minoritized scholars (Canagarajah, 2021). This translingual orientation guided our choice for the content and form of *How to Become the World's Most Not Racist English Teacher* (Figure 9.1), which emulated and remixed popular equity-oriented 'educational infographics' shared widely on the internet as the fade of the moment.

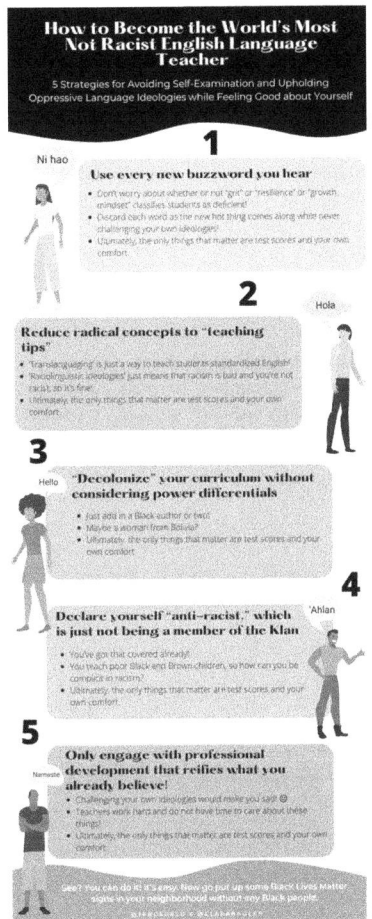

Figure 9.1 How to Become the World's Most Not Racist English Teacher

Our linguistic choices included what Gerald might call 'saying the quiet part out loud,' in other words, plainly stating what is implied by the lack of self-examination employed by far too many language teachers. For example, 'Decolonize your curricula without considering power differentials' would never be included in a real 'educational infographic,' yet that is somehow what always occurs. The distance between the cheerful visuals and the somewhat dark, direct diction is the space in which the humor exists. We also made a point to avoid using the word 'White' since a small hope of our project is that the predominantly White educators who are the target of the humor might see the error of their ways more effectively if they do not quite feel 'called out,' so to speak. We also make it very clear that we are not letting the targets off easy with a final line that, we believe,

Completed graphics:
1. Not Racist ELT
2. Why don't Black and Brown students succeed?

Possible future graphics:
- Diversity panel/ted talk (Nov 5th?)
- Call for DEI committee volunteers at a school/job (Nov 12th, **and also the day we promote the account**)
- Employee Self-Care/EAP (Nov 19th)
- Equity Strategies book(!) (Dec 3rd)
- Top Ranked school (Dec 10th)
- Reasons to move to Albaville (Dec 17th, to coincide with Christmas since Christianity is part of this)
- Protest for (white) parents' rights (Jan 7th)
- Celebrating MLK Day Event (Jan 14th, because it's right before it)
- Conference ad with keynote speakers on equity (Jan 21st)
- Academic job description (Jan 28th)

Figure 9.2 Timeline on Google Docs

twists the satirical knife. In this initial image, it reads, 'Now go put up some Black Lives Matter signs in your neighborhood without any Black people.'

We also made implicit and explicit semiotic choices to reflect a translingual orientation, especially using multimodality, that is, different symbols, images, and genres to unveil unjust racial relations and harmful language ideologies. For *How to Become the World's Most Not Racist English Teacher* (Figure 9.1), we selected a specific Canva template where diversity is superficially portrayed through the mere representation of people of assumed different skin color and cultural-linguistic backgrounds as they utter greetings in multiple languages. In fact, the infographic in its original iteration ends up reinforcing stereotypes and raciolinguistic ideologies, making implicit and explicit assumptions about race and language. Using that specific infographic perfectly matched our purpose to use emancipatory racial humor as a disarming pedagogical strategy to reveal hegemonic racism (Rossing, 2016).

Social media

We selected Twitter/X as the platform to share our work as we are already both on there, constantly sharing our ideas with like-minded peers in academia. Gerald has gained a significant number of followers due to his critical work with his podcast. Bauler is still growing her following. We have both felt that the platform fits the purpose of sharing ideas and pushing back against traditional educational practices due to its community by affinity nature, dialogic, thread-like textual medium and easiness of embedding images, GIFs and links.

Public engagement

Publication

We appealed to the fun, welcoming, and colorful nature of typical 'educational infographics,' which many teachers like and post in their classrooms, to draw attention to unexamined power relations and ideologies that nullify and exclude racialized multilingual students. At first glance, *How to Become the World's Most Not Racist English Teacher* (Figure 9.1) looks like any other colorful 'educational infographic,' but the message it conveys disrupts and challenges a series of actions that help perpetuate and enforce oppressive racial ideologies and unequal power relations. The scenography, that is, the visual design where the actors and situations unfold in a typical 'educational infographic,' remained the same, but the ethos, that is, the image and authority we wanted to convey, was of a humorous, satirical and critical interlocutor, who aimed to persuade the audience through sarcasm and revelation.

We utilized the ongoing social and historical nature of all discourses to 'remix' the 'educational infographic' into a disarming pedagogic strategy (Rossing, 2016). Figure 9.3 displays the original post made by Gerald on October 28, 2021. Gerald used humor to shed light on the common practice of sharing and enjoying colorful 'educational infographics' without deeply examining dominant and possibly harmful messages. In doing this, Gerald appealed to an ethos of a critical scholar that wants to disrupt hegemonic relations. https://twitter.com/JPBGerald/status/1453796830152646659?s=20

Reception

How to Become the World's Most Not Racist English Teacher seemed to have been received positively by our audiences on Twitter/X. Figure 9.4 shows the popularity of the tweet and 'misinfographic' with 198 likes, 59 retweets, and 25 quote tweets. Figure 9.5 includes some of the comments

JPB Gerald
@JPBGerald

 and I made our own colorful infographic.

Behold, 'How to Become the World's Most Not Racist English Language Teacher: 5 Strategies for Avoiding Self-Examination and Upholding Oppressive Language Ideologies while Feeling Good about Yourself.'

Enjoy and share! :)

Figure 9.3 Original publication of How to Become the World's Most Not Racist English Teacher

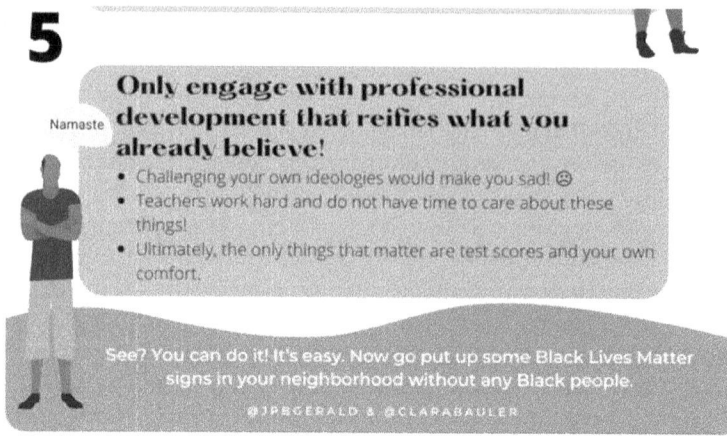

Figure 9.4 Reception of How to Become the World's Most Not Racist English Teacher

Figure 9.5 Comments to How to Become the World's Most Not Racist English Teacher

made to the original post, displaying the humorous effect with participants both using laughing emojis or by uttering how funny it was. The participants were teachers who are still part of our circle of Twitter/X friends and followers. The dialogic and affinity nature of Twitter/X provided us with a medium to share our work with our esteemed peers while receiving affirming feedback.

Creating Chaos

Our 'misinfographics' have helped us resist standardization and escape the H-Index via public engagement with a wider social media platform, the creative use of multimodality, and the possibility of enacting non-standard language. We worked together to use our 'misinfographics' to challenge dominant discourses while considering implications for more socially just public scholarship practices. In a way, @Graphics4Chaos became our own publication platform, which is completely independent of any sense of rejection or acceptance from H-Index measures.

Conclusions

We are told to aspire to inclusion within traditional academic spaces by following the established norms for publication, but if these archaic ideologies are prized, then what value is there chasing the value it supposedly confers upon a scholar's reputation? The H-Index and journal system is, in both definition and execution, a process of gatekeeping, of conferring relative value upon certain approaches and identities, despite the nominally objective nature of peer review. As we have mentioned, and by writing for (Gerald) and writing and editing for (Bauler) this volume, we are still participating in the academic publishing discipline to some extent. Yet, we feel as though we are finding a way to make a small, interconnected push towards justice through our knowledge of and experience in language spaces. All of which is to say, while anyone has the freedom to make jokes at the expense of the powerful, readers might question the 'legitimacy' of our efforts as scholarship. We simply don't care and keep doing what we believe is right.

Critical Discussion Questions

(1) What is your experience with additional academic writing practices? In what ways have your positionalities shaped your understanding of these experiences?
(2) What attempts have you made to break free from standardized academic writing? What more could you do to challenge the expectations of the H-Index?
(3) What single piece of scholarship has had the greatest impact on your ideologies? Define 'scholarship' as broadly as you would like.

(4) Do you agree with the authors in finding value in using humor to challenge hegemonic power relations, racism, and Whiteness? Explain the rationale for your position.
(5) If an educator, in what ways would you use the satirical graphics posted in @Graphic4Chaos on Twitter/X in your teaching practices? If a student, would you find value in following the work of @Graphic4Chaos on Twitter/X as a learning experience? Why?

Note

(1) Regarding our decision to use the word *standardized*, 'you can dispense with the idealization implied by the word 'standard' and use different descriptors.... You can... acknowledge the prominence of these small but mighty dialects by calling them versions of *standardized* English, because, for the time being at least, they do have a tight hold on our field, to the detriment of everyone except the small number of people' (Gerald, 2022: 92).

References

Baker-Bell, A. (2020) *Linguistic Justice: Black Language, Literacy, Identity, and Pedagogy*. New York: Routledge.
Bakhtin, M.M. (2010) *Speech Genres and Other Late Essays*. Austin: University of Texas Press.
Canagarajah, S. (2021) Diversifying academic communication in anti-racist scholarship: The value of a translingual orientation. *Ethnicities* https://doi.org/10.1177/14687968211061586
Ellis, C., Adams, T.E. and Bochner, A.P. (2011) Autoethnography: An overview. *Historical Social Research/Historische Sozialforschung*, 273–290.
Fairclough, N. (2003) *Analysing Discourse: Textual Analysis for Social Research*. London: Psychology Press.
Flores, N. and Rosa, J. (2015) Undoing appropriateness: Raciolinguistic ideologies and language diversity in education. *Harvard Educational Review* 85 (2), 149–171. https://doi.org/10.17763/0017-8055.85.2.149
Freire, P. (1996) *Pedagogia da autonomia: Saberes necessários à prática educativa*. São Paulo: Paz e Terra.
García, O. and Li, W. (2014) *Translanguaging: Language, Bilingualism and Education*. Cham: Springer.
Gerald, J.P.B. (2020) Worth the risk: Towards decentering whiteness in English language teaching. *BC TEAL Journal* 5 (1), 44–54.
Gerald, J.P.B. (2022) *Antisocial Language Teaching: English and the Pervasive Pathology of Whiteness*. Bristol: Multilingual Matters.
Hirsch, J.E. and Buela-Casal, G. (2014) The meaning of the h-index. *International Journal of Clinical and Health Psychology* 14 (2), 161–164.
Maingueneau, D. (2004) La situation d'énonciation entre langue et discours. *Dix ans de SDU*, 197–210.
Ramírez, C. (2013) Ethos and critical discourse analysis: From power to solidarity. *COnTEXTES. Revue de sociologie de la littérature* (13).
Rosa, J. and Flores, N. (2017) Unsettling race and language: Toward a raciolinguistic perspective. *Language in Society* 46 (5), 621–647.
Rossing, J.P. (2016) Emancipatory racial humor as critical public pedagogy: Subverting hegemonic racism. *Communication, Culture & Critique* 9 (4), 614–632.
Sawyer, R.D. and Norris, J. (2012) *Duoethnography*. Oxford: Oxford University Press.

Part 3
Through a Critical Incident Lens

10 When Daily Uses of Language, Identity and 'Power' Intersect with the Global (Center) versus Local (Periphery) Power Relations: An Interdisciplinary Study

Ribut Wahyudi and M. Faisol

In this chapter, Ribut and Faisol are engaged in dialogues about how to challenge the dominance of the West in the English classroom (viewed from North-South) and the dominance of the Middle East in the Arabic classroom (viewed from South-South) relation of power. Rather than using the traditional form of approach, we employed *collaborative autoethnography*, a postmodern type of research which emphasizes personal identity and ideology (Wahyudi, 2021). Our dialogues also reflect our positions as practitioner and researcher (Jain, 2013) and embedded in our subjectivities, agency and social activism.

Collaborative Autoethnography

We refer to (critical) collaborative autoethnography to connect our *teaching experiences* (Ngunjiri *et al.*, 2010) and the *personal* as *political* (Caldas & Heiman, 2021; Wahyudi, 2021) to our research process. Banegas' and Gerlach's (2021) article, through duoethnography of teacher educators revealed that *teacher educators' sense of social justice* and *responsibility* plays an important role in exerting their *agency* and *identity performance* as critical language teacher educators.

Through this collaborative autoethnography, our dialogues have multivocal dimensions because it reflects two authors' self-narratives rather than a single narrative and thus enhances research credibility as discussed by Hernandez *et al.* (2017). We refer to multiple data sources in our dialogues. The multiple data sources are (1) our bios, our reflections on Ribut's lecture notes and Faisol's course outline, (2) reflections on our teaching respectively, and (3) critical incidents in our classes. We define our *critical incidents* as moments where student(s) critically negotiate or contest our explanation in the classroom.

In our writing, we employ critical *reflexivity* through *storytelling* (Choi, 2013) by analyzing the data arising from our dialogues: such as the critical incidents in our classrooms, the similarity and difference of the theories (e.g. *Southern Theory* versus *Occidentalism*) we use, and the similarity and difference between our exercise of power and our performance of identities. The critical incidents were selected because they indicate the students' questioning of lecturers' authority (for Faisol) and act of disciplining one student in the classroom (for Ribut). In these incidents, the students could be seen as negotiating lecturers' exercise of power as explained by Foucault (Gallagher, 2008). In addition to collaborative ethnography, this chapter is shaped by our position as both practitioners and researchers as we both are teachers and also researchers.

Our Position as Practitioners and Researchers

This chapter narrates the overlapping space between our teaching practice and also our research. Jain (2013) explains that as a practitioner researcher we use our research to teach and vice versa make use of our teaching to do research. In that regard, our chapter in this project is the reflection for our position as practitioners and researchers. In the following, we foreground our dialogues from the initial, completion and revision process of this chapter as we believe that dialogue means personal and professional engagement, social interaction and knowledge construction.

Our dialogues during the writing and the revision process

Our dialogue started when Ribut came to Faisol (who is Ribut's Dean) with a proposal to co-author a chapter on the issues of language, identity and power. The subsequent dialogues take place during the writing and revision processes of the chapter.

In the first meeting, Ribut explained the scope and objective of the chapter and proposed using theories such as Foucault's theory of *power* (Gallagher, 2008) and Norton's (2013) *Theory of Identity as a research framework*. Ribut also asked Faisol about the possibility of using critical theories from the Middle East or by Middle East scholars. Faisol suggested two theories from Middle East scholars; M. Abid Aljabiri and Hasan Hanafi (cf. Faisol, 2010, 2011, 2017).

There is a dialogue constraint. It is partly due to the medium exposure to 'standard' English being limited for Faisol, and also inability to access Al-jabiri's and Hanafi's works (for Ribut) from the primary sources as he does not read Arabics.

In this context, Ribut took the lead in the research and initiative. This dialogue constraint is something which may not be easily imagined from the Global North (e.g. American and European). However, the dialogues did emerge through data collection, analysis and the revision process.

The dialogue also happened when we discussed the problem being addressed in this chapter, the dominance of Global North in the English Literature Department (explained by Ribut), and in *Philology* (explained by Faisol). Further, Faisol argued that the domination needs to be countered through Hasan Hanafi's Occidentalism. He also contends that the stagnation of Arabic thoughts which need to be reconstructed as suggested by M. Abid Aljabiri and concurrently he is critical to the West (in the *Approaches to Islamic Studies*, henceforth AIS). This problem is relevant for Ribut because he wants to create more democratic and dialectic knowledge production and for Faisol, it trains students to be responsible to care for manuscripts by local Ulama (in Faisol's Philology course) and to know the AIS course through a critical eye. The context for Ribut's course is *Interculturality in Language and Literary Studies* (ILLS) for undergraduate students, and for Faisol is *Philology* for the Arabic Literature Department and AIS for Masters' students majoring in Arabic Language Education. Both Faisol and Ribut are teaching at an Indonesian Islamic University in East Java, Indonesia. The goal for this chapter is to critically negotiate the Western dominance in the field (for Ribut) and decrease Western and Middle East dominance for Faisol. To locate our dialogues in the existing studies, in the following we discuss the relevant concepts.

The Concepts Underpinning Our Dialogues

Our dialogue is centered, among others, around our dialogue of critical theories adopted in our chapter and how the adopted theories share similarity and difference. Ribut uses Foucault's *concept of power* (Gallagher, 2008). Foucault conceptualized *power* as abstract, actions upon actions, relational (top-down or bottom-up) and embedded in different networks (Gallagher, 2008). Ribut also uses Norton's (2013) theory of *identities* as *multiple, non-unitary, a site of struggle* and *changing*. Furthermore, he proposes the use of *Language*, in Foucauldian terms, as *Discourse*. In this regard, *language as a discourse* has the capacity to shape students' way of thinking and acting (Walshaw, 2007). In capturing the Global North versus Global South relations, Ribut employs Connell's (2007) *Southern Theory*. This theory challenges the Global North's (Europe/North America) dominance in knowledge production and calls for diversification and democratization. Global North is generally meant to refer to North America and Europe where the modern social sciences are constructed, which are then claimed to be universal, whereas the Global South refers to Australia, as 'a colony of settlement' and postcolonial Africa, Iran, Latin America and India where the hegemony of the Global North has been challenged (Connell, 2007: viii). Pennycook and Makoni (2020) explain that this North/South divide is a world division made after World War II, where North is associated with the developed, and South is identified as the developing line.

Faisol introduces Hanafi's concept of Occidentalism and Al-Jabiri's epistemological critique to reconstruct the stagnation of Islamic world as shown in our dialogue in the first revision process:

> **Faisol:** 'Konsep Hasan Hanafi Occidentalism melihat Barat sebagai powerful yang harus dinaturalkan dengan melemahkannya sehingga Barat tidak lagi menjadi pusat. Barat menjadi Orientalist dengan membuat Islam jadi objek bukan subjek. Sedangkan dalam Occidentalisme, Islam harus jadi subjek itu sendiri'
> (Hanafi's concept of Occidentalism sees the West as powerful, and needs to be made natural by looking at its weaknesses so that the West is no longer the Center. Western becomes Orientalist by positioning Islam as object not as subject. In an Occidental perspective, Islam should be the subject rather than object (cf. Faisol, 2011).)
> **Ribut:** 'Menarik Pak Faisol, kalau untuk Aljabiri?' ('That's interesting Pak Faisol, how about Al-Jabiri?')
> **Faisol:** 'Al-Jabiri berargumen bahwa kemunduran Islam karena ketergantungan terhadap teks dalam arti bahwa keilmuan dalam Islam harus dikembalikan ke teks. Tidak ada ruang kritik di situ. Bagi Al-jabiri, Muslim tidak boleh terjebak dalam teks tapi tek-teks [suci] harus dikembalikan lagi ke konteksnya [masing-masing]. Al-jabiri menganggap bahwa masa lampau mempunyai warisan sejarah (intellectual heritage), yang harus dibawa ke masa kini dengan memberlakukan kritik sejarah dan kritik ideology. Dua kritik ini diperlukan untuk memutus mata rantai epistemologis sehingga kita bisa menjadi objektif dan tidak hanya terjebak oleh masa lalu'
> (Al-Jabiri argues that the setback of Islam is the reliance on the authority of texts in the study of Islam so that everything should be returned to texts. There is no criticism in that regard. For Al-Jabiri, Moslems cannot be trapped into texts only but rather the text(s) need to be understood from their contexts. Al-Jabiri argues that the past has an intellectual heritage which needs to be brought to the current context by enacting the critiques of history and ideology. These two critiques are needed accordingly to disconnect the epistemological link so that we can be 'objective', not only trapped by the past.) (cf. Faisol, 2010, 2017)
> **Ribut Wahyudi:** 'Menarik ini Pak.' (This is interesting, Sir.)

In that regard, we learned the domination of the West has both been challenged by scholars from the Global North such as Connell's (2007) *Southern Theory* (as Ribut explained formerly) but also by

Hasan-Hanafi's (Egypt) *Occidentalism* as Faisol explained. Ribut: 'Ini untuk menjawab feedback dari editor Pak Faisol yang menyebutkan analisis kita masih belum terintegrasi (disjointed), maka perlu, di antaranya perlu ditarik titik temu teori utama yang digunakan. Menurut saya Connell's (2007) *Southern Theory* dan Oksidentalisme Hasan Hanafi dan Kritik Epistemologis Al-jabiri mempunyai kemiripan positioning yaitu menentang dominasi Barat. Bagaimana menurut Pak Faisol?' (This is to answer the feedback from editor Pak Faisol saying that our analysis is still disjointed so that, among others, we need to draw a meeting point between the key theories used. In our opinion, Connell's (2007) Southern Theory, Hanafi's Occidentalism and Al-Jabiri's epistemological critique share similar positioning that is challenging the domination of the West, what do you think Pak Faisol?').

> **Faisol:** 'Ya benar, Hasan Hanafi menentang Barat dengan cara mencari kelemahannya' (Yes, right, Hasan Hanafi challenges the West by looking its weakness.)
> **Ribut:** 'Kalau perbedaannya Pak Faisol, dalam Occidentalism subjek yang terdominasi sesuai dengan penjelasan Pak Faisol adalah dunia Islam, sedangkan di Connell's (2007) Southern Theory yang terdominasi adalah Global South, yang mana keIlmuan Islam menjadi salah satunya saja. (The difference between Occidentalism and Southern Theory is (Pak Faisol) that, in Occidentalism, the subject being dominated in the Global South (as you explained) the is Islamic worlds, whereas in Connell's (2007) Southern Theory, the dominated is the Global South, where Islamic knowledge is one among other subjects)
> **Faisol:** 'Ya.' (Yes.)
> **Ribut:** 'Kalau Al-jabiri yang dikritik adalah kemunduran Umat Islam karena terjebak dalam teks tanpa memperhatikan konteks, tidak untuk mengkritik Barat?' (For Al-Jabiri, the one being critiqued is the setback of Islam because of being trapped in understanding text without considering contexts, not for critiquing the West?)
> **Faisol:** 'Ya, tetapi Al-Jabiri juga bisa digunakan untuk mengkritik dominasi Barat dengan menggunakan kritik epistemologis sehingga kita tidak mentah-mentah menerima interpretasi teks tanpa konteks dalam Islam dan juga tidak serta-merta menerima dominasi Barat, sehingga ada ruang kritisisme di situ' (Yes, but Al-Jabiri can be used to critique the West domination by employing epistemological critique so that we do not take for granted the interpretation of text without context in Islam, and do not take for granted the West domination as well, so there is a criticism space there.)

In the above dialogue, we see that both Connell's (2007) *Southern Theory* and Hanafi's *Occidentalism* share similar critical positions to interrogate the dominance of the Global North. However, the difference is that in Occidentalism (as elaborated by Faisol) the dominated subject is the Islamic worlds while in the case of Connell's (2007) *Southern Theory*, the dominated subjects are more the Global South where Islamic knowledge is only one part. While Al-jabiri's thought, which emphasizes the importance of contexts in understanding text in Islam, resembles Connell's (2007) *Southern Theory* which offers the critique of the universality of Western knowledge. In the Southern Theory, local indigenous knowledge is promoted.

The above dialogue resonates with Hernandez *et al.*'s (2017) explanation in 'Collaborative Autoethnography as Multivocal, Relational, and Democratic Research: Opportunities, Challenges, and Aspirations'. We discussed the conceptual relations between two different theories (Southern Theory and Occidentalism) which have a meeting point, that is both can be used to problematize the Western (in the case of English) and Middle East (in the case of Islam) in our dialogues.

Research Question

Overall, our dialogues aim to answer the following question:
In what contexts do the use of language, power and identity intersect with the global relations of power?

In the following, we make sense of our identities which are embedded in our teaching (see Wahyudi, 2021, 2023), how language functions as a discourse through deconstruction and how we exercise power and power negotiation through critical incidents in our classrooms.

The need to maintain identity

The following dialogue between Ribut and Faisol is based on Ribut's reflection on his lecture notes where he explained Jackson's (2011) article on *Cosmopolitanism and Intercultural Citizenship*, where a Chinese person conducted a sojourn in the UK where she maintained Chinese values but concurrently was open to accommodate the desirable values of the host country:

> She (the main actor in Jackson's article) has cosmopolitan skills and has become an intercultural citizen. She can operate herself within two cultures: Chinese and local English cultures. Apart from that the important point is that there are similarities at some points, good things I take, in the UIN (State Islamic University) context in الفقه [Islamic Jurisprudence] tradition, *something which is not good, we can ignore it* (Muhadjir, 2015). In the UIN context, interculturality, in the Islamic context, *in Al-Qur'an it is said that Allah (God) creates humans into different ethnicities, nations to know each other* (Quran Kemenag n.d.) [2]. Of course it is not only about a language but also cultures therefore it is closely related. In Islamic understanding, this intercultural understanding is necessary and is good to learn. *If that's good, the Western values we take ...*

if the Western values are not in line with our cultures, we just need to know them but of course we avoid the values and we do not implement the values.

(Dated 21 May 2021, Interculturality B Class)

Ribut contextualized his teaching with the institutional demand, that is, giving the Islamic values relevant to the topic being discussed (Wahyudi, 2021). The identity values promoted in the above quote was being firm on the Islamic values but also on being tolerant, open and accommodative to 'desirable' positive Western cultures (see Wahyudi, 2023). This is in line with the concept of identity as multiple and changing (Norton, 2013) and at the same time resonates with the *cosmopolitan skill* in intercultural language education (Jackson, 2011).

What Ribut explained above also illustrates an example of discourses, which is to shape students' way of thinking and being (Walshaw, 2007). The following is our dialogue on Ribut's reflection of the way Ribut taught above:

Ribut: 'Bagaimana pendapat Pak Faisol tentang pengajaran saya terkait kosmopolitanisme yang saya jelaskan bahwa mahasiswa perlu mempunyai wawasan global dan tetapi tetap berpijak pada identitas lokal seperti yang saya jelaskan di atas?' (How is your opinion about my teaching related to cosmopolitanism? I explained to students that they need to have a global mindset but still uphold local identities as I explained above?)
Faisol: 'Pak Ribut dipengaruhi oleh rujukan Barat (e.g. Cosmopolitanism), Barat telah memberikan perspective?' (Pak Ribut is influenced by the reference from the West (e.g. Cosmopolitanism); the West has provided a perspective.)
Ribut: 'Kalau tentang Fiqh dan Islam yang saya masukan?' (How about Fiqh (Islamic Jurisprudence and Islamic values which I inserted)?)
Faisol: 'Itu merupakan kosmopolitanisme lokal.' (That's local cosmopolitanism.)
Ribut: 'Apa itu kosmopolitanisme lokal?' (What's local cosmopolitanism?)
Faisol: 'Khasanah lokal yang masih bisa dipakai tapi banyak dikesampingkan oleh masyarakat umum.' (The local values which are still used but often ignored by public society.)

In the above dialogue, Faisol said that Ribut was influenced by Western reference on cosmopolitanism, and the Islamic values he commented as local cosmopolitanism, that is the local values often ignored by many peoples. From Faisol's comment, Ribut could learn a term of 'local cosmopolitanism', which Ribut had not yet encountered in his former readings.

As in the postmodern and poststructural context, language is understood as a discourse, in the following, we discuss the concept of *deconstruction* as an enactment where language operates as a discourse.

Deconstructing inferiority feeling

Our dialogue below is based on Ribut's reflection on Canagarajah's (2013) 'Agency and Power in Intercultural Communication':

> ... then the implication for us as Asians?, We prove that we have skills for example and we have particular selling points, therefore should we go abroad we would not feel inferior, feeling socially lower than them, no, we are equal, let alone if we have professionalism in our field. (May 7th, 2021, Interculturality B Class)

As there are still many people in our society which are still 'colonized' by Western superiority (see Alatas, 2003), Ribut aimed to disrupt Western hegemony (Wahyudi, 2016, 2018) to change subject position from 'inferior' feeling to 'confident' feeling (Walshaw, 2007). Through the above examples, we have encouraged students to take *critical positioning*, being confident that what makes a difference among people is professionalism, not because the people from the West are superior to people from the East (see Wahyudi, 2023). This example also reflects the spirit of *activism*, that is challenging the existing assumption that the West is superior (cf. Caldas & Heiman, 2021).

> **Ribut:** 'Tentang penjelasan saya ke mahasiswa supaya untuk tidak menjadi inferior?' (How about when I encouraged the students to not be inferior?)
> **Faisol:** 'Intercultural digunakan oleh Pak Ribut untuk mengubah identitas yang tunggal (inferior) menjadi multi-identitas (terbuka, superior)' (You use intercultural to change a single identity, which is inferior, into multiple (open) identities which is superior).

In this dialogue, while Ribut is of the position to believe in multiple identities, Ribut noticed from Faisol that the single identity is inferior and multiple identities are superior. Ribut realized that he needs to learn more about this difference for future reference. This suggests that this dialogue enhances Ribut's understanding of multiple identities as a superior subject position.

The background of Faisol plays an important role in how he performed multiple identities toward the students: his being an alumnus of an Islamic boarding school affiliated to *Nadhlatul Ulama* (the biggest Islamic moderate organization in Indonesia), his encounter with critical thinkers both from the West (e.g. Derrida) and Middle East (Hasan Hanafi, Abid-Al Jabiri), along with his former educational training in Islamic Philosophy and Islamic Studies, shapes the way he teaches in the classroom.

M. Faisol firstly *deconstructed* the common stereotype labeling the Arabic literature department as having no future prospect. He emphasized that students taking this department can contribute to social civilization.

The deconstruction of the status of students in Arabic Literature Department

Faisol deconstructed the common 'false' assumption of the status of being students in the Arabic Literature Department to reconstruct its important role:

> **Faisol:** '… Saya juga mengatakan saat anda menjadi mahasiswa Sastra Arab, ini bukan berarti kalian teralienasi, tidak. Tetapi sebaliknya, kalian mempunyai kesempatan yang besar'.
> **Ribut:** 'Kenapa teralineasi Pak?'
> **Faisol:** '… Ada asumsi yang muncul jika kuliah di Jurusan Sastra Arab itu tidak prospektif … saya jelaskan begitu supaya mahasiswa *tidak minder* [feel inferior] … Saya selalu mengatakan hal yang sama untuk mahasiswa yang menempuh mata kuliah saya …'

In the above dialogue, Faisol deconstructed the common assumption that Arabic language literature has no prospect by locating its contribution to civilizations. He did the deconstruction for the students to have 'future imagination' ('*tidak minder*/to kill inferior feeling)'. In that regard, he changed the subject positions (Walshaw, 2007) from an Arabic literature department as undesirable to a desirable position, and performed a spirit of activism (Caldas & Heiman, 2021).

We discussed how identities are embedded in our classroom as follows:

> **Ribut:** 'Kira-kira mata kuliah apa yang Pak Faisol bisa di dalamnya itu ada unsur identitas, ada unsur kuasa, kalau bahasa dan kuasa sudah jadi satu, mana yang kira-kira kalau dicontohkan menjual begitu'
> **Faisol:** 'Opo yo (Javanese phrase)? (berfikir).' (What is it? Thinking.)'
> **Ribut:** 'Saya yakin banyak, ini misalnya relasi egaliter di Barat tidak serta merta bisa diterapkan di kita misalnya kita strict di kelas dengan gaya konstruksi budaya Jawa dan Islam misalnya kan ndak masalah …' (I think many, for example the egalitarian relationship in the West cannot be taken for granted, for example we are strict in our classroom which is shaped by Javanese culture, and Islam is no problem …)
> **Faisol:** 'Nek itu saya bilang begini di kelas Philology misale.' (In that case, I said like this in my Philology class.)
> **Faisol continued:** '… harus ada sesuatu yang bisa dinikmati di akhir kelas Filologi ini yang berkontribusi terhadap perubahan sosial. Untuk itu masing-masing mahasiswa harus mengerjakan final project khususnya menulis tentang manuskrip Ulama Nusantara. Ini akan berkontribusi terhadap *perubahan sosial*' (There should be something which could be enjoyed at the end of this Philology class which contributes to social transformation. Therefore, each student should do the final project, especially writing the manuscript Nusantara Ulama (Indonesian Islamic scholars). This will contribute to social transformation.)
> **Ribut:** Apa yang dimaksud dengan tranformasi sosial? (What's meant by social transformation?)

Faisol: '... saat menulis ini kalian menulis tentang sejarah, dan ini akan dibaca oleh generasi setelahnya. Generasi yang akan datang bisa belajar dari perjuangan dari Ulama lokal dalam melakukan transformasi sosial ...' (Writing this, you are writing about history, and this will be read by the next generations ... the next generation(s) can learn from *perjuangan* [the struggle] of the scholars in doing social transformation ...)

Faisol: '... Awalnya mahasiswa tidak tahu apa itu Filologi. Lalu saya jelaskan merupakan data sejarah dan bila data ini dikaitkan dengan teori sejarah pemikiran berarti bahwa manusrip muncul saat itu karena ada kebutuhan sosial. Lalu saya jelaskan faktanya sekarang banyak manuskrip yang dilupakan. Untuk anda (mahasiswa) harus punya tanggungjawab untuk merawatnya. Lalu mahasiswa melakukan digitalisasi manuskrip'

(... formerly students did not know what Philology is. Then we explained Philology can be historical data. If these data are discussed in relation to *teori sejarah pemikiran* [theory of historical thoughts] which means manuscripts of the particular year exist because there was a societal need. From that Faisol explained that the manuscripts are ignored. When it is ignored [in the current society] then you have a responsibility to save them. The students did digitization (of manuscript) ...).

In the above dialogue, an example Ribut made (e.g. the fact that egalitarian patterns in the West should not be taken for granted) proves to be useful to generate Faisol's own example from his Philology class and his insightful elaboration. This shows that dialogue can be both a way to collect the data as well as to open up possibilities for interpretation and critical reflection.

Faisol's explanation of the important role of local Islamic scholars, as the role model for students, serves to resist the dominance of the Middle East Islamic scholars. For him learning Islam does not have to directly refer to the Middle East references but could be from manuscripts written by local Indonesian Ulama, who have made the summary or the interpretation of Islamic texts from Middle East while taking into consideration the local contexts as promoted by Al-Jabiri (see Faisol, 2011). For him the local Islamic scholars' works are not less contributive to social civilization than Islamic works written by Ulama from the Middle East. This act resonates much with Connell's (2007) *Southern Theory* which challenges the domination of the Islamic scholars from the Middle East and creates the space for multi-centered social sciences. Faisol's act also reflects the enactment of Hasan Hanafi's thoughts on Occidentalism and Abid Al-Jabiri on the role of context in understanding of Islam (see Faisol, 2010, 2011, 2017).

The contribution of local Indonesian Ulama

The following is our dialogue on the contribution of Ulama Nusantara:

Ribut: 'Apakah transformasi sosial juga menunjukkan identitas Nusantara?' (showing social transformation but also reflects Nusantara Identity'?) maksud saya jika dibandingkan dengan Ulama Nusantara?' (Showing Ulama Nusantara thoughts if contrasted to Transnational [Islamic] scholars?')
Faisol: ' Ya tentu, akhirnya begini, saat kita bicara transformasi sosial di Indonesia di mana Islam yang mayoritas, banyak Ulama lokal yang mempunyai peranan yang sama jika dibandingkan dengan masa lalu, Ulama tidak harus berarti Arab, kontribusinya ada di situ..'
(Yes, of course. At the end, it could be like this, when we talk about social transformation in Indonesia where the majority is Moslems, there are lots of local Islamic scholars [Ulama] who have the same role if we compare to the past. *Ulama do not have to be Arab, no*, the contribution is in that field).
Ribut: 'Dari sudut pandang post-kolonial saya bisa merasakan itu.' (From a post-colonial perspective, I can sense that.)
Faisol: '… Istilahnya ada Islam pusat dan periperi (the term is there is Center and Periphery Islam), kita lihat ini Islam periperi (we try to, this is Periphery Islam) e.g. Imam Nawawi, Syekh Mahfud Attremasi, faktanya banyak (In fact there are many other Indonesian Islamic scholars.)

The important point of what Faisol did was to localize the course subject to the local context, the equal role of Ulama from the Center and Periphery in creating social changes. The Centre-Periphery model refers to 'a spatial metaphor that describes and attempts to explain the structural relationship between the advanced or metropolitan "center" and a less developed "periphery", either within a particular country, or (more commonly) as applied to the relationship between capitalist and developing societies' (Oxford Reference Online). This is relevant to Connell's (2007) call for democratizing knowledge production from the Middle East dominance to Indonesian context. Concurrently, this makes the Indonesian Ulama a subject based on Hasan Hanafi's work (see Faisol, 2011).

On the point relating to identity, we share differences and similarities due to different disciplinary courses and each contextual need. As teaching in the English department, Ribut needs to instill the Islamic values in the ILLS course as required by the university and also his own initiative (Wahyudi, 2021) while for Faisol, it was done by promoting the works of the local flavor of Islam. The similarity lies in both our sense of activism (praxis; Kubota, 2021). Ribut promoted students' agency and deconstruction of students' inferior feeling by introducing students to critical works in the classroom. While Faisol did his activism by deconstructing the common 'false' assumption of Arabic Literature and also his promotion of local Islamic scholars' works as a way to challenge the dominance of Middle East scholars' works.

The lecturers' exercise of power

Following Foucault, we see 'power' as something to be exercised, not as an abstract entity and commodity (Gallagher, 2008). The following dialogue is relating to how we discipline the students through the exercise of power.

> A quote from Ribut's *ILLS* classroom:
> 'Only write the name in the presence list (in the online classroom) but not actively participating means zero.'

Ribut usually said this to the students because his online class is through WhatsApp, so he required the students to be active in the online classroom by posting their answers in response to his question or classroom discussion. If the students just wrote down their names but were passive, he would suspect them of not engaging in the online class as they could be away and doing something else instead of paying attention to the classroom interaction. Therefore, requiring students to actively post in the classroom means *surveillance* (Walshaw, 2007) and 'law-like' mechanism of power exercise (Lilja & Vinthagen, 2014).

Similarly Faisol in his Zoom classroom also necessitates the students to login in e-learning through the university website to ensure that students' presence is recorded:

> **Faisol:** Even though we meet in Zoom, you should be present.
> **Ribut:** Is there any firmer reminder, for example, failing to comply with this expectation will have an implication for mark?
> **Faisol:** Yes, of course, *if you for example join the Zoom meeting but the presence list* (via e-learning) *bolong-bolong* [often absent], *your mark gets decreased.* (translated from Indonesian)

The above quote also acts as *sovereign power* where the students could not say no (Lilja & Vinthagen, 2014), where the power differential is constituted in the university regulations which students should obey (Wahyudi, 2018).

In terms of exercise of power, we enacted sovereign power so that the students should obey the rules of the class. We consider it important to discipline students.

The Critical Incident

In the case of power, Ribut, considered it important to discipline students who were late joining WhatsApp group discussions due to Covid-19 situations. The following critical incident occurred when Ribut was teaching an Interculturality class online (through WhatsApp group) during the Covid-19 pandemic. He was a bit angry with a female student (A) who was often absent. Then one male student (FI), the leader of the students, responded politely, but defensively, explaining the many difficulties students faced to join the class during the pandemic:

> I beg your pardon sir, in several places, *[in] our friends' houses the signal is far from stable*. Some need to go out from their villages reaching a relatively long distance up to the city to get a signal. There are some friends who are able and brave to leave their houses and go to the city to search for a signal. But, some are afraid to do it because of the current condition [Covid19], sir. Indeed sir, we realize that we need to struggle more to study due to current conditions. It can be by spending the night in the relative's house in the city where the signal is good. But, in some friends' houses, *it could not be done* because *there is a restriction from the local village authority*. I beg your pardon sir, if you [do not] mind with my *curhatan* [confession]. *I am trying to convey the obstacles which are really faced by our friends* during the online class. Again, I apologize if [these] are inappropriate words for you. And if you do not mind my confession, *it can be of your consideration*. Thanks sir.

Ribut did not respond to the FI's aspiration verbally, but he considered it his discretion whether or not he should grant the female student (A) who was often absent and late a passing grade. In this regard, the student (FI) as the leader of his cohorts negotiates my exercise of power by explaining the difficult circumstances some students faced during the Covid-19 pandemic in meeting the class expectation. This critical incident suggests that in Foucauldian Discourse, power is not only exercised from top down but also resisted or negotiated from below (Gallagher, 2008).

The following is our dialogue on the critical incident happening in Ribut's ILLS classroom.

> **Ribut:** 'Bagaimana pendapat Pak Faisol tentang critical incident seperti yang sudah saya jelaskan di atas?' (What is your opinion Pak Faisol about the critical incident as I explained above?)
> **Faisol:** 'Bahasa yang Pak Ribut gunakan masih cenderung otoritarian dan itu justru menjadi masalah secara methodologis di kelas intercultural.' (The language used by Pak Ribut still shows authoritarianism and that is problematic methodologically in the Intercultural classroom.)
> **Ribut:** 'Kenapa begitu Pak?' (Why are you saying in that way Pak?)
> **Faisol:** 'Karena cenderung menutup alasan orang lain.' (Because it will close another's reason.)

In the above dialogue, Faisol pointed out that Ribut's way of teaching expects the students to be punctual in the online classroom (in the Covid-19 situation) and tends to be authoritarian as he did not quite welcome the student's explanation for joining late/being absent. However, Ribut, in his own defense, believes that in similar situations, while he needs to be more considerate, he is obligated to discipline the students, but not in a threatening way.

Student's challenge toward lecturer's explanation

The critical incident for Faisol was when he explained in his AIS course that there are a variety of approaches in understanding Islam.

> Faisol: When I taught AIS, that time I explained that to understand Islam for now we need to approach it from different perspectives. One of them is modern methodologies. When I offered that one of approaches is through epistemological critiques, I was questioned by one student, 'Isn't Islam كافة (comprehensive)? So no further approach is needed.' Then I explained firstly the term كافة is normative. Secondly, to understand text we need a set of tools. Nah, if Qur'an and حديث [words or actions from Prophet Muhammad or actions from his followers approved by him] are جامع مانع [final] that should be accepted. But the understanding of text from one thought to another could be different. And if there is no authoritative methodology to understand that *ya serampangan* [the interpretation would be unreliable]. ... This is once again very dangerous and this happens. The student's question meant a challenge for his authority. The student's act can also be seen as the student's negotiation of power, that is power starts from bottom up (Gallagher, 2008). The act of [the] student's questioning [of] his explanation by saying that 'Isn't Islam already كافة (comprehensive)?' reflecting the broader social debate between Puritan and Moderate Moslem respectively where the first tend to be textual and the latter is contextual in understanding Islam (Munawir, 2017).
> Ributt: 'Apa arti kritical incident di atas bagi Pak Faisol sendiri?' (What is the meaning of the critical incident above for you Pak Faisol?)
> Faisol: 'Critical incident provides me a chance to expose this typical student to a variety of perspectives as *mereka* (student) is the victim of indoctrination and should be countered by exposing students to different perspectives'.

Faisol's act also suggests his identity as *a poststructural informed lecturer* who accepts *multiple truths* (Grbich, 2004). His explanation does reflect different approaches to Islamic study as reflected in the teaching of Abid Al-Jabiri who is one of critical scholars we have discussed.

Both critical incidents in our classrooms share similarities and differences. Both students in our class negotiate our authority. However, the difference is that in Ribut's class, the student's negotiation was on the student's failure to be punctual in the online classroom due to the Covid-19 situation, while for Faisol's class, it was more about negotiating the lecturer's explanation on the course content. The incidents also consolidate the fact that dialogues promote interpretation and critical reflections for us.

Conclusion

The dialogue in action has been proven as rich sources of data generation, reflection/, insights and interpretation/analysis for our chapter on language, identity and power. Our dialogues reflect *multiple identities* which could be seen as the extension of the *global relations of power* between Global North and South (West versus Asia for the English classroom) and South–South (Middle East versus Indonesia for the Arabic classroom). Both in our classes, we tried to challenge the Western and Middle Eastern dominance as the reflection of *activism* and or *social responsibility*. In our classrooms the *power dynamic* emerged, where the operations of power can be both top-down (from us to students) and also bottom-up (from students to us). Thus, our use of languages can be both seen from the micro-classroom and macro-global levels. Our interdisciplinary (English and Arabic) backgrounds have facilitated our choice of critical theories (e.g. Connell's Southern Theory and Hanafi's Occidentalism) and have made richer analysis on the relationship between Global North and South in the context of English and Arabic classrooms.

Critical Discussion Questions

The followings are five questions which we think may inspire readers to engage in critical conversations especially for the topics relating to the intersection of language use, identity and power:

(1) What are the roles of dialogue involving how interdisciplinary backgrounds shape knowledge production?
(2) To what extent does the lecturer's use of language reflect their multiple identities and the exercise of power in the classroom?
(3) To what an extent is the lecturer's classroom teaching shaped by their subjectivity, identities and activism?
(4) How far can a Global South lecturer disrupt the Global North's (Europe/North America) or Middle East's dominance in their classroom teaching?
(5) In what way can a lecturer strategically handle the critical incident in the classroom, for example, when a student questions their authority or explanation?

References

Alatas, S.F. (2003) Academic dependency and the global division of labor in social science. *Current Sociology* 51 (6), 599–613. https://doi.org/10.1177/00113921030516003
Banegas, D.L. and Gerlach, D. (2021) Critical language teacher education: A duoethnography of teacher educators' identities and agency. *System* 98. https://doi.org/10.1016/j.system.2021.102474
Caldas, B. and Heiman, D. (2021) Más allá de la lengua: Embracing the messiness as bilingual teacher educators. *Journal of Language, Identity & Education* 20 (1), 58–70. https://doi.org/10.1080/15348458.2021.186420
Canagarajah, S. (2013) Agency and power in intercultural communication: Negotiating English in translocal spaces. *Language and Intercultural Communication* 13 (2), 202–224. https://doi.org/10.1080/14708477.2013.770867

Centre-periphery model. Accessed from: https://www.oxfordreference.com/view/10.1093/acref/9780199683581.001.0001/acref-9780199683581-e-239

Choi, J. (2013) Constructing a multivocal self: A critical-auto ethnography. PhD thesis, University of Technology Sydney.

Connell, R. (2007) *Southern Theory: The Global Dynamics of Knowledge in Social Sciences*. Crows Nest: Allen & Unwyn.

Faisol, M. (2010) Struktur nalar Arab – Islam menurut Abid al-Jabiri. *Jurnal TSAQAFAH* 6 (2), 335–359.

Faisol, M. (2011) Mensikapi tradisi: Membaca proyek pemikiran kiri Islam. In K. Faizin (ed.) *Menafsirkan tradisi dan modernitas: Ide-ide pembaharuan Islam* (hal: 25–42. Pustaka Idea.

Faisol, M. (2017) Hermeneutika kritis: Pembacaan Al-Quran Abed –Al Jabiri. *ISTIQRO* 15 (2), 383–399.

Gallagher, M. (2008) Foucault, power and participation. *International Journal of Children's Rights* 16 (3), 395–406.

Grbich, C. (2004) *New Approaches in Social Research*. London: Sage.

Hernandez, K.A.C., Chang, H. and Ngunjiri, F.W. (2017) Collaborative autoethnography as multivocal, relational, and democratic research: Opportunities, challenges, and aspirations. *a/b: Auto/Biography Studies* 32 (2), 251–254. https://doi.org/10.1080/08989575.2017.1288892

Jackson, J. (2011) Cultivating cosmopolitan, intercultural citizenship through critical reflection and international, experiential learning. *Language and Intercultural Communication* 11 (2), 80–96. https://doi.org/10.1080/14708477.2011.556737

Jain, R. (2013) Practitioner research as dissertation: Exploring the continuities between practice and research in a community college ESL classroom. Unpublished doctoral dissertation: University of Maryland.

Kubota, R. (2021) Critical engagement with teaching EFL: Toward a trivalent focus on ideology, political economy and praxis. In O.Z. Barnawi and A. Ahmed (eds) *TESOL Teacher Education in a Transnational World: Turning the Challenges into Innovative Prospects* (pp. 49–64). New York: Routledge.

Lilja, M. and Vinthagen, S. (2014) Sovereign power, disciplinary power and biopower: resisting what power with what resistance? *Journal of Political Power* 7 (1), 107–126. https://doi.org/10.1080/2158379X.2014.889403

Muhadjir, A. (2015) Islam Nusantara untuk Peradaban Indonesia dan Dunia. In A. Sahal and M. Aziz (eds) *Islam Nusantara: Dari Ushul Fiqh hingga Paham Kebangsaan* (hal: 61–68). Mizan.

Munawir (2017) Muslim puritan and Muslim moderat: Pembacaan terhadap kedudukan perempuan. *Fikrah: Jurnal Ilmu Aqidah dan Studi Keagamaan* 5 (1), 25–48. http://dx.doi.org/10.21043/fikrah.v5i1.2068

Ngunjiri, F.W., Hernandez, K.C. and Chang, H. (2010) Living autoethnography: Connecting life and research. *Journal of Research and Practice* 6 (1), 1–17.

Norton, B. (2013) *Identity and Language Learning: Extending the Conversation* (2nd edn). Bristol: Multilingual Matters.

Pennycook, A. and Makoni, S. (2020) *Innovations and Challenges in Applied Linguistics from the Global South*. New York: Routledge.

Wahyudi, R. (2016) Intercultural competence: Multi-dynamic, intersubjective, critical and interdisciplinary approaches. In F. Dervin and Z. Gross (eds) *Intercultural Competence in Education: Alternative Approaches for Different Times* (pp. 143–166). London: Palgrave Macmillan.

Wahyudi, R. (2018) Situating English language teaching in Indonesia within a critical, global dialogue of theories: A case study of teaching argumentative writing and cross-cultural understanding courses. PhD thesis, Victoria University of Wellington.

Wahyudi, R. (2021) A transnational TEGCOM practitioner's multiple subjectivities and critical classroom negotiations in the Indonesian university context. In R. Jain, B. Yazan and S. Canagarajah (eds) *Transnational Identities and Practices in English Language Teaching: Critical Inquiries from Diverse Practitioners* (pp. 240–258). Bristol: Multilingual Matters.

Wahyudi, R. (2023) Example of practice: Designing and teaching a course that matters: Going beyond business as usual. *Intercultural Education* 34 (2), 199–202.

Walshaw, M. (2007) *Working with Foucault in Education*. Rotterdam: Sense Publishers.

11 A Critical Dialogue Among Participants in a Professional Learning Community

Luciana C. de Oliveira, Destini Braxton, Jia Gui and Tara Willging

This chapter presents a continuing dialogue among participants of a research group entitled 'Multilingual Learners in Schools'. We represent different linguistic, racial/ethnic backgrounds, and home languages. In addition, we have teaching and learning experiences in global contexts. This research group represents a professional learning community (PLC) that has served a dual purpose in promoting collaboration among university faculty (Luciana/Dr D) and doctoral students (Destini, Jia and Tara). We propose to engage in a dialogue about language learning and teaching as we work together as collaborators as part of this research group. We attempt to provide insights for doctoral students as new scholars in education with a particular focus on collaborating, preparing to present and publish together, and engaging in other scholarship opportunities.

This PLC has opened a space for scholars to collaborate on different research projects and presentations. Throughout this chapter, we explore this PLC, unique in both its contextual features and its approach to collaborative learning. Then, drawing from our experiences, successes, and challenges, we participate in a critical dialogue to reflect on our roles, responsibilities, and engagement in the PLC.

Professional Learning Community (PLC)

This chapter is grounded in a sociocultural theoretical perspective of PLCs as 'a group of people sharing and critically interrogating their practice in an ongoing, reflective, collaborative, inclusive, learning-oriented, growth-promoting way; operating as a collective enterprise' (Stoll *et al.*, 2006: 223). Some basic characteristics are present in the majority of the PLC definitions proposed by different scholars, such as shared goals and reflective dialogues (Prenger *et al.*, 2018; Stoll *et al.*, 2006). The following five interconnected variables define the concept of a PLC in a broad approach so it can be applicable to varied settings: (a) reflective dialogue, (b) deprivatization of practice, (c) collaborative activity, (d) shared goals, and (e) a collective focus on student learning. Reflective dialogue refers to a discussion and exploration of issues and challenges using reflection as a guide. Deprivatization of practice explores practice as an open and public endeavor. Collaborative activity refers to ways we engage with each other and collaborate to reach common goals. Shared goals refers to what we share as objectives as part of the PLC. A collective focus on student learning placed students at the center of our discussions.

The next section provides short narratives that tell parts of the stories of each member of our PLC and focuses on the following components: (1) Identity; (2) Teaching experience; (3) Critical incident; (4) Role in this research group. Critical incidents refer to something which we interpret as a problem or a challenge, an event that is not a routine occurrence and is often personal; they refer to any unplanned and unanticipated events that occur during a professional's career (Richards & Farrell, 2010). We use each author's voice and therefore each section is a narrative written in first person.

A Research Group as a PLC

Introductions and critical incidents

Luciana/Dr D

I am a Latina who is multilingual and multicultural. I was born in Brazil, the largest country in Latin America and grew up speaking Brazilian Portuguese at home. I started learning English at age 12 in private language schools in Brazil. At age 18, I started college at a local university in my hometown, Araraquara, in the countryside of the state of São Paulo. It is one of the highest ranked universities in Brazil. My major was Languages (Portuguese and English) and I got a minor in German. During my first year in college, I also started teaching English in a private language school and taught children, adolescents, and adults from Level 1 (beginners) to Level 5 (advanced) and this experience was an incredible opportunity for me to grow both personally and professionally. I learned to work together as a team with other teachers and saw the amazing benefits of collaboration with colleagues. My critical incident is related to this first teaching experience – that initial experience as a teacher was instrumental later on when I did my Master's and started a PhD program and was part of many wonderful collaborations. One such collaboration was in my PhD program in Education at the University of California, Davis. I started collaborating and writing for publication with my mentor Steven Athanases who showed me how to go through all the steps to submit manuscripts to journals – from selecting an appropriate outlet, writing the manuscript itself, writing a cover letter, to writing a response to reviews and making revisions to the manuscript, among many other tasks. I learned so much by being part of his research team and by working closely with him that I wanted to do the same for my own students – anyone interested in working with me on issues related to teaching multilingual learners in K-12, my area of research and teaching. I had my first research group when I was an Assistant Professor at Purdue University. This research group led to several publications, including a book project (de Oliveira & Yough, 2015). Later, when I moved to the University of Miami after a short time at Teachers College, Columbia University, I started a new research group with students from the literacy and language program area which again led to another book project (de Oliveira & Smith, 2019). I continued to collaborate with doctoral students throughout my 15-year career in higher education and find this to be one of the most exciting and wonderful experiences we can have as faculty members and advisors.

When I got to Virginia Commonwealth University (VCU) and started to work in the School of Education, I wanted to follow the same path I pursued in the past – start a research group. I have an incredible opportunity to work with graduate student research assistants in this amazing research group we developed and we collaborate on many scholarly activities, including presentations and publications. This chapter is one such activity that is part of our PLC. The members of this PLC and many of my current and former students call me 'Dr D' – short for my last name 'de Oliveira' – which I find really cute and interesting so that is why I included this above before my introduction!

Destini

I am a Black woman, and with that comes the identity of a Black educator, researcher, student, and mother. I have mainly identified as a Black mother when my advisor, professors, and research team members asked me what they could do to better support me or what additional support I needed from them. I chose this identity because it is the role that takes priority over an educator, researcher, and student. In my mind, I feel as if having the needs of a mother met and the understanding of the obligations that a mother has, the better it would be for me to function as a student, researcher, and educator.

I was raised in Woodbridge, Virginia, in a very diverse community. I had the opportunity to apply to a specialty program called the Center of International Studies and Languages (CISL). This program allowed me to travel to Italy and France as an exchange student for a week and host three exchange students, one of whom I still stay in daily contact with since 2010, and we consider each other 'international sisters'. During this program, I was also able to take foreign language courses. I took four years of Spanish and two years of Arabic during my high school career. Developing knowledge of a second language is to me a critical incident that has had a major influence in my professional life – little did I know that taking four years of Spanish would later hold a lot of importance in my life as a teacher.

I moved to Richmond in 2013 when I began my undergraduate studies in Mathematics, later changing to Psychology at Virginia Commonwealth University (VCU). Richmond was where people truly saw me as Black and not just the 'mixed girl' or the girl who 'looked Black but acted White'. Hearing people, who looked like me, describe me as if I was different played a significant role in how I identified myself. It wasn't until I began my journey as an urban educator, teaching special education in a school that served Black, Latinx, and multilingual students, that I developed a sense of belonging without questioning my identity. In 2018, I earned my Master's of Education in Special Education through the VCU Richmond Teachers Residency (RTR) program. I am in my fourth year of teaching at Richmond City Public Schools. I currently serve as a Special Education, now referred to as Exceptional Education, middle school teacher. I teach sixth-grade Mathematics. The population of my school is made up of Black and Latinx students. The Latinx student community primarily identifies as multilingual, with Spanish being their primary or home language. Throughout my four years of teaching, I have engaged with and advocated for students who are considered to be dually-identified English learners (DIEL). DIELs are students who are English language learners and receive special education services. Through my teaching experience, I have developed my research interests and that is why I believe I am an asset to my research group.

I began my PhD journey in 2019 at VCU. I am currently in my third year of the PhD in Education, Educational Psychology Concentration, program. Within my first year, I gave birth to my son. Just one day after giving birth to him, I was interviewed virtually for an opportunity to become a member of the VCU Holmes Scholars program. This, to myself and interviewers, showed that I was truly dedicated and passionate about being a part of this program. This program's mission is to provide support, resources, professional development, and mentorship to underrepresented students pursuing their PhD. Joining this program allowed me to develop a sense of belonging within an academic setting while continuing to develop my sense of self and identity. Through this program, I was introduced to Dr de Oliveira and my current research team members. My research interests are motivation, emotion, teacher trust, and teacher-student relationships for students with learning disabilities belonging to underrepresented groups in Mathematics. I examine how motivational beliefs, emotion, and teacher trust, impact the *teacher-student relationships and the determination of students with disabilities belonging to underrepresented groups in Mathematics while positively addressing the overrepresentation of Black and Latinx students with learning disabilities in Mathematics.*

Jia

I am a Chinese international student pursuing a PhD. degree in the United States. I was raised and educated in China from kindergarten to undergraduate education. In China, English is a foreign language. I have been exposed to English since grade two. My dad was an English professor, and he would offer English classes once a week for kids at the same age as me who lived in our community. My official English learning experience started in middle school when English was considered the main course. However, I did not realize the importance of English until the last year of my undergraduate studies. I came to the US through a short-term college exchange student program. The new environment exposed me to topics around race and diversity. Later, I studied in the United Kingdom for a master's degree in Teaching English to Speakers of Other Languages (TESOL). During the master's study, my English proficiency was strengthened, and that was when I considered myself bilingual. Now, I speak English and Mandarin in everyday life. I am proud of my accented English (speaking English with a perceived Chinese accent) and feel like I can confidently speak the language fluently.

My first official teaching experience was as a volunteer Chinese teacher serving in Thailand. Besides teaching Mandarin Chinese to elementary and middle school students, I was invited to teach English for a while. My students learned Mandarin and English from me, and I learned Thai from them. I started to consider myself and my students multilingual learners as we were all learning more than two languages. Later, I joined the College Board Volunteer Chinese Teacher Project and became an elementary school Chinese teacher serving at Old Bridge, New Jersey, for a year. During that year, I traveled from school to school (a total of 12) every day and met students who were first-generation, new immigrants from all over the world. For example, some students came from Mexico, Colombia, North Macedonia, Ukraine, Italy, Germany, Pakistan, Iran, India, Singapore and China. Having so many students from different racial and cultural backgrounds, I tried to create a multicultural environment and design class activities embracing students' home cultures. Returning from the US, I started to work as a College English Teacher in my hometown in China. I taught English professional courses and College English courses. My teaching experiences have made me interested in multilingual learners and language teaching.

As I mentioned above, my recent English teaching experience was teaching in English professional courses to English major (EM) students and College English courses to non-English major (NEM) students in a private college in China. These students have been learning English for more than eight years. Some of them speak dialects in everyday life besides Mandarin. The school required English courses to be taught only in English, regardless of students' majors. No Mandarin (first language, L1) should be used in the classroom. The goal of giving English-only instruction is to create an immersive environment to enhance learners' language acquisition. The comprehensible input could help students acquire the language naturally and quickly (Krashen, 1982). However, did students really receive comprehensible input? What if students' English proficiency limited their understanding of the input? What if the teacher did not provide comprehensible input? According to the input principle (Krashen, 1982), learners acquire a language when they receive understandable messages in the target language or comprehensible input. Therefore, when students do not receive comprehensible input, they feel forced to use the second language. This would just frighten them away. It turned out that my point seemed correct because the non-English major students were strongly against the English-only instruction and asked me to use L1 to help them engage in the class. Unlike NEM, English major students were comfortable with English-only instructions. I also found that most NEM students' motivation differed from the EMs'. The NEM students claimed that they would not have a chance to use English in their future careers and daily life. They only wanted to pass the College English Test and final term tests to obtain the degree. This teaching experience I just reported is a critical incident in my professional life – I learned from the comparative teaching experience that one teaching mode or teaching pedagogy does not apply to all multilingual learners. Differentiated teaching will work best for students. Respecting students' needs and culture will bring them more benefits. This perspective was confirmed after I learned about culturally sustaining pedagogy from our professional learning community, which comprises three PhD. students (the second, third, and fourth author of the paper) and my advisor (the first author of this paper). We should draw on students' home languages and cultures to maintain the practices of students (Paris, 2012; Paris & Alim, 2017).

Tara

I am a white cisgendered woman, from the United States. My parents both have bachelor's degrees and my mother is a practicing teacher (as am I). My family heritage is of European descent, specifically German and Italian, and while both my parents had exposure and opportunity for learning more languages, they did not. My family's experience influenced my learning and understanding of languages in different ways. My paternal grandmother grew up speaking Italian with her mother, but was not encouraged to pass it on to her children. My maternal grandfather was born and raised in Germany and has an affinity for learning languages, but again, did not engage my mother in multilingual dialogue – she learned German grammar through writing, but it was not spoken. The critical incident I want to report on is my recall of my first experience with the concept of multiple languages in a middle school Spanish 'foreign language' class. My lack of metacognition in English grammar, despite it being my only language, affected my ability to understand grammar in a second language. The duality of language learning had me hooked since then. I continued Spanish language classes as a graduation requirement but never felt comfortable enough to speak in class or with other students, especially native Spanish speakers.

I attended James Madison University for my bachelor's degree in health sciences and public health education. I also earned a minor degree in Italian, in history and language. Similar to my experiences learning Spanish in an English-speaking environment, I felt nervous and acquired a false confidence in my abilities because I was still able to complete the minor degree requirements successfully. Throughout my minor courses, I developed a close relationship with the professors, who came from Italy to teach language and history at the university. While they attempted to teach only in Italian, the students were all native English speakers and we worked around the need to rely on language acquisition skills, such as the productive struggle in the zone of proximal development ZPD (Lantolf & Appel, 1994). The professors supported our learning but acknowledged the lack of a language-rich environment once we left the classroom. The director of the program encouraged me to participate in the summer study abroad program in 2012 and 2013 in Reggio di Calabria.

After graduating in 2013, I moved to Florence, Italy to be an au pair. I lived with the family that hosted my experience and had an incredible experience. My host family sponsored the enrollment for courses in Italian at the Centro Internazionale Studenti La Pira. All of the students were multilingual but all learning Italian, therefore we could only communicate in Italian. Language learning is a tremendous and vulnerable adventure. From my own journey, I aspire to work with compassion for language learning in schools.

I returned to Virginia and enrolled in the master's degree program in TESOL. I began working in Stafford County Public Schools soon after, first as a provisional teacher and once I was certified, as a licensed postgraduate teacher. I enjoyed the rigorous practice as a new teacher by day and student by night. Now, in my sixth year of teaching students in our ESOL program and finishing the second year of my PhD in Education program, with a concentration in Curriculum, Culture, and Change at Virginia Commonwealth University, I appreciate the opportunity to learn from our research group and recognize how our personal histories impact our work with multilingual students.

Research Processes and Practices

To guide our reflections and dialogue exchanges, we used the following questions:

(1) How has this research group helped enhance our knowledge about multilingual learners as a researcher?
(2) How have we grown as researchers since joining this PLC?

Collaborative autoethnography

We used collaborative autoethnography as the research methodology for this chapter. Collaborative autoethnography (CAE) was developed from autoethnography and refers to a team of researchers pooling their lived experiences on specific issues to uncover commonalities and differences (Chang, 2013). While autoethnography only focuses on analyzing individual narratives, collaborative autoethnography emphasizes analyzing narratives of a duo or team as it involves more than one researcher engaging in the research process (Blalock & Akehi, 2018). We implemented CAE as the methodology for our chapter for two main reasons. First, it allowed us to narrate our personal and unique experiences as members of this research group individually, collectively, and reflectively. Also, it enabled us to highlight our dialogue among ourselves, drawing on each other's experiences to reflect on lessons learned from this PLC.

Data collection and analysis

The collaboration among us in writing this chapter was initiated by Dr D. She received the 'Call for Proposals' and recognized the possibility of gathering the four of us for contributing to this edited volume. Thus, Dr D made this a project part of the research group activities. We mainly used shared Google Documents and emails for collaboration and data collection. We also followed the process presented in Figure 11.1 for data collection and analysis. As the most experienced writer, Dr D was responsible for pulling the chapter together at the end of the process and ensuring the full manuscript followed the guidelines provided by the editors. The collaboration allowed the four authors to peer-review each other's writing prior to submission to the editor. Revisions were made after the entire collaborative process.

What Did We Learn? Presentation of Findings and Discussion

This section presents an explanation of how this particular PLC works in practice and then our dialogue among our PLC with a focus on what we have learned about multilingual learners and ourselves.

Preliminary Data Collection	↓	Individual writing and reflection
		Group sharing and asking questions
Subsequent Data Collection	↓	Individual writing and reflection
		Group sharing and initial analysis
Data Analysis and Interpretation	↓	Individual data review and coding
		Group analysis and theme development
Writing of Results		Individual analysis and outlining
		Group writing

Figure 11.1 Collaborative autoethnography as concurrent collaboration (Adapted from Ngunjiri et al., 2010)

This PLC meets twice a month, typically every other week, on Zoom. Since we started the PLC during the pandemic and given that two of the four members are practicing teachers, we decided that meeting online later in the day (4:30–6:00 PM) on a day in which the members do not have classes was the best choice for the group. The meetings are semi-structured in that we typically have items to discuss but also leave new additions open for all to contribute. Luciana typically leads the meetings with things they need to discuss, but everyone contributes equally to the discussion. The topics for inclusion are negotiated prior to the meeting. We have a running agenda that Jia is typically responsible for updating; however, everyone has access to it and adds information during the meetings. We keep the agenda open during each meeting so we know what will be discussed, and review notes taken by members during and after the meetings. We also keep a calendar of when things are due (such as presentations and publications) so we are all on track. Luciana also sends out calendar invites for the meetings and due dates so nobody is caught by surprise when things are due. Something that is unique to our PLC is how we start each meeting, with about 15 to 20 minutes of a mental health check-in time, especially important for Destini and Tara, two practicing teachers who often just need to discuss some issues of practice that are in their minds as they are teaching on a daily basis. This check-in time was especially important during the pandemic, when they were dealing with challenges that they wanted to share and get other group members' perspectives and ideas.

Question 1: How has this research group helped enhance our knowledge about multilingual learners as a researcher?

During this dialogue, the members of the PLC engaged with each other to reflect on and explain how this research group has helped them explore new perspectives, strategies, and practices to better support and advocate for multilingual learners. The members of the PLC authentically responded to each other throughout the dialogue.

Dialogue section and answering questions about the PLC

Luciana/Dr D: *One of the best things about this PLC is the opportunity to work with emerging scholars and especially those who have an interest in, and experience [of] working with multilingual learners in K-12, including practicing teachers such as Destini and Tara, and international students such as Jia who are learning a lot about K-12 education through our work together. In addition to discussing research issues, we also discuss issues of practice that are happening in schools daily, including most recently the need for substitute teachers and how Destini and Tara are being pulled to other classrooms. This is an emerging issue in K-12 schools and a major area of concern, especially for teachers of MLs.*

Destini: *I chose to join this PLC because I saw it as an excellent opportunity to build on my knowledge and experience working with students who identify as multilingual, with students' first language being Spanish. I also saw this as an opportunity to implement new strategies and practices as a special education teacher who often had dually-identified English learners (DIELs) placed on my caseload. DIELs are students who are classified as both having special needs and also classified as someone who is in the process of learning English. It became disheartening that I constantly had DIELs each year labeled as having a learning disability due to language barriers. When it came time for their triennial re-evaluations, I often noticed that I advocated for them the most because I saw that they did not need special education services. They mostly only displayed difficulty understanding the academic language and content due to their first language being Spanish. As I continued to be a part of this PLC, I was able to explore research findings and strategies that could enhance my professional career as a special education teacher. Working on various projects focusing on multilingual learning has strengthened my understanding of why it is vital to promote equity in my classroom and school. I have learned new equitable and practical strategies to implement within my teaching practices and become a better advocate for multilingual students. In addition, I have the opportunity to specifically learn how to implement equitable and effective practices using the language-based approach to content instruction (LACI) model* (de Oliveira, 2016). *LACI is a teacher education model developed over the past 20 years in classrooms with teachers of multilingual learners by Dr de Oliveira.*

Jia: *I love my PLC because it is a very diverse and open-minded group. We all come from different racial groups holding various teaching and learning backgrounds, bringing different expertise to this community. It is the PLC that helped me gain a better understanding of the definition of multilingual learners. I used to believe that students who are learning more than two languages are identified as multilingual learners. However, after collaborating with my PLC members on WIDA (World-Class Instructional Design and Assessment) projects and other works* *relating to multilingual learners (MLs), I realized that students who engage with and/or are exposed to languages other than English on a regular basis are considered multilingual learners. The clarification of MLs expanded my view on English language teaching and learning and gave me new ideas on research. Under the mentorship of Dr de Oliveira (author 1), I learned the LACI framework that focuses on equity and culture to develop multilingual learners' academic language proficiency. I am using this approach as a theoretical framework and research method in studying K-12 MLs for my dissertation. In the future, as I am planning to teach college-level students in the US context, I plan to use LACI to study adult college multilingual learners.*

During one of our collaborative sessions, we conducted data analysis of classroom observation transcripts using LACI. One member of our community was unsure if the way she coded the C of Community and Collaboration and C of Classroom Interactions [was] accurate. So, we reviewed all our analyses and found that we all mixed examples of these two Cs while doing the analysis. Recognizing that we might have misconceptions about these two concepts, we added comments and concerns to the examples and discussed them with Dr D in the next meeting. By confirming that some of our codes were correct, she clarified the differences between these two Cs by giving us more examples from the texts. The experience highlights the importance of collaboration and peer review in a professional learning community as well as the value of having a mentor who can provide guidance and clarification. By working together and seeking input from an expert in the field, we were able to ensure the accuracy of our analysis and deepen our understanding of the LACI framework.

Tara: *Joining the group as a first-year doctoral student was an incredible opportunity, not only to better understand higher education and research but also how our group collaborates and supports each other. I was introduced to Dr de Oliveira because of her experience with TESOL International Association and research on multilingual learners and culturally sustaining teaching practices (CSTPs). She shared one of her recent books, Focus on Grammar and Meaning (de Oliveira & Schleppegrell, 2015) to help us develop our own academic writing. I particularly enjoyed our recent project based on her work of CSTPs and how it could transfer into my own practice. I work with classroom teachers and work with multilingual students. I find the research and dialogue from our team to be invaluable! I remember our first meeting when I was made aware of the negative framing I used when speaking about multilingual students, that they should only use English in school. The work from our group helped me understand and change my own language to use an assets-based approach and see the strengths of my students and teachers. I am learning to think critically about my own teaching practices. We often discuss the teaching practices that focus mainly on front loading vocabulary for multilingual learners and now I understand that the systems of language functions can be taught within the context of learning. We read and discuss ideas with Dr de Oliveira and others in her network. We research topics that connect our interests, experiences and* readings. I can ask for any advice or support in helping my practice focus on student abilities and the strengths of multilingualism. I read a lot about translanguaging in a project, and now I use a translanguaging stance when I teach math and reading. Through our research, I recognize the need for clear language practices through content objectives and write many examples of lesson plans and analyses. We continue to help each other learn through book studies, sharing our ah-ha moments and hard questions. I feel comfortable discussing the complexities of language and teaching with our group.

Question 2: How have we grown as researchers since joining this PLC?

The following dialogue will explore how each member of the PLC has grown as a researcher. In addition, each member will reflect on their experience, scholarship opportunities, and reflect on the achievement of their goal(s). It was essential to draw on and reflect upon the collaboration amongst the PLC members to promote personal growth, professional development as a researcher, while focusing on multilingual learning and experience(s) with various scholarship opportunities and publications.

Dialogue section and answering questions about the PLC

Luciana/Dr D: *This PLC has contributed tremendously to my sanity these past three years at VCU. Because my position is 100% administration, I deal with problems on a daily basis. I say that I am the problem-solving associate dean – if there is a problem, that problem comes to me! I really enjoy my work but it is a tough one. This research group helps to keep me grounded as a researcher and keeps my productivity a high priority while I also attend to my administrative duties. I absolutely love the diversity of our PLC with a Latina woman, a Black woman, an Asian woman, and a White woman all sharing and learning from each other. I could never have expected that by opening my student researcher positions I would end up putting together this amazing group of individuals, individually and collectively.*

Destini: *When reflecting on my experience as a member of this PLC, I have grown so much as a researcher! I have been able to present at the 2021 Virginia TESOL (VATESOL) Conference, receive my first publication as a second author, and work on various manuscripts. Some of the skills I have strengthened are: transcribing interviews, writing a manuscript from start to finish, and working on literature reviews. It is also important to mention that whenever I had a question, Dr de Oliveira was always readily available and willing to answer my questions. For example, she has developed my understanding of discourse analysis and the use of language when advocating for multilingual learners as I continue to teach middle school students. This has played an important role in my research because I am now able to confidently implement discourse analysis around the use of language within my* *qualitative dissertation study. She was also always looking for ways to collaborate with the members of the PLC to ensure that we received the best academic experience possible while pursuing our doctorate. Being a part of this PLC has allowed me to achieve many of my research goals that I wanted to accomplish before earning my PhD, some of which have been mentioned above. I love being able to collaborate with each of the PLC members because of the fact that we are all racially diverse! That was definitely a bonus because I love learning from different perspectives.*

Jia: *I totally agree with Destini! I gained tons of knowledge and experiences through collaboration opportunities in publication and conference presentations with my PLC colleagues. The co-authoring opportunities strengthened my academic writing skills and boosted my confidence in journal writing. I had no publication experience in the US, so when I first read the 'Call for Papers/Chapters' of this book, I was not clear about the expectations from the editor and the group. As our mentor, Dr de Oliveira walked us through the whole publication process. She led us to read the call thoroughly and picked up a topic. After that, she drafted a proposal and assigned literature review searching tasks and writing sessions for each member. We all worked on our own parts and had a few debriefing sessions via emails, Zoom meetings, and WhatsApp for instant communications. Dr de Oliveira also showed us how to communicate with editors and meet reviewers' requirements. As a non-English native speaker, I cherish every single interaction with my group members in verbal or written form. For example, I learned language patterns used in academic writing by reading their writing pieces; I could imitate the language they used in the conferences. The PLC helped me quickly grow as a researcher!*

Tara: *When the research group invited me to participate, I was impressed and a little overwhelmed by the professional projects on their agenda. However, through the conversations about learning and teaching, I understood the* why *behind their work. During our meetings, we uncover how each researcher brings a new perspective and insight to our common interests. We discuss our experiences as doctoral students and candidates and share personal moments along the way. Considering the context of the Covid-19 pandemic, I am so fortunate for the flexible environment to commit to this group work remotely, but we also cannot wait to meet and work together in person, one day. Despite the challenges of remote research collaboration, I find that everyone is very efficient in communicating and acknowledging the time it takes to build projects together that we are proud of. We are courteous when communicating in the evening and weekends, and respect our group members when they have to say 'no' to an extra project. Working from home, our PLC was able to present two projects at this year's VATESOL conference and we are in the process of publishing them, of which I will be a second author. I learn more every time about the potential for publishing and even the expectation for doctoral students to complete before they become a candidate or defend their dissertation. I am inspired by the* *women I get to work with and learn so much about being a student, working remotely, balancing work, school, and research that I will be forever grateful for this time together!*

Final Thoughts (Not Quite Final)

This chapter presented a dialogue among members of a PLC that highlights our identity, language experiences, and collaborative research activities. Throughout this collaborative process and dialogue exchange, the group members' learning and development as new researchers were highlighted throughout our exchanges. This collaboration has also culminated in our own growth and development as researchers and practitioners, as we have learned more about multilingual learners and their experiences in K-12 schools. In addition, because two of our group members are language learners of English themselves (Dr D and Jia) and the two other members (Destini and Tara) are learners of other languages, we personally share language learning ideas and experiences with the group and invite others to share their learning experiences. It is our hope that, by showcasing these experiences, others involved in or thinking about developing research groups can see the many possibilities for these unique PLCs and will inspire other educators to develop such collaborations in the future.

Critical Discussion Questions

(1) How does a professional learning community such as the one described in this chapter help novice scholars learn more about multilingual learners and experience scholarship opportunities?
(2) What are some other types of professional learning communities that could be started with a focus on multilingual learners and other diverse students?
(3) How can new faculty 'pay it forward' and create these types of PLCs within their new positions in higher education?
(4) What are some challenges and opportunities of PLCs such as the one described in this chapter?
(5) What other ideas might you have for this type of PLC you can share with the research group members?

References

Blalock, A.E. and Akehi, M. (2018) Collaborative autoethnography as a pathway for transformative learning. *Journal of Transformative Education* 16 (2), 89–107. https://doi.org/10.1177/1541344617715711

Chang, H. (2013) Individual and collaborative autoethnography as method. In S. Holman Jones, T.E. Adams and C. Ellis (eds) *Handbook of Autoethnography* (pp. 107–122). New York: Routledge.

de Oliveira, L.C. (2016) A language-based approach to content instruction (LACI) for English language learners: Examples from two elementary teachers. *International Multilingual Research Journal* 10 (3), 217–231.

de Oliveira, L.C. and Schleppegrell, M.J. (2015) *Focus on Grammar and Meaning*. Oxford: Oxford University Press.

de Oliveira, L.C. and Smith, B. (eds) (2019) *Expanding Literacy Practices Across Multiple Modes and Languages for Multilingual Students*. Charlotte, NC: Information Age Publishing.

de Oliveira, L.C. and Yough, M. (2015) (eds) *Preparing Teachers to Work with English Language Learners in Mainstream Classrooms*. Charlotte, NC: Information Age Publishing and TESOL Press.

Krashen, S. (1982) *Principles and Practice in Second Language Acquisition*. Oxford: Pergamon Press.

Lantolf, J.P. and Appel, G. (eds) (1994) *Vygotskian Approaches to Second Language Research*. Westport, CT: Greenwood Publishing Group.

Ngunjiri, F.W., Hernandez, K.A.C. and Chang, H. (2010) Living autoethnography: Connecting life and research. *Journal of Research Practice* 6 (1), E1–E1.

Paris, D. (2012) Culturally sustaining pedagogy: A needed change in stance, terminology, and practice. *Educational Researcher* 41 (3), 93–97.

Paris, D. and Alim, H.S. (eds) (2017) *Culturally Sustaining Pedagogies: Teaching and Learning for Justice in a Changing World*. New York: Teachers College Press.

Prenger, R., Poortman, C.L. and Handelzalts, A. (2018) The effects of networked professional learning communities. *Journal of Teacher Education* 70 (5), 441–452. https://doi.org/10.1177/0022487117753574

Richards, J.C. and Farrell, T.S.C. (2010) *Professional Development for Language Teachers*. Cambridge: Cambridge University Press.

Stoll, L., Bolam, R., McMahon, A., Wallace, M. and Thomas, S. (2006) Professional learning communities: A review of the literature. *Journal of Educational Change* 7 (4), 221–258. https://doi.org/10.1007/s10833-006-0001-8

12 Ebbs, Flows, What's New is Old: A Collaborative Autoethnography of Three EFL Educators in Turkey

Edmund Christopher Melville, Rasha Ashkar and Nicholas Douglas

As English as a Foreign Language (EFL) educators in Turkey who were raised in the cultures of colonized countries, we occupy the margins in higher education. Melville is Brooklyn-born and was raised in the Guyanese tradition; he is currently employed in the US. Ashkar is from Syria and is employed as an international classroom teacher in Turkey. Douglas is from Jamaica and taught previously in Turkey. This collaborative autoethnography involved these three EFL teachers - the three authors of this study – who worked together at a school in Turkey. Surveying our work as educators in the current era enabled us to connect and become thought partners. We conceived this collaborative autoethnography as an inquiry rooted in the politics of our representation with the aim of deconstructing the unequal power relations often created by ideological distortions of social identities in academic discourse. First, we used reconstructed dialogue to make our voices visible and dispel some falsehoods that are presented as truths in many research texts about educators like us. Second, we have examined our histories, our experiences, and our embodied realities in a new and previously unexplored light as we reflexively examined our roles as EFL educators in Turkey. We also applied methodological ingenuity by focusing on the dialogue central to the construction of this collaborative autoethnography. This investigation allowed us to explain and consider our views relative to each other's views and our shared institutional and cultural context.

In summary, we hoped to contribute to academic discourse regarding EFL educators and expand the sociological imagination inherent in the current literature as we represented ourselves as multidimensional (not monolithic), reflexive, inquisitive and collaborative EFL educators via our reconstructed dialogue.

Context

English was introduced to the Ottoman Empire through British trade relations around the 1530s. The Tanzimât period (1839–1876) was marked by the Westernization of Turkish education and severe economic and political setbacks (Kirkgöz, 2005). To construct a Western educational system, Mustafa Kemal Atatürk, the founder of the Turkish republic, sought out foreign experts, such as John Dewey (Korkmaz, 2020). Since then, ELT has undergone many politically motivated changes (Kirkgöz, 2007). Learning English gained popularity from the 1950s to the late 1970s. Political, economic, and commercial relations with the West and the introduction of a liberal economy provided opportunities for Turkish free enterprise, particularly after 1980 (Dogançay-Aktuna, 1998). In 1997, English learning was introduced to students in grades four and five, shifting from secondary to primary school to provide children with more exposure (Kirkgöz, 2009). In 2012, compulsory education increased from 8 to 12 years, and weekly English language study increased from three hours to four (Uztosun, 2013). Selvi (2011) argued that English language learning attracts considerable attention in Turkey, despite the absence of a historical colonizer-colonized relationship, as English is widely used.

Fault Line Spaces: Capital and Habitus Emerge in the Field

Bourdieu's theories can be used to examine the geopolitical and power dynamics surrounding the field of ELT, which is still approached from a colonial perspective, although we are in a new global era. By exploring the interrelationship of 'capital,' 'habitus' and 'field', we elucidated the geopolitical and historical aspects of English teaching and how English has acquired symbolic and economic power (capital). Further, as its status as a lingua franca affects English teaching and learning as a social practice (habitus), value (symbolic, social and monetary) and social standing are conferred through accumulated knowledge of English.

Cultural capital

According to Bourdieu (1986), *capital* is the embodiment, materialization, or institutionalization of effort that is incorporated or implemented such that holders can acquire potentially scarce information. Depending on the context, capital may consist of non-financial assets such as physical appearance and dress style, appreciation of art forms currently defined as elite - such as opera or ballet – academic qualifications, and even grade point averages (therefore, it is akin to habitus).

Habitus

Habitus consists of the appreciation, perceptions, and behaviors created by a society that are internalized by members of that society, thereby forging their dispositions. Habitus relates to views, such as whether ambition is seen as reasonable or unreasonable, a particular commodity is considered accessible or inaccessible, or a particular action is deemed suitable or unsuitable. These viewpoints, in turn, are governed by the prior experiences that have shaped an individual's perceptions (Bourdieu & Wacquant, 1992).

Bourdieu brokered his notion of caste, which highlighted the socially constructed power inequity in French international governance that gave rise to the notion of field. In his ethnographic and sociological research during the Algerian War of Independence, Bourdieu (2003b) saw the brute power behind colonialism, despite the French state's assertion that they were in Algeria to ensure progress (Calhoun, 2006). These experiences led to his conception of 'habitus' as the 'disposition toward the world and towards others' (Wacquant, 2004: 391). Even when displaced Algerians were forced to surrender their habitual way of life, they maintained their traditions and culture. Habitus thus became the mediating category, straddling the divide between the objective and the subjective that enabled Bourdieu to capture and depict the troubled and double-sided world of crumbling colonial Algeria (Wacquant, 2004: 3).

Likewise, we connected our purposeful social practices to the educational field in Turkey, as they also determined how we experienced reality. The collective experience of reality is predicated on perceptions of the self in specific places, at particular times, among certain people and is, therefore, partially defined by the external – hence the need for the mediation of habitus.

Notion of fields

Fields are described as arenas of struggle for control over valued resources or forms of capital. They comprise broad areas in which agents are located according to their social positions – the social spaces wherein individuals pursue their own goals, interact, and compete with one another. Bourdieu argued that the social structure of a given field is premised on dominant and subordinate positions, which form a 'state of relations of force between players that defines the structure of the field' (Bourdieu & Wacquant, 1992: 99).

Bourdieu's notion of fields may have been developed to expose the dynamic forces tearing at the social and mental fabric of the caste society he encountered in colonial Algeria (Wacquant, 2004). He speaks of Algeria as a 'site of logic' that was important to understand because it displayed the 'relationship of domination' and 'racial segregation system' at the foundation of colonial societies (Go, 2013). Bourdieu emphasized that this system based on race and class supported the political privilege of the White French colonizing elite (Go, 2013) and was founded on 'the relation of force whereby the dominant caste maintains the dominated caste under its rule,' keeping it locked in collective 'humiliation' (Wacquant, 2004: 394). Bourdieu's conception of the colonial situation in Algeria unearthed his later notion of 'field'; he saw the dominant and subordinate positional relationships as 'specific and irreducible, much like the relationships between the colonizer and the colonized that formed the colonial situation' (Bourdieu & Wacquant, 1992: 97). In our collective and respective circumstances in the field of ELT in Turkey, we complied with or resisted norms of dominance (school administrators, parents) according to our views and lived experiences.

Bourdieu also (2004) stated that one cannot survive unless one exerts permanent practical reflexivity, which is indispensable for interpreting and assessing a situation and mobilizing consciously. Adams (2006) emphasized that habitus is always related to the field and that, although dispositions become transposable between fields, a lack of fit is always possible, even probable. This lack of fit constitutes the space where reflexivity can emerge, particularly during times of crisis (Bourdieu & Wacquant, 1992: 131).

Epistemic reflexivity describes how the researcher's knowledge must include the sociological conditions of existence and illuminate the 'reflexive analyses to the unthought categories of thought which delimit the thinkable and predetermine what is actually thought' (Bourdieu & Wacquant, 1992: 40). Bolton (2010: 13) writes that reflexivity 'is finding strategies to question our own attitudes, thought processes, values, assumptions, prejudices, and habitual actions to strive to understand our complex roles in relation to others.' In short, reflexivity may become personal and requires a social context.

Bourdieu's notions unearth the complexities of social disadvantage, including their colonial dimensions. Following Bourdieu, in this study, we approached reality as a social concept wherein 'social existence' and what we consider 'real' are related to those around us. Social fields have specific internal power relations defined and maintained by habitus (individual and collective).

We integrated Bourdieu's theories with literature by Turkish scholars on teaching English as a foreign language (EFL) due to the complexity of investigating this study through a single discourse. Our study aimed to collaboratively develop knowledge within our specific context, while simultaneously reconciling our capabilities. The theoretical framework influenced our methodology by acknowledging the importance of logical categories that guide unconscious mental functions, as well as the dialectic between social structures and the dispositions that shape and transform cognitive schemas (Bourdieu, 1990: 41). His theoretical model is rooted in the effort to dialectically surpass divisions between objective and subjective realities.

Research Questions

Arising from the rationale for this study, the questions for this collaborative autoethnography were as follows:

RQ 1: How does our dialogue address the intersection of language, identity, and power for us as EFL teachers in Turkey?

RQ 2: How do we, three EFL educators from culturally and linguistically different backgrounds, perceive our roles and how are we perceived where colonialism is camouflaged in the discourse of global competitiveness?

Methodology

Bourdieu believed that through a dialectical methodology, a social scientist could justifiably leap over the binary modes of thought without being either strictly subjective or strictly objective. With this in mind, we employed Chang's (2013) notion of collaborative autoethnography (CAE) to explain the relational networks between the three authors and their collective struggle against dominant forms of power to make social influence more pronounced.

The key components of the methodology follow:

(1) *Self-focus*: 'The researcher assumes the dual role of the researcher and the research participant' (Chang, 2013: 22).
(2) *Researcher visibility*: 'The researcher turns the lens inward to make thoughts and actions visible and transparent to the audience' (Chang, 2013: 22).
(3) *Context consciousness*: Continual juxtaposition of self and context is crucial. Similarly, social knowledge is formed by the relationships between the researcher and others (Chang, 2013).
(4) *Critical dialogue*: In CAE, dialogue is enriched by team members' occupation of dual spaces of researcher and participant via the dialogue that is created in a community (Chang, 2013).

We sought to co-construct holistic and multiple realities, wherein biography and history intersect as detailed, rich descriptions of contextualized behavior as the context (institutional, cultural and temporal) that both shape and are shaped by an individual's language and actions in a community of others. We believe this is part and parcel of the multivocality inherent in the collaborative process of CAE. This approach, like Bourdieu's work, pulls from the dialectical nature of structure and action and allows one to gain a sense of how actors in various fields live the structures that define them (the habitus).

Our backgrounds

Melville

I am a former professional dancer. I also taught middle school for three years in New York City while earning my first master's degree, followed by six years in Turkey teaching Pre-K to Grade 4 EFL in the elementary division with Ashkar and Douglas. (Melville's reflexive journal)

Douglas

I taught for a combined 10 years in the US, where I earned my master's degree in education. Although I wished to become an entrepreneur rather than pursue teaching, the necessary schooling was too expensive for my mother (my father had died). Thus, I attended a teachers' college that offered scholarships, making it more affordable. (Douglas' reflexive journal)

Ashkar

I studied under the French system; the French colonized Syria, but they called it a mandate. I earned my bachelor's degree in English literature in Syria, a teaching license in Lebanon, and a master's degree from the University of Bath in the UK. Before coming to Turkey, I had dreamt of becoming a teacher since I was 7. My native language is Arabic; I am also fluent in Turkish and English. (Ashkar's reflexive journal)

Collecting reflexively

Data collection, which occurred in three successive phases, comprised pulling information directly from our professional dialogues and interactions:

Phase 1

Orientation and overview – In the first phase, we each kept a reflexive journal – a diary within which the investigator recorded information about themself daily (or as needed; Lincoln & Guba, 1985). Next, during our weekly meetings, we described aspects of our embodied capitals to one another thereby enabling us to see, judge, and act in the world in different ways. We strove to have valid, legitimate, and authentic exchanges throughout our collaborative endeavor. Our conversations were characterized by descriptions of complicity in the allocation and exercise of power – either toward or by each of us – in a loop of self-discipline (Bourdieu & Wacquant, 1992). According to Bourdieu, to 'produce and reward reflexive scientific habitus, it must, in effect, institutionalize reflexivity in mechanisms of dialogue' (1992: 41). Likewise, Chang (2013) contends that CAE emphasizes collective and cooperative self-interrogation among team members.

Phase 2

Focused exploration was based on my readings about Bourdieu, and we incorporated the second phase after-meeting debriefings. We discovered that the debriefings prompted us to share critical incidents – acts of observable behavior sufficient to permit inferences about the observed (Flanagan, 1954) – that served as tools for collecting and analyzing autoethnographic data. This observation reflects Chang's (2013) contention that questioning and probing others adds a unique depth to personal interrogation. Moreover, Tripp (2012) expanded the definition to include commonplace yet 'not necessarily obvious' happenings, and Erlandson *et al.* (1993) contend that using critical incidents (CIs) to understand social context and uncover constructed realities may lead to rich insights.

Phase 3

Member checks and closure was based on Ngunjiri *et al.*'s contention that 'cooperative data collection is key to collaborative autoethnography' (2010: 6) and Chang's (2013) description of CAE participants complementing, contradicting, and probing each other as critical peers. Thus, we reviewed our accounts to dispel misapprehensions, triangulate data, validate sources through comparison, and sustain the trustworthiness of the data (Guba & Lincoln, 1994b).

Back and forth

The data analysis strategy was inspired by constant comparative analysis methods (Glaser & Strauss, 1967), wherein incidents, events and activities are identified and continually compared with emerging categories. We applied these methods to achieve the right fit by constantly comparing old and new data from our recorded dialogues and shared entries from our individual reflexive journals. This back-and-forth movement is characteristic of autoethnography: participants move 'between self and others' to interpret and analyze data (Chang, 2013). Moving between our reflexive journals, CIs, and research questions allowed us to identify recurring themes in the data and infer the capital – the elements that contribute to how we view the world (habitus).

Finally, member checks were again used to ensure fair and balanced interpretation and analysis (Lincoln & Guba, 1985) and facilitate shifting power dynamics by enabling each of us, as participants and researchers, to control our presentation. Each of us provided clarifications and changes as needed to correct any inaccuracies in how we were represented.

Representing Ourselves

Relaying networks

We three formed relational networks to mount a collective struggle against dominant forms of power. To do so, we represented our self-focused, researcher-visible, context-conscious, critically dialogic (Chang 2013) selves via our jointly reconstructed dialogue. Throughout our collaborative ethnographic process, our dialogue equipped us to question each of our beliefs, thoughts, practices, and, most importantly, our mindsets in relation to ourselves and others in context. We selected the CI below to represent the starting point for the research processes: our professional activities. Our dialogue is presented in the following CI, which drove our collaborative inquiry and answered RQ 1: how does our dialogue address the intersection of language and identity and influence us as EFL teachers in Turkey?

With two teachers in each elementary classroom – one Turkish and one international – Ashkar, a Grade 2 international teacher, Douglas, a Grade 3 international teacher, and I (Melville), the Director of Language and Learning Support, began our weekly meetings to discuss the students who were struggling to learn the English language and those having difficulty grasping various concepts as evinced by in-class and out-of-class assessments.

To support struggling learners, Ashkar, Douglas, and I reviewed writing samples from our struggling learners to clarify their needs and revise the instructional plans and assessments. The rubrics the institutions required us to use were given to us. One item states that a satisfactory teacher 'demonstrates current and appropriate knowledge.' Douglas, who arrived in Turkey a few months earlier, asked, 'How are we supposed to know what "appropriate knowledge" is since we are new here and are unfamiliar with the learning outcomes put forward by the Turkish Ministry of Education.' I replied with a knowing and, I hoped, consoling nod and said to him, 'That's the reason we're meeting today, to speak about the learning outcomes that are only published in Turkish. We are asked to use a scale of 1 to 4.' '1 to 4 of what? I. Can. Not. Read. Turkish!' Douglas exclaimed. Ashkar interjected, 'I can translate them from Turkish to English so that this process actually makes sense' 'Great!' I said to Ashkar, 'That would be very helpful for us to be able to accurately measure areas that the students need to improve in, and any incoming international teacher would be able to see our comments and guide them.' (Critical incident)

Ashkar said, 'It would be great if the incoming international teachers were able to read the objectives in English to take their students to the next level.' Melville replied, 'Perhaps then there would be fewer students who are struggling. But, ultimately, student success is tied to teacher belief.' Douglas, in agreement with both Ashkar and Melville, nodded his head while tapping his finger on the table and asked, 'What if we continue this discussion during Monday's meeting?' It was a Friday afternoon.

Ashkar, over the weekend, translated the rubric we used to determine which students required remediation support. She began this meeting by turning her laptop toward us as, in order to work cooperatively, we sat around a table on chairs designed for eight-year-olds. The translated learning outcomes for English language proficiency were displayed on the whiteboard so that Melville and Douglas could critique them and make suggestions for revisions.

After taking in the whiteboard, Melville said, 'This looks great! I have been looking into English language standards used in similarly developing countries and would like to change a couple of the indicators so that teachers from all over could connect with the language used.' Douglas responded, 'I think it is fine as it is; it seems clear to me.'

Ashkar stated, 'I have also explored other schools right here in Turkey! And, I worked really hard on this translation, Melville, and it will be a lot more informative for international teachers than when it was in Turkish.' 'What's behind this? Why are you so interested? Why are you so bent on introducing this tool when you might not even be here to see it through?' Feeling uneasy with the sharpness in Ashkar's voice, Melville replied, 'I know firsthand what it's like for teachers to teach what they think I need as opposed to what I really need.' 'And we don't?' Douglas interjected. 'Look, I am leaving because I would like to work in an institution that might value what I have to offer instead of aiming to humiliate me by seeing that my knowledge and skills are being depreciated. We three are surrounded predominantly by White teachers from North America, over 50 of whom have only bachelor's degrees. While we teach, perform research for our degrees, and participate in every school activity, we watch less qualified teachers rise to leadership positions, yet senior administrators fail to consider our repeated requests. Did senior administration ask you to fill in for the early childhood coordinator position? Did anyone mention Douglas's name when a grade-level lead was sought? I am dually certified and working toward my doctoral degree and not getting a very high rate of return on my educational investments. But our work is less about me and more about the students who receive lower grades because they may have a thick Turkish accent.'

Douglas, with a hoarse voice, said, 'We are not enemies, and if we continue like this, then we are only talking the talk but not walking the walk. We've let these people make us argue amongst ourselves. That is the oldest trick in the book. I come from a line of Black Jamaicans, and I saw so much fighting between the Black, Indian and Chinese Jamaicans, while everyone spoke the same Jamaican patois.' Melville said, 'Right! We are drinking the Kool-Aid. It is the same thing in Guyana, or at least from what my mother told me. She always told us stories of the racial strife between the Indians and Blacks in British Guyana. From as far back as I can remember, there have been race riots between the Indians and the Blacks especially … the Brits brought both groups over, and we began to compete over the limited resources, both groups trying to become more powerful than the other.' Douglas replied, 'You make it sound like they brought them over for a holiday. Britain imported indentured labor, mainly from India, when buying and selling us became illegal.' 'The French did the same thing!' Ashkar added, 'In Syria, our textbooks called it an occupation. We are all products of countries that fought for power.'

We turned our lenses inward to investigate our thoughts and actions and the intersection of all three of us as we assumed the dual roles of researchers and participants in our reconstruction of dialogue for the joint authorship of this chapter. CIs led us to communicate what we thought and how we felt so we could act as a network. Thus, the CIs aligned with Bourdieu's (1990: 56) notion of habitus (embodied history) and provided practical means of documenting our views, experiences and circumstances as EFL educators in Turkey. As individuals, writing and reading what we had written provided a stark reminder of how our views of identities were continually juxtaposed to the context of the school in which we worked. Most importantly, we were reminded of the fragile ways in which our identities were constructed, in part, by our school.

In sum, we found that our use of dialogue as a 'method' addressed our individual and collective intersections of language, identity, and power as EFL educators in Turkey and enabled us to navigate the ways we think, feel, and act in contexts we encountered and are likely to encounter within systems and structures that are not prepared to recognize us as individuals but may struggle to ignore us as a collective.

I view my role as being …

In late summer, given the high rate of attrition, we were all mildly surprised that we each were back. As EFL educators, we continuously rely on previously acquired and accumulated knowledge about teaching from other contexts to educate our students. Below, our dialogue and reflexive journals reveal how we perceived our roles as EFL educators in Turkey. Collectively, we answered RQ 2: how do we, three EFL educators from culturally and linguistically different backgrounds, perceive our roles and how are we perceived where colonialism is camouflaged in the discourse of global competitiveness?

While packing up to leave the classroom after leading a meeting, I (Melville) told Douglas, 'I am glad to see you back.' Douglas replied, 'Yeah, last year was difficult for me; parents were complaining about their kids not understanding me because of my accent. Some parents have a narrow view of who native speakers of English are and what they look like.' I replied, 'Yeah, neither of us has the face of English from the parent's perspective. Many parents would ask if I would teach private weekend lessons because of my American accent.' Douglas added, 'If you remember, many parents complained to the principal and told them they were paying for native speakers to teach their children.' I replied, 'I do remember.' Douglas continued, 'Parents insisted that Jamaicans are not native English speakers; they expected to get what they were paying for, which is native-sounding speakers of English … if my accent were like yours, there would be no problem.'

Matching the theoretical framework, Douglas' statements in our dialogue reflect what Bourdieu (1990: 114) referred to as 'linguistic capital,' which is embodied in language and refers to one's proficiency in and relationship to language, including pronunciation and accents. Based on this concept, the personified speaker of English would be a White American, not Douglas, a Black Jamaican, who is a native speaker of English but does not have the 'face of English' (Melville 2012). Thus, the symbol of the native speaker defined the linguistic boundaries that position the non-native English speaker as bankrupt (Gill, 2012) and externally predetermined Douglas' role as an EFL educator in Turkey.

I considered Bourdieu's (1992) comments regarding the commodification of language, wherein ELT is referred to as a 'linguistic market,' and my experiences in Turkey. I also thought about Baugh's (2005: 158) linguistic profiling based on 'auditory cues that may include racial identification but can also be used to identify other linguistic subgroups within a given speech community.' In the Turkish ELT market, Douglas' Jamaican-accented English was devalued by some parents, whereas my American English was heralded. Baugh (2005: 164) states that 'the dominance of US culture and the economy has evoked the full continuum of scorn to envy'. In Turkey, there is 'linguistic adoration' of American-accented English; parents complimented my 'beautiful speech' as a positive linguistic attribute they wanted for their children.

The following conveys how Douglas' internal view of his role is unlike the external view presented in our previous dialogue.

> I have always viewed my role as ensuring that my students have a love for learning. It is important for me that my colleagues and I help our students solve real-world problems. Specifically, my key role here is related to my teaching and my students' learning of English. (Douglas's reflexive journal)

Linguistic profiling is usually associated with stereotypical views of racial discrimination; it is common in Turkey based on the preference for hiring teachers from the US, then the UK. Ashkar shared her view of her role and expressed it in her reflexive journal as follows:

(Ashkar's reflexive journal)

Below is an excerpt of Melville's view shared with Douglas and Ashkar:

> My role in large part has been to teach English to students whose parents are most interested in them learning from American teachers. (Melville's reflexive journal)

All of these examples point to what Howey and Zimpher (2006) refer to as the trend in universities connected to PK-12 schools of having 'boundary-spanning' positions; they describe 'boundary spanners' as 'individuals who [blur] the lines of responsibility traditionally assumed by those in universities and schools' (2006: 5). I, along with other 'border crossers' – those crossing the traditional boundaries of professional role responsibilities (Howey & Zimpher) – invoke notions of a third space where migrants become hybrids and liminal positions emerge, reflecting the hybridity theory that individuals of in-between geographic locations and roles draw on multiple discourses to make sense of the surrounding world (Bhabha, 1994).

Collective Self Appraisals

The reconstruction of our dialogue around what tool we might use as a stratagem to effectively assess and further facilitate the English language acquisition of our students and our 'member checking' enabled us to see how our discourse addressed the intersection of language, identity, and power for us as EFL teachers in Turkey. We realized that our power in this context resided in the networks that we formed with each other as professionals and how we rationalized teaching English in Turkey. Power does not reside in individual circumstances but in our systematically interconnected relationships. Our speaking back-mounted a collective struggle against the dominant forms of power, beginning with discourse and leading to ideologies, institutional and national.

Through the member checking and joint authorship of this text, we recognized how we each struggled for recognition within the country and that our school's organizational culture was, based on our perceptions of both, more powerful than each of us. We agreed during this write-up that we regarded our circumstances in Turkey as symbolic violence (Bourdieu, 1990) – a cultural scheme that appears natural but is power-based. This perception shifted as we began considering our job in the field through our relation network while deploying our individual skill sets to act as a collective with an aim to not reproduce the inequities that had become part of our embodied histories. We also now inhabit the 'in-between' (Bhabha, 1994) space, with a reflexive habitus that Bourdieu contends mediates a field that enables greater awareness of the organizational, cultural and social expectations of us as EFL educators.

We similarly saw that EFL educators in Turkey are seen as transmitters of knowledge gained from prior institutions and training, just as we had viewed ourselves. We all expressed a deep commitment to the needs of the students. Melville's perceived role of 'teach[ing] English to students whose parents are most interested in their children learning from American teachers,' Ashkar's 'teaching English and celebrating and bringing together all aspects of my students' cultures,' and Douglas's commitment to 'ensuring that my students have a love for learning' and to 'solve real-world problems' express a dual commitment – first to our students; second to the wider society of Turkey.

Our views, in total, suggest that, as EFL educators, we needed to source information from our prior experiences in education and everyday lives to fulfill the primary role of teaching English to Turkish students. Though we needed to draw from the school in which we worked, our roles required us to draw more from our past experiences and skill sets. This was especially clear when Ashkar expressed her view of the social structure in each setting (ELT, specifically in Turkey) as premised on dominant and subordinate positions, as Bourdieu and Wacquant (1992) attested. This is evident in the social structure of ELT in Turkey today in the set standard of non-native EFL educators measuring themselves against their native English-speaking counterparts, thereby perpetuating a hierarchy. The linguistic capital of non-native educators is easily misconstrued. They are primarily seen as subordinate to the dominant native EFL educators' linguistic capital, as reflected in Douglas's responses.

These recognition patterns or misunderstandings are easily recognizable in social structures in Turkey and elsewhere. Such inequities led Melville to recognize that his 'beautiful speech' positions him as a 'reflexivity winner' (Hey, 2005: 864). Adams (2006: 517) further observes, 'Reflexivity is bounded in advance by social structure limits as embodied in one's habitus.' Thus, individuals can be only as reflexive as their circumstances, cultures and societies permit them to be. Consequently, winning the game of reflexivity in the field is typically group-specific and context-dependent, and those who succeed generally are from a dominant social class.

In ELT in Turkey, English as a global language separated us within our positions as non-native or native EFL educators and bound us to use English as a shared tool that sustained us in our social, cultural, political, and economic needs. The back-and-forth dialogue between Ashkar, Douglas and I revealed our perceptions of the role of English and our role as educators. We recognize that we, as EFL educators, provide English education as the global commodity that it is within the monopolized linguistic marketplace.

The three authors have come to know that we are products of the ebb and flow of the historical discourses and current dialogues that continue to shape EFL educators as facilitators for spreading the 'global commodity' of English (Pennycook, 2007: 112). Going forward, as Melville lives and works in Iraq, Douglas in the UAE and Ashkar in Turkey, we have made the commitment to each other to continually examine how and why our practices may have been altered in our current contexts as a result of this dialogic collaborative endeavor. We also committed to a future joint presentation.

Conclusion

As a profession, EFL education has diverged from its origins in colonialist expansion's promotion of the global use of English. Now, possibilities for individual expansion abound. As English is used as a bridging language, or *lingua franca*, enhancing global tourism, linguistic migration, and more, the reasons for adopting English have changed. Learning English is in people's best interests owing to their relationship with globalization rather than explicit coercion. As EFL educators, we simultaneously celebrate our students' English proficiency successes while facilitating some globalization effects of which we may disapprove, such as multinationalism and homogenization.

Autoethnography (collaborative or otherwise) is ethnographic owing to the intent to gain cultural understanding (Chang, 2013). Through dialogue, CIs, and reflexive journals, we realized that distinctive 'cultures,' which we believe are created by people's perceptions and actions concerning extant social systems, produce circumstances that empower some and disempower others. This realization led the three authors to understand that, had we all remained at the same institution in Turkey, this chapter might have been very different due to the ways society and institutions influence our views.

Critical Discussion Questions

(1) Who has the earned/unearned privilege to validate your educational qualifications?
(2) Where do you position yourself in terms of your identity and role as an ELT educator?
(3) What theories (or theoretical frameworks) support an understanding of the role of the EFL teacher working in low- and middle-income countries in an era of uncertainty and inequality?
(4) How do geopolitics and power dynamics affect the role of EFL educators?
(5) How do your perceived realities relate to those of others in your current context?

References

Adams, M. (2006) Hybridizing habitus and reflexivity: Towards an understanding of contemporary identity? *Sociology* 40 (3), 511–528. https://doi.org/10.1177/003803850663672
Bhabha, H.K. (1994) *The Location of Culture*. London, Routledge.
Baugh, J. (2005) Linguistic profiling. In A. Ball, S. Makoni, G. Smitherman and A.K. Spears (eds) *Black Linguistics: Language, Society and Politics in Africa and the Americas* (pp. 167–180). Routledge.
Bolton, G. (2010) *Reflective Practice: Writing and Professional Development* (3rd ed.). Sage.
Bourdieu, P. (1986) The forms of capital. In J. Richardson (ed.) *Handbook of Theory and Research for the Sociology of Education* (pp. 241–258). Greenwood Publishing Group.
Bourdieu, P. (1990) *The Logic of Practice*. Stanford university press.
Bourdieu, P. (2004) *Science of Science and Reflexivity*. Polity.
Bourdieu, P. and Wacquant, L.J. (1992) *An Invitation to Reflexive Sociology*. University of Chicago Press.
Chang, H. (2013) Individual and collaborative autoethnography as a method: A social scientist's perspective. In S.H. Jones (ed.) *Handbook of Autoethnography* (pp. 107–122). Left Coast Press, Inc.
Dogançay-Aktuna, S. (1998) The spread of English in Turkey and its current sociolinguistic profile. *Journal of Multilingual and Multicultural Development* 19 (1), 24–39.
Erlandson, D.A., Harris, E.L., Skipper, B.L. and Allen, S.D. (1993) *Doing Naturalistic Inquiry: A Guide to Methods*. London: Sage.
Flanagan, J.C. (1954) The critical incident technique. *Psychological Bulletin* 51 (4), 327. https://doi.org/10.1037/h0061470
Glaser, B. and Strauss, A. (1967) *The Discovery of Grounded Theory: Strategies of Qualitative Research*. London: Weidenfeld and Nicholson.
Go, J. (2013) Decolonizing Bourdieu: Colonial and postcolonial theory in Pierre Bourdieu's early work. *Sociological Theory* 31 (1), 49–74. https://doi.org/10.1177/0735275113477082
Guba, E.G. and Lincoln, Y.S. (1994b) Competing paradigms in qualitative research. In N.K. Denzin and Y.S. Lincoln (eds) *Handbook of Qualitative Research* (pp. 105–117). London: Sage.
Hey, V. (2005) The contrasting social logics of socialit and survival: cultures of classed be/longing in late modernity. *Sociology* 39 (5), 855–872. https://doi.org/10.1177/0038038505058369
Howey, K. and Zimpher, N. (2006) *Boundary Spanners: A Key to Success in Urban P-16 Universityschools Partnerships*. Washington, DC: American Association of State Colleges and Universities.
Kirkgöz, Y. (2005) Motivation and student perception of studying in an English-medium university. *Journal of Language and Linguistic Studies* 1 (1), 101–123.
Kirkgöz, Y. (2007) English language teaching in Turkey: Policy changes and their implementations. *RELC Journal* 38 (2), 216–228. https://doi.org/10.1177/0033688207079696
Kirkgöz, Y. (2009) Globalization and English language policy in Turkey. *Educational Policy* 23 (5), 663–684. https://doi.org/10.1177/0895904808316319
Korkmaz, S. (2020) The position of physical education in John Dewey's report of education in Turkey. *European Journal of Education Studies* 7 (5). https://oapub.org/edu/index.php/ejes/article/view/3092/5729
Lincoln, Y.S. and Guba, E.G. (1985) *Naturalistic Inquiry*. London: Sage.
Ngunjiri, F.W., Hernandez, K.A.C. and Chang, H. (2010) Living autoethnography: Connecting life and research. *Journal of Research Practice* 6 (1), E1.
Pennycook, A. (2007) The myth of English as an international language. In S. Makoni and A. Pennycook (eds) *Disinventing and Reconstituting Languages* (pp. 90–115). Clevedon: Multilingual Matters.

Tripp, D. (2012) *Critical Incidents in Teaching: Developing Professional Judgment*. New York: Routledge.
Selvi, A.F. (2011) The non-native speaker teacher. *ELT Journal* 65 (2), 187–189.
Wacquant, L. (2004) Following Pierre Bourdieu into the field. *Ethnography* 5 (4), 387–414. https://doi.org/10.1177/1466138104052259

13 Critical Listening: A Teacher-Scholar Dialogue on the Challenges of Linguistically- and Culturally-Centered Coursework

Julia E. Kiernan, Joyce Meier and Xiqiao Wang

This chapter argues for a meta-reflective concept we call *critical listening*, which is an often-overlooked aspect of pedagogical dialogue; as this chapter illustrates, *critical listening* is central to the development and implementation of responsive, critical pedagogies. It entails listening to one another as we describe our teaching and name challenges that emerge in our classrooms, and reflecting back on and analyzing what we hear; such feedback, in turn, helps us see ourselves, better understand complicated classroom situations, and apply this knowledge to subsequent teaching. *Critical listening* involves studying ourselves, as well as one another. Thus, this chapter brings together action research and teacher dialogue, as tools to illustrate how nuanced understandings and interpretations of entangled teaching moments can be situated within the intersectional identities of ourselves and our students. Accordingly, the responsive pedagogies we offer are informed by our own self-reflexive, layered dialogue around problematic scenarios that arose in our classrooms.

This work is primarily informed by the joint dialogue of three faculty who taught a first-year bridge writing course at a large US post-secondary institution. Within this self-study, the concept of *critical listening* evolved out of discussions around a course consisting of mostly multilingual students – a course in which we worked collaboratively to create coursework that centered students' languages and cultures as assets and resources for learning. We ask:

- How might recursive teacher dialogue surface the complex ways that our pedagogical choices can both elevate the rich linguistic and cultural gifts of diverse learners *and* engender friction, exclusion and injustice?
- How might recursive teacher dialogue help us see that racism, sexism, and classism can still emerge across international lines of difference, even in pedagogies that intentionally challenge the linguistic and cultural racism expressed through the valorization of standardized English?
- How might recursive teacher dialogue itself become a resource for teachers' learning as they work to understand the relationships of identity and language across various teaching and learning situations?

In seeking to answer these questions, we used collaborative and recursive pedagogical approaches to respond to the complexity of our own attitudes and responses as well as those of others (e.g. students, pre-service teachers, graduate students, non-tenured faculty, tenured faculty, etc.). We argue that closer attention must be paid to the many layers of dialogue that occur within teaching: multiple perspectives, experiences, and approaches are necessary in order to not only make visible the competing undercurrents of learning environments, but also to make room for a richer understanding of classroom dynamics. These moves can lead to the development of sustainable and nuanced pedagogical practices, particularly those that acknowledge the many manifestations of diversity, equity and inclusion across lines of difference.

Theoretical Framework: Intersectionality, Linguistic Justice and Critical Listening

Scholar-teachers in our home discipline of rhetoric and composition have long argued for Students' Right to Their Own Language (CCCCs 1974, 2003, 2006, 2014) and for students to express themselves using their own linguistic and multimodal repertoires (especially in, but not exclusive to, theories of translingualism – see Horner & Lu, 2011); yet, this theoretical shift is not fully experienced by many of our diverse students. While our disciplinary focus on language and communicative practices lends itself towards issues of linguistic racism, our students embody myriad visible and invisible personal and academic intersectional identities (such as race/ethnicity, indigeneity, gender, age, ability, etc.) that can obstruct their access to learning. Building upon the work of others (Crenshaw, 1989; Collins, 1990), Hankivsky defines an intersectional perspective as one where 'inequities are never the result of single, distinct factors. Rather, they are the outcome of intersections of different social locations, power relations and experiences' (2014: 2). Intersectionality is recognized as a dynamic of oppression in which power-invested and mutually constructed structures intersect to marginalize (Collins & Bilge, 2020; Inoue, 2015), an intersectional approach supports a way of understanding and analyzing the world that accounts for the complexity of human experience. However, attending to only one or two (often visible) facets of identity can render other, and broader, oppressive structures invisible. As Kishimoto (2018) suggests, such single-minded focus can flatten or obscure other important axes of difference. We situate intersectionality as central to framing *critical listening*, but do so while acknowledging that depending on institutional demographics, the full spectrum of the theories that inform intersectionality may not always be at play.

One such theory is linguistic racism; April Baker-Bell (2020) reminds us that US culture (and Western culture more broadly) is infused with Anti-Black Linguistic Racism, which she defines as the 'linguistic violence, dehumanization, and marginalization that Black Language speakers experience in schools and in everyday life' (2020: 3). Linguistic racism influences teacher perceptions of student ability for both US and non-US students. Dumas and Ross (2016) explain that 'linguistically marginalized' students are regularly categorized by educators as 'linguistically inadequate.' Consequently, the standard English reified by teachers across Western educational settings works to construct students who speak languages other than English and/or non-standard varieties of English as racialized others – a situation that has prompted Franquiz and Ortiz (2017) to, as De Costa *et al.* (2021) put it, equate the 'acquisition of standardized language codes with acquisition of Whiteness' (2017: 3).

While linguistic practices and language usages that deviate from privileged English are often not always easily apparent and, therefore, can manifest as invisible markers of oppression, race and culture can provide visual markers that are used to ascribe student ability. In recognizing these histories and experiences there has been a recent move across our home discipline to attend to translingual and transcultural themes within coursework, much of which is a direct response to shifting student demographics. This chapter contends that translingualism (and transculturalism) align with intersectionality in their attention to 'situating oneself in liminal social spaces and drawing from values and practices of diverse cultures to constantly reconstruct one's identity and social belonging' (Lee & Canagarajah, 2019: 4); the dialogues we offer in later sections of this chapter illustrate ways that teachers can use *critical listening* to practically apply these theories in efforts to accept, honor, and validate the many colliding identities of the many members of our learning communities.

Critical listening embraces all these theories in its attempt to make space for multiple dialogues, particularly those that enable instructors to draw upon rhetorical listening, which acknowledges the 'cultural logics' of others as well as the relationships to larger ideologies and institutions.

Rhetorical listening is central to what we define here as a *critical listening* approach; it includes and recognizes the 'privileges and non-privileges' (Ratcliffe, 2006: 32) of all members of a classroom. Marty (2008), building upon Ratcliffe, identifies four moves of rhetorical listening: '(1) promoting an understanding of self and other; (2) proceeding within an accountability logic; (3) locating identifications across commonalities and differences; and (4) analyzing claims as well as the cultural logics within which these claims function' (2008: 75). Informed by theories of linguistic racism, anti-racist pedagogy, and intersectionality, a *critical listening* approach can enrich pedagogical dialogue that encourages teacher reflection on the complexity of student identities and experiences – each with its own shifting axes of privilege and marginalization. Proponents of the aforementioned theories support work in the contact zone (Pratt, 1999), as such a framework entails a self-understanding of one's many intersecting identities. This approach invokes Jacqueline Jones Royster's (1996) questioning: When do we listen (or not)? How do we listen? How do we demonstrate that we honor and respect the person talking (1996: 38)? Such moves, we argue, enact 'rhetorical listening' as a 'trope for interpretive invention and as a code of cross-cultural conduct' that 'signifies a stance of openness that a person may choose to assume in cross-cultural exchanges' (Ratcliffe, 2006: 1).

In the context of this chapter, a *critical listening* approach within teacherly dialogue is essential in recognizing moments of identity conflict that are felt by all members of the learning community (teacher and students). *Critical listening* is always intersectional, but also recognizes the value and juxtaposition of a specific perspective, as 'all people ... have a stake in each other's quality of life' (Ratcliffe, 2006: 31). At the heart of *critical listening* is the goal of shifting mindsets in order to surface the voices, perspectives, and experiences of diverse students. This approach aligns with action research through enabling recursive and responsive pedagogy that leads to recommendations for curricular and social change across post-secondary contexts. It intentionally resists flattening out differences *or* ignoring/veiling racism and other specific components of discrimination that manifest in the everyday classroom experience. In advocating for *critical listening*, we acknowledge its ongoing, unfinished nature, and that the work forward may be imperfectly done.

Methodology: Dialogic Inquiry Approach to Critical Listening

Institutional context

Like many institutions of higher learning across the US, the university where this research is situated has witnessed a rapid and drastic increase in international students; for a five-year period, growth in the number of international students rose from 5% to 8% annually. In 2017, roughly

10% of our undergraduate class (and 20% of our graduate class) were from non-US countries (Office for International). Moreover, the writing department, where this research is grounded, and especially the bridge course, Preparation for College Writing (PCW), which is the primary nexus of dialogue within this chapter, is home to large numbers of non-US multilingual students (roughly 80% of the students), US multilingual students (e.g. the children of migrant workers and other immigrants) and US BIPOC students. As an academic unit that introduces diverse learners to formal language practices at the university, PCW has become a hub that supports pedagogical innovation and curricular revision informed by asset-based pedagogy; this course enables collaborative research into diverse students' literacy experiences, and provides space for related teacher training and dialogue.

Instructor positionalities

The three authors in this article were colleagues who taught numerous sections of PCW. Joyce had been serving as the Associate Director of First Year Writing (FYW) for two years and Xiqiao and Julia were newly hired by the program. Our positionalities, as transnational individuals with divergent experiences of teaching, learning, language, and language negotiation across disciplinary fields, inform the approaches we take when working through our data.

Julia's academic and personal background, while monolingual, is firmly grounded by the bilingual and multilingual structures of her home country: Canada. When Julia moved from a small, Eastern monolingual and primarily working-class province to graduate school in the largest and most culturally diverse province of Canada, the sheer abundance of diversity was initially shocking, but has since shaped all aspects of her professional career and personal life. Beginning with her dissertation research, Julia sought to better understand the affordances and constraints of linguistic diversity for allophone Canadians – citizens, usually immigrants, whose first language is not English, French, or an Indigenous language (according to the 2016 census, roughly 22.3% of the Canadian population would be considered allophone). However, when she moved her professional career to the US her focus shifted towards multilingual US and non-US students – not stemming from a lack of interest in Canadian linguistic diversity, but due to a need for teachers prepared to work with diverse multilinguals. While herself cisgendered and monolingual, Julia's children attend Francophone schools where many students are immigrants, some from war-torn countries. Her children are exposed to class, language, and culture in ways that she could never have imagined growing up in a small, isolated region of Canada, yet Julia feels that these experiences are helping to shape her children to be empathetic citizens who see intersectional differences as normative and expected.

As her first-year writing program's Associate Director, Joyce has extensive experience observing and mentoring colleagues, and organizing monthly faculty workshops that enable her to identify common themes and innovative pedagogical practices. These experiences are deepened by her teaching of community-based courses, as well as a college freshman writing class in summer 2015, at the Harbin Institute of Technology in China (HIT). Indeed, after her time in China, Joyce returned to facilitate a faculty workshop in which she presented, illustrated, and unpacked a range of the taken-for-granted cultural practices she had encountered there, as she was convinced these practices manifested themselves in the expectations and assumptions of many of her Chinese students in the US (for example, Harbin's use of classroom monitors – student leaders who acted as 'translators' to mediate between the Chinese students and the US teachers; the highly hierarchical classroom structure of the HIT classroom as evident by the teacher's raised dais and extensive podium, with the student seats arranged below, in church-like pews). In addition, Joyce's background growing up in a working-class, bilingual (Polish and English) household helped sensitize her to the particular struggles linguistically diverse students face. Finally, as a White woman, she has nonetheless engaged in multiple, collaborative, interracial community projects that supported local schools and other institutions, such as a two-year Underground Railroad project highlighting the unique contributions of Michigan conductors of color, and a 10-year 'Life-Stories' project, whereby her university students co-facilitated writing workshops with Detroit elders and children.

Xiqiao's background as a biliterate scholar and an international student have helped her identify problematic scenarios that embody the intersectionality of minority writers; her ethnographic research into the literacy practices of Chinese international students and her role as principal investigator in a cross-disciplinary research study have allowed her to engage with diverse perspectives for interpreting and assessing asset-based pedagogy in her classroom. Having come to the US in her early twenties from a working-class family in China, she shares the same struggles as most of her students for adding English to her linguistic repertoire; at the same time, she attends to noticeable differences between her own class background and those of her students, most of whom come from positions of privilege in their home countries. Such similarities and differences provide a unique lens for attending to intersectional identities through ongoing dialogues with her students and colleagues.

Dialogue as methodology

The work discussed in this chapter has been ongoing for the last decade, with support from various departmental and institutional grants. Beginning in 2012, the authors participated in a program initiative that involved a cohort of six teacher scholars designing asset-based pedagogy in accordance with translingual and transcultural principles; the group's second goal was to re-imagine PCW to better serve linguistically and culturally diverse students. This initial collaboration set off a constellation of dialogues that have led to continuously expanding initiatives. It is in this institutional context that this project emerged. The teaching scenarios discussed in the following section were identified from an evolving composite of data streams drawn from fieldnotes, memos, and audio recordings that captured the richness of our PCW-related dialogues, as the six original instructors (including the authors) met monthly over a two-year period; then the three authors of this article, continued to meet at least once a month, over the next six years. Herein we focus on the pedagogical conversations surrounding two of the six scenarios we originally developed for a departmental faculty workshop, as each embodies, albeit differently, the complexities of intersectional identities that go beyond linguistic and cultural difference.

Pedagogical Dialogues

Each of the included teaching scenarios is affiliated with a single instructor and cohort of PCW students; however, both scenarios describe an arc of dialogue among the authors, much of which occurred outside the classroom space. The included scenarios begin by describing instances of student conflict that emerged within a specific teaching moment, move to discuss how these moments reified into broader and recurring classroom themes, and close with a brief example of pedagogical dialogue. Important to each scenario is attention to how a single moment of conflict, when validated and listened to critically, is able to shape the learning community and engender opportunities to recognize the nuanced and layered complexities of intersectionality. In both cases, dialogue among teachers provided the vehicle through which teacher awareness and learning occurred – learning that the teachers were each able to take with them back into the classroom. First, we present scenario one and our analysis that reveals how classed identities could mask the complexity of racial discourse in transnational contexts, this is followed by scenario two, which reveals how conversations around gendered identity can surface opportunities for learning.

Scenario One: Critically listening to discomfort

Over the course of several class periods, Joyce invited students to share objects of cultural significance with others, which led to subsequent conversations (amongst Joyce, Xiqiao, and Julia) concerning the intersectional identities of PCW students. The authors were especially interested in discussing a student exchange that occurred when a female Chinese student shared her umbrella; when the student explained the main purpose of the parasol was 'to keep her skin white,' a Dominican American student responded: 'Are there no dark people in China then?' With this simple question, the Chinese students in Joyce's class burst into conversation among themselves, mostly in Mandarin, as they worked through the quandary of how to respond.

This teaching moment is central to our chapter's discussion of difference and intersectionality because it captures an instance of clashing identities as reflected materially and linguistically, via a cultural object. The moment provided an opportunity for further collective inquiry (for both Joyce's students and with other teachers) into class-based, gendered and racialized discomfort – a discomfort that embodies the complexities of intersectional identities.

After describing this vexing teaching moment with Xiqiao and Julia, the latter noted that it was not uncommon that in a classroom so heavily populated by international students, US-identified students of complicated racial and national backgrounds (e.g. Delvin, as a Dominican American) might be overlooked. As a scholar of color, Xiqiao helped Joyce understand more fully – as indeed Delvin had – the complexity of Delvin's racial identity, rendered invisible in a class session that focussed on celebrating students' (national) cultures, but not necessarily on race. Indeed, the discussion with Xiqiao and Julia helped Joyce (as a White woman) realize that centering students' languages and cultures could obscure a focus on other aspects of student identity. Teacherly discussion helped illustrate that while the first-year writing curriculum was experiential and story-based, the stories and assumptions that students (and teachers) brought with them to class were anything but neutral and, instead, linked to institutional and ideological systems of oppression.

Joyce's discussion with Xiqiao and Julia also informed subsequent class periods, where Joyce engaged her students in discussions of how racism occurs transnationally and materially (e.g. linking the umbrella to the ideal of White feminine beauty). That such examples cross national lines was indicated when some of the Chinese students drew upon a popular internet trope to talk about students from privileged backgrounds as 'fair, rich and beautiful,' which is often used with another phrase to describe young men from privilege as 'tall, rich and handsome.' Such conversations helped Joyce's students understand how classed and racialized identities might be conflated with gendered biases, how they occur both similarly and differently across national borders, and how such biases manifest in linguistic labels such as 'fair' and 'rich'; class discussions also centered around how various cultural perspectives impacted perceived definitions of English words such as 'beauty,' and how such words might be defined differently by different cultures. Informed by teacher conversation with Xiqiao and Julia, Joyce's subsequent classroom discussions came to reveal and unpack taken-for-granted ways that students may fail to acknowledge linguistic difference, when phrases, tropes, and idioms become implicated with ideologies that bear the weight of social and economic inequalities. Indeed, as Lippi-Green writes, ideology 'is most powerful when its workings are least visible' (2012: 79); surfacing these assumptions is particularly important for privileged students (and yes, teachers) who may not be aware of, or attuned to, their (often invisible) participation in oppressive ideologies that manifest through person-to-person, often implicit, microaggressions. While having such conversations may be difficult, they are essential, as they invite us all to engage in conversations that critically engage with intersectional identity challenges that differ for each member of a given community.

Dialogic reflection

Through her discussions with Xiqiao and Julia, along with others, Joyce has come to realize that despite all the positive changes enacted in the PCW classroom over the past nine years, it nonetheless can still surface and circulate complex identities, assumptions and viewpoints that exist in often uneasy and even contentious relationships, in which one person's stance is presented or represented at the expense of another's.

Xiqiao: There are so many material aspects here. Incidents like these entail a cultural assumption or status that the object, like the parasol, carries. But these meanings are perceived so differently!

Joyce: Exactly. And conversations about the implications of these objects, and how these objects may be described differently in different languages, becomes so important. At the same time, such moments also suggest that a curriculum that centers objects as signifiers of others' cultures and languages can open up a space for misunderstanding.

Julia: Yes! For the surfacing of how cultural and linguistic assumptions can be experienced as microaggressions – I never thought of that before.

Joyce: The 'contact zone' of the classroom not only provides an opportunity to view differences through a positive lens, but also invites and reveals assumptions about others that could be more negative.

Xiqiao: As an Asian person of color, I can understand why Delvin might feel invisible in this class, because race is not something we talk about much, if at all, in PCW. And it's hard to talk about. I didn't even know race was such a thing, as it is constructed here, before I came to the US. If I were in that classroom, I wouldn't even know how to react.

In discussing a vexed teaching moment with this article's co-authors, Joyce came to realize that teachers, like students, could be better equipped to recognize such moments as they occur, and to be nimble in their response. As a result, she has since brought up both instances in ongoing departmental workshops, engaging in pedagogical conversations and using these scenarios as opportunities for others to propose and examine an array of possible responses. She has also participated in multiple anti-racist discussions and dialogues that have helped provide more theoretical frameworks and cogent examples; she is currently engaged in collaboratively co-writing (with others in her program) a workbook on anti-racist pedagogical approaches to first-year writing, that unpacks and presents some of these ideas and scenarios. Ultimately, she acknowledges that this work is ongoing, and that when moments like these are listened to in the classroom and then shared with other teachers, not only does the instructor continue to learn, but this learning also impacts the teaching and mentoring of others. Accordingly, engaging in teaching dialogue is central for both students and teachers; through listening critically, teachers can learn to reflect collaboratively, making sense of the insensible. In her work, Joyce supports both faculty and students (as well as herself) in becoming more rhetorically attuned to the effects of their taken-for-granted assumptions of self and others.

Scenario Two: Critically listening to difference

Albina, a Women's Studies major from Ghana, is the only daughter from a family of 12 children to complete her K-12 education through the sponsorship of an international NGO. In the PCW classroom, Albina actively collaborated with her peers to complete a series of assignments that surfaced language and cultural differences. From an assignment that invited students' sharing of cultural texts, Albina worked with an ethnic minority woman from China to discover a theme they continued to explore through a series of activities and assignments: women's autonomy in marriage. The juxtaposition of cultural differences, manifested in how spouses were chosen, was enabled by a translingual and transcultural curriculum, which not only positioned cultural texts chosen by students as objects of analysis, but made listening – specifically, *critical listening* – a mainstay for learning. Here, such cultural inquiries into romantic rituals across cultures carried forward into a classroom skit; Albina and her peer enacted a consultation between an advocacy worker and a victim of domestic abuse. The two women provided a gripping representation of the tragic circumstances of a young woman in an abusive relationship, ensued by a short exchange that involved the advocate's attempts to comfort and encourage the victim to reveal the physical abuse. The survivor, performed by Albina, produced a monologue where she expressed her desire to pursue a meaningful career. Student reactions ensuing from the skit gave rise to a few young men questioning the victim's motive to leave her husband because of her lack of access to financial and social resources. A few young women, on the other hand, argued that immediate departure was a legitimate response to physical violence. The nature and consequences of domestic violence were further complicated as various students offered nuanced understandings of gender roles in connection to professional opportunities and domestic abuse.

Dialogic reflection

What is particularly noteworthy from this cross-cultural and cross-linguistic dialogue are the complex ways in which gender scripts were maintained and disrupted. It is helpful to remember this conversation took place at a large US university in 2017 among freshmen students from diverse cultural and linguistic backgrounds. In particular, a male student, who vocalized the view that domestic violence might need to be tolerated for financial security, received much encouragement and support through his peers' laughter. Despite the student's oblivion to his male privilege, Albina's sharing of female divorcees being considered as 'secondhand' – even in the context of domestic violence – made space for a discussion of gender inequality that may not have surfaced otherwise. The skit and the ensuing conversation provided a space to promote students' understanding of self and other across commonalities and differences (Marty, 2008), thereby supporting students' ongoing inquiry into how cultural logics and norms work through their own claims and linguistic choices.

The transformation of this classroom event into pedagogical dialogue was later discussed by the authors of this essay. This conversation incrementally surfaced the complexity of the intersectional identities manifested in language embedded in this teaching moment.

Xiqiao: My conversation with Bree (graduate field researcher) helped me realize that we had such different views of power dynamics that are motivated by gender. She noticed how the young men were essentially silencing Albina and defending male privilege. Bree was suggesting that her reading in feminist theory made the gendered biases and assumptions that I, or other students didn't hear. I don't think many of us have the language to name and discuss these issues.

Joyce: It is interesting that the curriculum we are developing, one that emphasizes the value of linguistic and cultural diversity, and the safe space we helped to build, could also silence Albina.

Julia: But they [the students] are learning to listen to differences, right? Even when some of their ideas are clearly biased. And at least it's a learning community that encouraged Albina to speak her mind.

Xiqiao: Yeah. I think part of the reason I didn't jump in to shut the male students down was because I wanted them to know

	speaking up is expected, respected, and valued. But this is difficult to do when many students come from educational settings where speaking up is discouraged.
Joyce:	So a central problem is how do we respond when what students share is aggressive, harmful, or disrespectful?
Julia:	What did you do, Xiqiao?
Xiqiao:	I was literally biting my lips but I was so worried about damaging the safe space.

At this moment, the reflective conversation went quiet; the authors paused to consider comparable teaching moments in their own classrooms, particularly those that were lost. Julia mentioned fear and apprehension in making a complicated situation worse, while Joyce brought up the possibility of engaging in microaggressions that could have alienated students further. This dialogue illustrates that although Xiqiao focused her energy on prompting students' discussion of ideas grounded in the skit, the presence of a graduate researcher – a White US woman with invested intellectual interests in gender equality – was crucial in surfacing the need to attend to the juxtaposition of multiple perspectives, to reflect on and reconsider pedagogical choices for scaffolding productive conversations. From this dialogue, the teacher and field researcher determined a teaching objective that they pursued in the next class: inviting students to further discuss cultural assumptions and practices of romantic pursuit. Such conversations engendered a productive sharing of language practices embedded within cultural jokes, pick-up lines, and dating practices that were connected to cultural norms and assumptions students often critiqued as inequitable. Dialogue was further mobilized when Xiqiao participated in a departmental workshop, where she used this scenario to invite pedagogical conversations about the challenges of respecting linguistic and cultural differences while critically engaging with biases and stereotypes that might surface during cross-cultural conversations.

Critical Listening in Practice

As the above scenarios suggest, even despite the expertise of seasoned teachers, and the best intentions of an asset-based curriculum that features students' languages and cultures as sites of inquiry and resources for learning, problematic moments in the 'contact zone' of our classrooms will continue to emerge. As the teacher dialogues offered above indicate, these moments can feel paralyzing to a teacher, who 'in the moment' may find herself at a loss on how to respond. This is why dialoguing with other teachers is so important. Dialogue provides a space in which instructors can talk through the many complexities and implications such moments raise, and then apply the new ideas, understandings, and lessons to subsequent teaching. In these layered conversations, the constellation(s) of students' classed, gendered, and racialized identities (as well as those related to transnational cultures and languages) become sites for inquiry, as students and teachers alike began to examine identities as interconnected, layered, and shifting – historically and cross-culturally. *Critical listening* across difference surfaces the powerful ways social dynamics of oppression intersect. Learning to listen with empathy and patience renders visible the inequitable social mechanisms that are at play in translingual and transcultural classroom spaces. Just as discussing these issues with their colleagues moved Xiqiao and Joyce to a deeper understanding of vexed classroom moments, follow-up conversations in the classroom moved their students toward a recognition of, and ongoing inquiry into, how interlocking systems and structures of sex, language, race, and class shape ideology and experience.

Thus this chapter argues for a stance of ongoing *critical listening* – an attunement to the endlessly variable shifts in students' (and teachers') self-expressed identities, beliefs, and assumptions that have the potential to lead to classroom microaggressions. As the conversations following both teaching scenarios illustrate, becoming sharply attuned to the complex intersectional aspects of identity and attitudes that emerge in our classrooms, and devising how to respond, can be supported by ongoing dialogue among ourselves as teacher-scholars: as we question, examine, and share such moments. This sharing is necessary if we are to truly commit to better preparing ourselves in not just recognizing and responding, but also anticipating and preparing students in advance, so that they too are more likely to *see* themselves and their experiences and those of others within larger institutional and societal contexts that discriminate on the basis of race, class, and gender (to name a few). In other words, this chapter seeks to develop better *critical listening* skills in our students *and* in ourselves, to the multiple differences that exist (both singly and intersectionally); we work to cultivate ongoing awareness of the manifestation of hierarchies (that position White over dark, male over female, moneyed over not, etc.); and we invite all members of the learning community to engage in ongoing dialogues that question the taken-for-granted assumptions about difference that we carry. We argue for the need to develop a rhetorical sensitivity to the positionalities of others who differ from ourselves – one that moves beyond only one or two particular frameworks (as in our case, language and culture) – and to engender similar sensitivities in our students, so that they may be more likely to *see* and *hear* others from the perspectives of others – which inevitably entails deep questioning of one's own views as well as learning spaces that invite uncomfortable conversations.

A curriculum that encourages collaborative inquiry into differences has the potential to create a space for students to recognize their own intersectionalities, suspend familiar assumptions, and develop strategies for critical listening – but only if the instructor herself is also attuned. Such attunement may be reinforced by a robust teaching community that values collaborative, recursive and generative dialogues that make it axiomatic, rather than exceptional, that instructors reflect on moments of identity conflict within their classrooms, so that they can adjust their teaching practices accordingly. In each of the instances described above, meaningful teaching moments emerged as objects of pedagogical reflection, conversation, and juxtaposition. Space for change was made through the convergence of dialogue, these listening/sharing practices. Furthermore, teacherly dialogue can motivate additional learning: here, for example, through the three authors' shared examination and discussion of related theories of intersectionality; or via-a-vis other venues (e.g. Xiqiao's conversations with a field researcher or Joyce's with other colleagues, through her university's anti-racist dialogues).

So we ask: How might teachers approach their classrooms, to engage with the many institutional structures of oppression that pervade Western education? How might teachers anticipate and prepare for such moments? How might teachers prepare students to better consider the perspectives of others? These questions, seemingly pedagogical in nature, have compelled our team to engage with scholarship on intersectionality and linguistic racism, and to develop models for using critical listening to address various forms of oppression based on race, gender, class, and other oppressive constructs.

Critical Discussion Questions

Throughout this chapter we have sought to affirm that teacher dialogue is necessary in order for all members of a learning community to identify, articulate, and mobilize conversations that critically and thoughtfully recognize and unpack differences. We close with a series of critical discussion questions that we encourage readers to consider as they move through pedagogical dialogues that are unique to their own learning communities.

(1) Who are the members of our classrooms and teaching communities? What identities might not be heard and how can we create learning spaces that invite multiply inflected experiences with difference, as well as opportunities for reflection on and questioning of the implications of one's own taken-for-granted assumptions about others? In other words, how can we create productive critical listening opportunities?
(2) How might critical listening be a central tenet of both disciplinary and interdisciplinary dialogue?
(3) When, where, and how do we intervene in low-stakes discussions of difference?
(4) How might attending to and sharing classroom-level dialogue, in all of its complexity, help teacher-practitioners engage in pedagogical innovation and theoretical dialogue?

(5) How might dialogue with other instructors about our teaching experiences deepen our own understanding of and contributions to complex moments in the 'contact zone' (Pratt, 1991) of the classroom?

References

Baker-Bell, A. (2020) *Linguistic Justice: Black Language, Literacy, Identity, and Pedagogy*. New York: Routledge.

Conference on College Composition and Communication (1974) Students' right to their own language. *College Composition and Communication* 25 (3), 1.

Collins, P.H. and Bilge, S. (2020) *Intersectionality* (2nd edn). Cambridge: Polity Press.

Crenshaw, K.W. (1989) Demarginalizing the Intersection of Race and Sex: A Black Feminist Critique of Antidiscrimination Doctrine, Feminist Theory and Antiracist Politics. *University of Chicago Legal Forum* 1989, 138–67.

De Costa, P.I., Green-Eneix, C., Li, W. and Rawal, H. (2021) Interrogating race in the NEST/NNEST ideological dichotomy: Insights from raciolinguistics, culturally sustaining pedagogy and translanguaging. In R. Rubdy and R. Tupas (eds) *Bloomsbury World Englishes Volume 2: Ideologies* (pp. 127–140). London: Bloomsbury Academic.

Dumas, M. and Ross, K.M. (2016) 'Be real Black for me': Imagining blackcrit in education. *Urban Education* 51 (4), 415–442.

Franquiz, M.E. and Ortiz, A.A. (2017)'Co-editors' introduction: Who are the *transfronterizos* and what can we learn from them? *Bilingual Research Journal* 40 (2), 111–115.

Hankivsky, O. (2014) Intersectionality 101. *The Institute for Intersectionality Research & Policy, SFU* 36.

Inoue, A.B. (2015) *Antiracist Writing Assessment Ecologies: Teaching and Assessing Writing for a Socially Just Future*. Anderson, SC: Parlor Press LLC.

Kishimoto, K. (2018) Anti-racist pedagogy: From faculty's self-reflection to organizing within and beyond the classroom. *Race Ethnicity and Education* 21 (4), 540–554.

Lee, E. and Canagarajah, S. (2019) The connection between transcultural dispositions and translingual practices in academic writing. *Journal of Multicultural Discourses* 14 (1), 14–28.

Lippi-Green, R. (2012) *English with an Accent: Language, Ideology, and Discrimination in the United States* (2nd edn). New York: Routledge.

Marty, D. (2008) Rhetorical listening. *The Review of Communication* 8 (1), 74–77.

Pratt, M.L. (1991) Arts of the contact zone. *Profession* 33–40.

Ratcliffe, K. (2006) *Rhetorical Listening: Identification, Gender, Whiteness*. Carbondale: SIU Press.

Royster, J.J. (1996) When the first voice you hear is not your own. *College Composition and Communication* 47 (1), 29–40.

14 Curiosity Matters: Envisioning Intercultural Dialogue in Qualitative Research Practice

Wing Shuen Lau and Kristine Mensonides Gritter

Synopsis

In this chapter, we highlight our dialogue as we interpret the meaning that two Chinese immigrant educators who were educated partially in China and partially in the US make use of their culturally responsive practices. Notably, minimal research exists on how educators integrate their cross-cultural educational experiences into US classrooms and how their intercultural knowledge contributes to building relationships with students and other teachers from diverse ethnic backgrounds. Since these educators have substantial cross-cultural experiences in China and the US, their teaching identities are likely shaped by both Eastern and Western cultures and values. The first author identifies herself as an immigrant educator; the second author does not, but does identifies herself as an educator concerned with the training of immigrant educators.

Behind the Scenes: How Did Our Collaborative Research Begin?

With the growing diversity in American populations over the decades, the perceptions of teachers of color, especially those who are first-generation immigrants, have barely appeared in conversations on culture and identity in the field of literacy and curriculum. Immigrant teachers are underrepresented in K-12 education due to various barriers such as licensing, educational requirements, and work authorization (Furuya *et al.*, 2019). Recent data from the 2020–21 National Teacher and Principal Survey (Institute of Education Sciences, 2022) showed that about 80% of K-12 school teachers in the US were White; 9% were Hispanic; nearly 6% were Black; 2% were Asian; less than 0.5% were Native Alaskan or American Indian; less than 0.5% were Native Hawaiian or Pacific Islander.

The first author is a female Chinese immigrant teacher, who belongs to less than 3% of the teacher population; the second, with the 80% of White, largely female teachers in the US. We are specifically interested in unpacking the impact of our identity and dialogue while interpreting our qualitative research data – the cross-cultural instructional experiences of Chinese immigrant teachers.

Wing Shuen's positioning

I came to the US to pursue a Master's degree in Teaching English to Speakers of Other Languages (TESOL). I was born and raised in a multilingual and multigenerational family in Hong Kong. Most of my older relatives converse in Chinese dialects, spoken across Nanchang and Yantai. My parents speak Mandarin as their first language while I speak Cantonese. During my teenage years, I studied at a co-educational, subsidized, Christian secondary school where academic subjects were taught in English.

Over the years, I have earned experience working with students across levels, from preschool through postsecondary, in various educational settings (e.g. intensive English language programs for international students, after-school enrichment programs for immigrant and refugee students, and the English language learners program in two local school districts). In recent years, my study and teaching have centered on a culturally responsive framework, which seeks to promote integrate social-emotional skills and identity work in literacy instruction for younger students whose first language is not English in the US.

Kris is a core faculty member and prolific professor in my PhD program. Together, we have engaged in several qualitative research projects on teaching practices and textual discussions in children's literature.

Kris Gritter's positioning

I am a second generation Dutch-American. My parents left the Netherlands as young children after World War II. Their families assimilated into US culture so much that both speak little Dutch. My family enjoys arguments or showing how clever we are with language. We tend towards loud talk when discussing something of passion.

I am also a White, Feminist professor at a faith-based university where I have worked for 15 years after receiving a PhD from a Research 1 institution. When I was hired, no women served on my White, male, six-member search committee, no woman was tenured within the School of Education, and untenured women in my school had far less scholarly mentoring than men, perhaps because of research interests, but perhaps because male professors were expected to not show undue interest in a female colleague. Prior to working in higher education, I taught middle school language arts for ten years and specialized in adolescent literacy during my PhD experience.

In time, in part by producing adequate scholarship, I became a full professor, a core doctoral faculty member (with reduced workload for mentoring doctoral students), so I dedicate much of my time working with doctoral students. Wing Shuen is one of those students. She is also my graduate assistant.

Our positioning

In examining our findings on culturally responsive teaching, we argued that both emic ('insiderness') and etic ('outsiderness') perspectives have shaped our inquiry, and we adopted the argument that 'researchers are not necessarily insiders or outsiders, but edge and margin navigators who locate the gaps and trace the moving and movable margins' (Beals *et al.*, 2020: 600). Our positioning as qualitative researchers is to create a space to embrace our emic and etic perspectives that empower us to find a new way to perceive our identities and cultures. Using our own expressions of dialogue, we analyzed our thoughts about culturally responsive teaching of two Chinese immigrant teachers and found that we responded very differently from each other.

A Bird's Eye View: What is the Role of Intercultural Dialogue in Educational Research?

Dialogue processes allow educators 'to excavate and bring to the surface their own personal biases and prejudices in order to transform classroom conditions into equitable learning spaces for all students' (Adams & Buffington-Adams, 2019: 155). Internationally, research on intercultural dialogue has been growing in the field of teacher education. For example, Skrefsrud (2016) discussed how intercultural dialogue is deemed an essential component of teacher training in Norway. Another study in Malaysia underlined the need to prioritize teachers' professional development on practicing intercultural communication in daily living (Othman & Ruslan, 2020).

To understand intercultural dialogue, education researchers should attune to their agreements, shared leadership, and discussion protocols because dialogue demands reflexivity to change. This practice requires 'critical friendships' that are 'organized, planned for, and facilitated' by the members engaging in dialogue (Adams & Buffington-Adams, 2019: 157). Critical friendships are based on agreements to ensure that all members in a dialogue group feel safe and can speak honestly and can revisit prior thinking. Agreements might include Singleton and Linton's four rules of courageous conversations: 'Stay engaged, speak your truth, experience discomfort, and expect and accept non-disclosure' (2006: 58–65). As such, intercultural dialogue begins with connecting differences, considering alternatives, and constructing new meanings.

Intercultural dialogue enables historically silenced researchers examining closely with historically privileged researchers to dismantle the prescribed ways of shaping ideas and opinions from dominant-culture perspectives. In this way, individual stories can 'build on one another and expand not only in quantity but also in depth' (Ngunjiri & Hernandez, 2017: 398). Dervin (2015: 84) proposed a 'post-intercultural' approach to teacher education based on his premise that identity is in flux and not set, that power relations are central to examining what is happening in classrooms, that teachers play a role in marginalizing certain students, and that knowing the context of dialogue is central to knowing what is happening and deciding how to react.

Theoretical concepts of intercultural dialogue

When people do not understand what is happening to others in a given situation, they often blame their lack of understanding as a lack of understanding culture rather than acknowledging that unequal power and/or structural inequalities may be exacerbating the situation. Johnson and Bhatt (2003) observed that examining identity as relational creates spaces where social justice can be examined and prevail. The intercultural exchange should be 'one from which we learn and influence each other in ways that undermine privilege and oppression' (Johnson & Bhatt, 2003: 231).

Intercultural dialogue goes beyond being bilingual or trilingual. It involves more than linguistic knowledge but also the desire and the know-how to engage in intercultural discussion in practice with others who may be quite different from oneself (Ponomarenko *et al.*, 2017: 90). This kind of discussion requires cultural cosmopolitanism defined as 'a commitment to the sharing of different cultures and the values that inform them as the basis for international independence' (McNiff, 2013: 501). Cosmopolitanism grows through intercultural dialogue. Cosmopolitans seek out other cultures through dialogue; locals stay home. True cosmopolitans take in the coexistence of cultures and allow them to become part of their personal identities (Hannerz, 1990).

Elias and Mansouri (2020) suggested four key dimensions of the intercultural framework that can be used to identify dialogue: (1) the relational dimension (interactions in which one critical friend directly responds to another critical friend's question or comment); (2) the integrative dimension (interactions in which values are shared and the dialogue seek to facilitate social integration); (3) the transformative dimension (interactions in which critical friends engage in expanding knowledge and skills by proposing their ideas and existing thoughts); and (4) the normative dimension (which addresses and acknowledge the value of cultural diversity and seeks to understand the other critical friend's perspective). We regard these four dimensions as additive in dialogic depth. In other words, without the relational dimension, two researchers engaged in intercultural dialogue will probably not be able to have dialogue at the normative dimension. The first two dimensions bring critical friends together by noting what is common between them. The second two dimensions honor and name cultural differences between intercultural friends.

Much of what has been discussed in prior theoretical studies described the core aspects of intercultural dialogue, while very limited empirical studies in the US context were conducted to provide insights into how intercultural dialogue plays a critical role in interpreting qualitative data in the field of education. Our chapter aims to expand the literature on the use of intercultural dialogue in research collaboration.

Research Questions

Our dialogue revolved around three research questions:

(1) Under what communicative contexts is our dialogue in agreement as two trained educators of language committed to being critical friends?
(2) What are the reasons for our differing interpretations of data?
(3) How do our emic/etic perspectives shape our role in qualitative research?

We especially wanted to note how we came to honor each other's viewpoints that were different from our own because of insider or outsider status and represented different viewpoints about teaching than our own.

Flashback: How Did We Process Our Dialogic Data?

We coded and analyzed our intercultural dialogue (dialogic data) based on our responses to each other's viewpoints made on the interview data that we had collected from teacher participants in a multi-case study (Lau & Gritter, 2022). That qualitative study included questions asked of immigrant teachers about their views of culturally responsive teaching and pedagogy. Our coding of the dialogic data (see Table 14.1 below) was grounded in the four key dimensions of intercultural framework: Relational, integrative, transformative, and normative (Elias & Mansouri, 2020).

In addition to the four intercultural dimensions, we also coded comments according to the nature of our responses: if we made a comment or an assertion or if we asked a question.

Data collection

The dialogic data came from our responses to the two interviews with Chinese immigrant educators about how they try to teach with a culturally responsive lens. Participant 1 or 'Jiang' (a pseudonym) teaches three levels of Chinese at a public middle school in an affluent city in the Pacific

Table 14.1 Coding process

Adapted Definitions of Four Dimensions	Coding Process of Dialogic Data
Relational: The direct response we deliver to each other.	We counted the number of times we directly addressed each other's response.
Integrative: Social integration and adaptation that center on constructing values together and looking for shared ground.	We looked for our responses that showed shared values to facilitate social integration.
Transformative: Exchange perspectives that promote knowledge sharing in a meaningful and inspirational way.	We coded the responses that we made to expand intercultural knowledge and skills as well as propose our ideas on the topics that we identified in our dialogue.
Normative: Mutual understanding and acceptance of diverse views.	We focused on how we affirmed the value of cultural diversity and understood each other's differences when we coded dialogue as normative.

Northwest. Participant 2, who was given the pseudonym, 'Xi', is a university professor of Chinese in an undergraduate linguistics program at a four-year university. Her duties include teaching language classes and Chinese culture classes.

For the first interview with Xi, Kris (the interviewer and the first commentator) responded with the first comment, and Wing Shuen responded with the second comment. For the second interview with Jiang, Wing Shuen (the interviewer and the first commentator) responded with the first comment and Kris responded with the second comment. The first comment was in reference to a response the interviewers gave about their interpretations of what teacher participants remarked on culturally responsive teaching. The second comment was made based on the first comment. Coding of the dialogic data referred only to the second comment made by either Wing Shuen or Kris. We met through an online meeting tool regularly to code our responses and analyze our findings based on the dialogic data. We also discussed our interpretations of the dialogic styles used in our responses to each other's comments. To be precise, we emphasized that the dialogic data collected for this chapter were based on the dialogue of the two researchers conducting the study and not on the interview data (responses of the two immigrant teachers).

Zoom-In Views: What Do the Data Analysis and Findings Tell Us?

Research Question 1

(1) Under what communicative contexts is our dialogue in agreement as two trained educators of language who are also committed to being critical friends?

KG: Wing Shuen and I often agreed about what sounded like good teaching when we read the transcripts of our participants talking about culturally responsive teaching or pedagogy. However, Wing Shuen tended to ask questions, and Kris to make assertions, which we viewed as a hierarchy in our discussion. We made relational comments in response to our critical friend/researcher's comment in that we directly responded to each other for every response. Wing Shuen's questions about my comments or about the interviewee's response showed greater curiosity about culture. We often agreed about what we thought was good teaching or good preparation for teaching as both 'Xi' and 'Jiang', the two participants of our multicase study, described their teaching. For example, Jiang described her education as follows:

> I majored in English language and literature at college when I was in China. I completed my Master of Education with a specification in second language acquisition at the University of Sydney, Australia. I was a college teacher who taught English in China. My teaching and research direction were all related to English language education. After I moved to the US, I completed [the] Startalk Certification Program. I began to teach Chinese in the US.

To this, Wing Shuen commented, 'My educational background is similar – second language acquisition. I spent some time in Lyon (France) and Sydney. Studying overseas has broadened my [worldview].' I agreed with Wing Shuen, by noting, 'Travel is a good thing for teachers to understand cultures.' This comment was coded relational, integrative, transformative, and one of my few normative statements. The relational coding showed I was responding to Wing Shuen's comment about traveling. The integrative coding showed we both agreed that travel was important for teachers to develop wider cultural understanding. The transformative coding was because Wing Shuen proposed her idea that travel broadens worldviews. The normative coding was because I valued Wing Shuen's perspective.

WSL: When Xi responded to a question about her teaching approach, she stated, 'We have an old saying about teaching from Confucius. Teachers are not just to teach knowledge but actually to journey with students and work on some confusion that students have in their life.' Kris first commented, 'She loves to learn with people. I think she really likes culture. I like the journey metaphor. I think that too.' I connected with Kris in the description of Xi's teaching and added my interpretation by sharing common beliefs of Confucianism as follows:

> Yes, I agree with you. I like the term 'journey' too. I like how she (Xi) cares about her students and makes teaching reciprocal. Confucian values are deeply rooted in East Asian countries such as China, Korea, and Japan. There is another saying, 'It takes 10 years to grow a tree, but it takes 100 years to cultivate a human being.' It truly takes time to journey with someone to make an impact on their lives.

This response was a typical example of other transformative responses I made to Kris in Xi's first and second interviews. It was coded as relational, integrative and transformative. Most of my transformative responses revealed the background of Chinese culture and personal schooling experiences related to Chinese and American education.

(II) Under what communicative contexts is our dialogue in disagreement?

KG: My transformative comments (those where it was clear to both of us that I was honoring Wing Shuen's lens of teaching as a cosmopolitan transnational teacher) tended to be about general teaching pedagogy because I cannot claim expertise in transnational teacher training. My comments tended not to broach the normative dimension which acknowledges the importance of cultural diversity and, therefore, did not often show appreciation for Wing Shuen's perspective and experiences as an immigrant teacher who had studied education and language around the world. For example, Jiang tended to organize [curricula] around festivals, and she stated, 'In the curriculum some topics are covered by at least six lessons, such as Mid-Autumn festival, Thanksgiving, Christmas, Chinese New Year, Halloween and Tomb Sweeping Day. Students prefer festivals, some important festivals.' Wing Shuen responded, 'I think she chose to include many festivals in the curriculum because these festivals can make culture more visible.'

I responded to Wing Shuen by noting, 'But it [a focus on festivals] does seem to be more shallow culture. However, it is a starting place.' This comment was coded 'relational' (it was a direct response to Wing Shuen), 'integrative' (some of the festivals seemed to be similar to US holidays), and transformative (in that I proposed an idea about a shallow culture that I later realized was untrue). Wing Shuen was correct, in fact. Lacking curiosity about culture, I made a premature and erroneous assertion about organizing a curriculum around festivals. In retrospect and upon reflection of my own written words, I am surprised by this because I have participated in religious and other festivals that get to the heart of my own identity and are not at all shallow to me. Wing Shuen's follow-up question allowed me to stop and reflect on my easy judgment in a respectful, non-judgmental, thoughtful way. I realized that I needed to ask more questions also.

My assertion conflated festivals with food or having a party (although parties, too, can be quite meaningful and celebrate culture in joyful ways I realize, upon reflection). I then assumed that festivals were 'shallow' without recognizing that I did not understand community values behind a festival like Tomb Sweeping Day. Because we took the time to transcribe our comments in reaction to research participants' questions (our thinking about their thinking) with Wing Shuen responding first because she knew more about transnational teaching, I was able to have an insight about my narrow thinking as I reflected on how Wing Shuen and I communicated. Wing Shuen has an identity I do not have and critical language I do not possess around that identity. Therefore, it was important for me, as a person of power in our current professional roles, to give more power to her in order to learn to get past my own shallow thinking about festivals as parties.

WSL: My responses to the comments Kris made on Xi were mostly constructed in a way to open doors for more substantial and deeper dialogues. Since the aim of my qualitative research with Kris was to examine how immigrant teachers' perceptions of their language use, personal and social identities, and cross-cultural education experiences would determine their implementation of culturally inclusive practices in US classrooms, I was keen on learning more about Xi's pedagogical practices. Keeping this purpose in my mind, my responses tended to be inquisitive rather than affirmative when compared to Kris. For instance, Xi introduced how she selected books that helped her share her culture with students. She said:

> In the traditional health and behavior class, I use a textbook. That textbook is at the introductory level, so the students know Chinese medicine, some history, maybe must-know knowledge and terms. In Spring Quarter, I will pilot a new class, Japanese and Chinese food history, a food culture. We will use a textbook as well. That textbook focuses on Japanese food. I think I will add some Chinese articles to supplement that class.

Kris noted, 'Her (Xi) text choices sound interesting' and 'I like how she (Xi) uses texts'. I was more eager to seek the reasons why Xi uses those texts, so I made quite different comments, 'It is worth exploring how teachers of color select culturally relevant books for their students. What makes them choose those books?' I also shared my assumptions, 'There may be fewer options for Chinese medicine books written in English. I wonder how her (Xi's) students responded to the required readings.'

When Kris responded to Xi's use of comparisons that engaged students in sharing their cultural experiences, she commented, 'She (Xi) loves to learn using comparisons.' On the other hand, I was interested in how the strategies Xi used to implement cultural comparisons could impact students' learning, so in my comment, I stated, 'compare and contrast is commonly used to teach cultures, but I hope to know how teachers can motivate students to bring their cultural experiences and knowledge in the discussions.' I asked more follow-up questions in my comments regarding the interviewees' culturally inclusive practices. As I had a similar cultural background with Xi and Jiang, most of the time my own teaching was relevant to elaborate their ideas, so I tended to share more about my learning and teaching experiences and observations as an immigrant educator when responding to the first comment that Kris made. If we had not committed to transcribing and coding our dialogue around the research we were doing, we would not have realized how emic status helps insiders to a culture understand more fully the culture they are describing. Dialogue can help researchers become critical friends and reduce some of the existing power structure through examining the language of those in power.

Research Question 2

What are the reasons for our differing interpretations of data?

KG: Wing Shuen has similar educational experiences with the two interviewees because three of them used to be Chinese international students in Western countries. She knows Jiang as a friend and Xi as a former instructor. I am older and sometimes have a position of power at the university where Xi works, so hierarchies existed in the interviews. Wing Shuen was much more likely to ask clarifying questions; I was more likely to make assertions and relational responses such as 'Right,' 'Yes, it is,' and 'I agree.' I conclude that is an indication of my relative power to *not* have to think deeply in truly integrative or normative ways. I am also the second author; this is not my original research; this research would not have occurred to me because it is outside of my teaching experience. I also conclude that Wing Shuen knows more about the topic and so asks better questions. Elias and Mansouri's four key dimensions for developing an international framework were revelatory. We could do the relational quite easily by responding to each other. Because Wing Shuen commented first on the participants' responses, I had an extra layer of context that allowed me to respond. The integrative layer was more difficult. I do not know the values of the immigrant teachers except that they prize cosmopolitanism more than I do because they left their home country and could operate as highly trained professionals because of their transnational education. I found Wing Shuen's transformational comments where she explained her ideas and thoughts about education in China the most interesting, however. Those were the moments when I could take on a normative stance to appreciate her additional knowledge about teaching around the world.

WSL: When I read our dialogue in response to our participants' responses, I began to engage in self-analysis and to reflect on my professional training. I sensed the influence of the Western perspectives on my question-asking behavior. When I first started my master's study in the US, I realized that asking and answering questions was a key colloquial and instructional component in a classroom. My P-12 schooling experience, which was mostly teacher-centered, and past learning behaviors, which emphasized self and inner reflection, did not prepare me to speak up in class to express my doubts and ideas. The practices in my research studies and teaching in the US have made me become more eager to propose new viewpoints and less afraid of losing face since I have learned that expressing personal ideas and seeking affirmation through sharing ideas and questioning the content are norms to demonstrate the understanding of learning material in American education. Because of that, I regarded asking questions as a constructive and necessary way to participate in my dialogue with Kris to express my thinking. I am inclined to ask more questions for clarification, and through questioning I reflected more on my current knowledge about Chinese and American schooling. For example, when Kris pointed out that Xi's response 'sounds like teaching is more learner-centered in the US,' I replied,

> The class size is an important variable for the implementation and effectiveness of teaching strategies. I agree that students in the US are more culturally diverse, so teachers need to be good at communicating their expectations with parents and students. I wonder what 'different needs' that Xi referred to in her response.

Overall, analyzing the differences in how we interpreted our dialogue and data collected from the interviews with the other two teachers helped me rethink the American and Chinese pedagogical practices I have adopted. The other reason for our differing interpretations stemmed from our schooling experiences and perspectives about culturally responsive teaching.

KG: I admit I was not raised in a culturally responsive P-12 environment. As a child and adolescent, I attended small Christian schools where the vast majority of students were White, working class, American, monolingual, and world language instruction was not provided for students. Even though my doctoral program had a think tank that investigated comparative Chinese-American educational systems, I learned very little about the Chinese educational system in my doctoral studies. I do recall reading one text comparing mathematical instruction in China with instruction in the US with the author's thesis stating that mathematics was taught better in China because Chinese teachers understood basic mathematical principles such as addition and subtraction much better than American teachers based on their mathematical vocabulary.

WSL: Neither Kris nor I studied in a vastly diverse classroom throughout our P-12 education, while in our dialogue, we realized how our viewpoints of teaching-learning environments are vastly shaped by our schooling experiences in different educational systems. I was raised in Hong Kong, a British colony from 1841 to 1997. Although both Chinese and English are official languages in Hong Kong, Cantonese remains the dominant language in people's daily living. Since 1997, the political transition has brought a series of educational reforms including the language policies of 'biliteracy and trilingualism' and 'mother-tongue teaching'. Under the new policies, I learnt to be biliterate (writing in English and Chinese) and trilingual (speaking English, Cantonese and Putonghua). However, the implementation of these language policies varied significantly from school to school. While I acquired academic English at an early age, I was taught in the stages of learning by a typical Chinese-teaching style which included 'memorization, understanding, application, and questioning or modifying what they (Chinese students) have learned' (Pratt *et al.*, 1999: 253). I was accountable for paying attention and answering teachers' questions.

Research Question 3

How do our emic/etic perspectives shape our role in qualitative research?

KG: We both realized an emic perspective is valuable when it comes to interviewing immigrant teachers. The interview conducted in the home language of the teacher (Jiang's interview) yielded a longer interview with a more in-depth description of her culturally responsive teaching. If one wishes to create critical friendships that explore intersectionalities, it makes sense to have the critical friend/research partner with more intersectionalities (race, gender, and a common home language) interview and respond first in dialogue. The second person to respond should take on a questioning stance and try not to make easy but erroneous assertions without understanding how culture or other variable was at work. Friendships are less critical than the critical friendships needed for scholarship. I believe I am pretty close friends with Xi, as she counseled me through a health scare. I noted this at the end of the second interview, 'Her worldview changed my perspective. I cannot say I understand how she thinks all the time (or that she understands me), but she cares about me, and I care about her. Sometimes the best friends are much different than us because they add to our lives.'

WSL: A Chinese term for 'doing scholarly work' is *zuòxuéwèn* 做學問. This term consists of three characters, 'do' (zuò), 'learn' (xué), and 'ask' (wèn). This term has summarized how I engaged in intercultural dialogue as a qualitative researcher. In our research, my emic viewpoints on Chinese education enabled me to share cultural knowledge with Kris and answer questions related to the Chinese educational experience. At times, I noted that my etic perspectives of American culture helped me better conceptualize the idea of culturally responsive teaching and generate new insights with Kris based on each other's responses. For instance, Jiang said her goals were to foster students' global citizenship when she explained why culturally inclusive teaching was important to her. I, then, added, 'I wonder whether American students are familiar with the ideas of "Global Citizenship" because this concept is emphasized in China.' Kris replied, 'I am not familiar with the term or what it means. It is not emphasized here except to help nations in war, to the best of my knowledge.' Through dialogues, I saw opportunities to distill vague thoughts and underdeveloped ideas into clear and essential statements, and I embraced the value of asking clarifying questions in information-seeking discussions with Kris.

Future Dialogues: Identity, Language and Power in Research Collaboration

Intercultural dialogue allows the collaboration to examine our emic/etic perspectives, identities, linguistic assets, and power difference so that we as researchers and educators, especially when we do not operate as institutional equals, can synergise our effort to create richer and more balanced narratives (Blalock & Akehi, 2018; Roy & Uekusa, 2020). The different dimensions of intercultural dialogue enables us to carefully reflect on ways to address power dynamics and existing hierarchies in research, so that critical friendships can be established and stories can be shared in safety. This practice lets the more powerful in the present learn from those with more experience about the topic. Such listening is critically important as school populations change in terms of ethnicity and cultural values. For teachers and their students to flourish, student and teacher cultures need to become more explicit to be understood and valued.

We both agree that we conducted qualitative research projects out of curiosity as we are inquisitive people. We care enough about the research topic to investigate because we believe that more needs to be known about immigrant teachers and their culturally responsive pedagogy and what intercultural dialogue or post dialogue looks like for the flourishing of all involved. Our desire for intercultural collaboration and dialogues was fueled by the process of learning and seeking new knowledge to be better teachers or to better describe better teaching. However, we needed to respectfully argue with each other when we made uninformed assertions about teaching practices because of time constraints and/or preconceptions about China or the US which might reflect culture or some other power difference at play.

Epilogue

Even though we have a clear propensity to ask questions as we are in a researcher role, we adopt a different way of asking and answering questions in our dialogue when interpreting the data we obtained from the interviews. Wing Shuen found that the preference of 'asking questions to learn' and showing curiosity is impacted by cultural beliefs and educational traditions across countries. For Kris, engaging in dialogue with a PhD student driven by curiosity with much background knowledge was a humbling experience. She realized she should have asked more questions after seeing Wing Shuen's responses. Curiosity nudges researchers to ask questions before they make assertions about culture or culturally relevant pedagogy. This is a reminder to both of us that culturally responsive teaching involves assessment of self, dialogue with insiders of a culture, and reflection, leading to greater learning about culture, and, incidentally, of self.

Critical Discussion Questions

(1) After perusing a 'diversity' syllabus at your university or school, what percentage of knowledge taught in the class deals with cultural conflict issues that Asian or Pacific Islander students are likely to face in schools versus what African-American or Hispanic students are likely to face?
(2) During your teaching and learning experience, what conditions or challenges (such as language proficiency and cultural differences) in conversations might have affected how you interpreted the identity and culture of others?
(3) How might festivals and traditions be taught in a diverse classroom in a way that deeply explores cultural values in intercultural discourses?
(4) In dialoguing with a partner with a different culture and worldview, when does it make sense to ask a clarifying question? When does it make sense to make an assertion?
(5) How does intellectual curiosity present itself in dialogue? How can intellectual curiosity be presented in classes where some students are less inclined to speak publicly than others?

References

Adams, S. and Buffington-Adams, J. (2019) Processes and protocols for creating and sustaining cross-racial dialogue among K-12 educators. In J.A. Heybach and S. Fraser-Burgess (eds) *Making Sense of Race in Education* (pp.155–168). Gorham, ME: Myers Education Press.

Beals, F., Kidman, J. and Funaki, H. (2020) Insider and outsider research: Negotiating self at the edge of the emic/etic divide. *Qualitative Inquiry* 26 (6), 593–601. https://doi.org/10.1177/1077800419843950

Blalock, A.E. and Akehi, M. (2018) Collaborative autoethnography as a pathway for transformative learning. *Journal of Transformative Education* 16 (2), 89–107. https://doi.org/10.1177/1541344617715711

Dervin, F. (2015) Towards post-intercultural teacher education: Analysing 'extreme' intercultural dialogue to reconstruct interculturality. *European Journal of Teacher Education* 38 (1), 71–86. https://doi.org/10.1080/02619768.2014.902441

Elias, A. and Mansouri, F. (2020) A systematic review of studies on interculturalism and intercultural dialogue. *Journal of Intercultural Studies* 41 (4), 1–32. https://doi.org/10.1080/07256868.2020.1782861.

Furuya, Y., Nooraddini, M.I., Wang, W. and Waslin, M. (2019) *A Portrait of Foreign-Born Teachers in the United States*. George Mason University Institute for Immigration Research. https://d101vc9winf8ln.cloudfront.net/documents/29869/original/Teacher_Paper_FINALWebVersion_012219.pdf?1548268969.

Hannerz, U. (1990) Cosmopolitans and locals in world culture. *Theory, Culture & Society* 7, 237–251. https://doi.org/10.1177/026327690007002014

Institute of Education Sciences (2022) *Characteristics of 2020-21 Public and Private K-12 School Teachers in the United States: Results from the National Teacher and Principal Survey*. https://nces.ed.gov/pubs2022/2022113.pdf

Johnson, J.R. and Bhatt, A.J. (2003) Gendered and racialized identities and alliances in the classroom: Formations in/or resistive space. *Communication Education* 52 (3–4), 230–244. https://doi.org/10.1080/0363452032000156217

Lau, W.S. and Girtter, K. (2022) Hidden voices: How Chinese immigrant educators implement culturally inclusive practices in U.S. classrooms. *Educational Research and Development Journal* 25 (1), 65–81. https://eric.ed.gov/?id=EJ1361385

McNiff, J. (2013) Becoming cosmopolitan and other dilemmas of internationalisation: reflections from the Gulf States. *Cambridge Journal of Education* 43 (4), 501–515. https://doi.org/10.1080/0305764X.2013.831033

Ngunjiri, F.W. and Hernandez, K.C. (2017) Problematizing authentic leadership: A collaborative autoethnography of immigrant women of color leaders in higher education. *Advances in Developing Human Resources* 19 (4), 393–406. https://doi.org/10.1177/1523422317728735

Othman, A. and Ruslan, N. (2020) Intercultural communication experiences among students and teachers: Implication to in-service teacher professional development. *Journal for Multicultural Education* 14 (3/4), 223–238. https://doi.org/10.1108/JME-04-2020-0024

Ponomarenko, L., Zlobina, I.S., Galitskih, E.O. and Rublyova, O.S. (2017) Formation of the foreign language discursive competence of pedagogical faculties students in the process of intercultural dialogue. *European Journal of Contemporary Education* 6 (1), 89–99. https://doi.org/10.13187/ejced.2017.1.89

Pratt, D.D., Kelly, M. and Wong, K.M. (1999) Chinese conceptions of 'effective teaching' in Hong Kong: Towards culturally sensitive evaluation of teaching. *International Journal of Lifelong Learning* 18 (4), 241–258. https://doi.org/10.1080/026013799293739a

Roy, R. and Uekusa, S. (2020) Collaborative autoethnography: 'Self-reflection' as a timely alternative research approach during the global pandemic. *Qualitative Research Journal* 20 (4), 383–392. https://doi.org/10.1108/QRJ-06-2020-0054

Singleton, G.E. and Linton, C. (2006) *Courageous Conversations About Race: A Field Guide for Achieving Equity in Schools*. Thousand Oaks, CA: Corwin.

Skrefsrud, T. (2016) *The Intercultural Dialogue: Preparing Teachers for Diversity*. Münster: Waxmann.

Index

academic publishing 125, 137
activism xxiii–xxiv, 19, 141, 148–149, 151, 155
Additional Language Teaching 18, 26,
affinity identity 61, 70
African American 32, 34–38, 41, 50, 91, 99, 217
agency 19, 27–28, 94, 104, 130, 141, 148, 151
Asian 8, 63–64, 68, 110, 148, 169, 197, 204, 210, 217
authority 10, 36, 99, 109, 126, 135, 142, 144, 153–155
autoethnography xxii, 19–21, 45, 61, 65, 79–80, 110, 141, 146, 165–166, 173, 177, 179, 186

Bakhtin xix–xx, 95, 128
belonging xx, 3, 12, 21, 27, 42, 45, 48, 50, 57, 64, 70, 87, 91–93, 111, 161–162, 191
bi/mutlilingual identities 116
bias xxiii, 39, 61–63, 65, 68–69, 71–72, 83, 116, 196, 199–200, 206
BIPOC xxiii, 91–94, 96, 98–104, 193
Black women 45, 47–48, 50, 52–58,
blended culture 64
border xxii, 3, 6, 79, 128, 131–132, 184, 196
Bourdieu 174–178, 182–185
Brazil 3, 17–18, 20, 22, 26–28, 55, 159

Canva 134
center – periphery 151
code-switching 51
collaboration xxii, 21, 34, 65, 114, 126, 129–132, 158–159, 165–166, 168–171, 195, 208, 216
collaborative autoethnography xxii, 19–20, 45, 61, 65, 141, 146, 165–166, 173, 177, 179

collective experiences 6, 20,
colonial xix, 12–13, 17–18, 42, 79, 99, 114, 144, 151, 174–177, 182, 186
commodity 152, 175, 185–186
communities of practice (CoP) 107
community 4–6, 13–15, 17, 21, 24, 35, 37, 41, 52, 54–55, 57–58, 61, 64–67, 70–71, 78–81, 83–88, 105, 107–111, 114, 118, 120, 134, 158, 160–163, 167–168, 171, 177, 183, 192, 194–195, 197, 199, 201–202, 211
community cultural wealth 4, 6, 13
composition instruction 60–61, 64, 71–72
contextualized 147, 177
critical consciousness 18–22, 24–27, 130
critical dialogue xxii, 21, 23–25, 27, 32–34, 36, 39, 42, 95, 108, 158, 177
Critical Discourse Analysis 24, 126, 131–132,
critical educators 19–20, 26–27, 35
critical incidents xxi, xxiii–xxiv, 33–35, 39, 49, 66, 97–98, 142, 146, 154, 159, 179
critical race theory 91, 103, 117, 123,
cross-cultural 45–47, 54, 71, 192, 199–201, 204–205, 212
cultural adjustment 45–47, 54
cultural capital 174

data analysis 21, 65, 168, 179, 209
data collection 65, 97–98, 143, 165, 178–179, 208
decentering Whiteness 42, 125
decolonial research 18
dialogue xix, xx–xxiv, 3–8, 10, 12–15, 21, 23–25, 27, 32–34, 36, 39, 42, 47–49, 54, 56, 60–61, 65–68,

70–71, 77, 81, 84, 87, 91–92, 95–99, 101–104, 107–111, 119, 126, 128–129, 131–132, 141–150, 152–154, 158–159, 164–169, 171, 173–174, 177–180, 182–186, 189–195, 198–202, 204–209, 211–216
difference 5, 10–11, 14, 33, 40, 45, 54, 63, 65–66, 69, 86–87, 95, 100, 103–104, 108, 142–143, 145, 148, 151, 154, 165, 168, 190–202, 206, 208, 214, 216
discourse identity 61
discussion questions 15, 28, 43, 58, 72, 104, 137, 155, 171, 186, 202, 217
diversity 8, 24, 31, 58, 60, 65, 78, 93, 104, 109–110, 115, 119, 134, 162, 169, 190, 193, 199, 204, 207, 211

emancipatory education 17, 19–21, 27,
emancipatory racial humor 130, 134,
engagement xxi–xxiii, 65, 83, 91, 93, 104, 111, 115–116, 119–120, 126, 130–132, 137, 142, 158
English as a Foreign Language (EFL) 173, 176
English Language Teaching (ELT) 107
epistemological pluralism xx,
equality 61, 72, 200,
equity xxi, 58, 99, 129, 132, 167–168, 175, 190
erasure of identity 8, 93, 96, 98

Foucault xx, 142–143, 152
Freire xix, 3, 14, 17–19, 22–23, 26, 130
gender 4, 7, 22–24, 27, 46, 49, 51, 55, 58, 61, 64, 71, 96, 104, 108, 113–114, 190, 199–202, 215

Global North 143–145, 155
Global South 143–145, 155
globalization 186
Guyana 181

habitus 174–179, 182, 184–185
hierarchies 18, 125, 201, 213, 216
home culture 64, 66, 69, 162
host culture 63–64

identity xix, xxi–xxiv, 5–7, 10, 12–13, 18, 20, 22–23, 27, 31–33, 36–42, 45–46, 48–49, 51–52, 54–56, 58, 61–62, 64, 66–71, 77, 80, 91–104, 107–109, 117, 123, 130, 141–142, 146–148, 151, 154, 159–161, 171, 177, 180–182, 184, 190–192, 195–197, 201–202, 204–205, 207, 211–212
inclusion 6, 58, 71, 120, 124, 137, 166, 190
inquiry xix–xxii, xxiv, 6, 91, 102, 111–112, 131, 173, 180, 192, 196, 199–201, 206
institutional identity xxii, 6, 60, 147, 173–174, 177–178, 184, 191, 193–196, 201–202, 216
intercultural dialogue 206–208, 215–216
interdisciplinary 24, 155
intersectionality 4, 7–8, 22, 61, 91–94, 96, 98, 190–192, 194–196, 202
Islam 143–154

Japan 45–48, 50–58, 99, 210
joint effort 71
justice 13, 18, 23, 27, 68, 71, 83, 114, 122, 130, 137, 141, 190, 207

knowledge construction xix–xxi, 79, 142

language xix, xxi–xxiv, 4, 6, 8–13, 18, 20, 23–27, 32–37, 39–40, 42, 45, 47, 49–53, 57–58, 60, 62–63, 65, 67, 77–86, 91–93, 94–98, 100–101, 103, 107–120, 122–130, 133–134, 137, 141–143, 146–147, 149, 153–155, 158–164, 167–171, 173–174, 178, 180–186, 189–191, 193, 196–201, 205, 208–216
language education 26, 88, 117, 122–126, 130, 143, 147, 210
language ideology 62, 79, 84
language learning xxi, 13, 35, 42, 47, 49, 58, 77, 79, 92, 124, 129, 158, 164, 171, 174,
legitimacy 39, 61, 99, 137
legitimate peripheral participation 91–120
linguistic discrimination 8, 10, 12, 52, 77–81, 83–87, 108, 110, 116, 130
linguistic identity 32–33, 40–41

marginalization xxii, 64, 108, 191, 192
meaning-making 91, 92, 95
minortized viii, ix, 3, 5, 12, 13, 32, 33, 40, 41, 42, 47, 54, 57, 78, 93, 101, 103, 108, 110, 122–124, 125, 132, 159, 164, 198
modalities xxi, 115, 116, 129
monolingualism 21, 42, 79, 83, 109, 110, 113, 119
multilingualism xiv, xxi, 8, 71, 78, 79, 80, 83, 84, 85, 108, 109, 115, 116, 123–124, 126, 169

narrative xxii, 21, 28, 40, 43, 80, 91, 98, 99, 101, 103, 142, 159
nature-identity 61
navigation 4, 14
negotiation xv, 16, 31, 41, 92, 104, 146, 154, 193
network 168, 182, 184
non-binary 45, 46, 48, 50, 52, 54, 55, 57, 58
non-native English-speaking writing instructors (NNESWIs) xiii, xiv, xv, 60
non-standard 37, 81, 85, 126,

otherness 9, 55, 63

participation xxiv, 32, 69, 77, 78, 79, 80, 81, 87, 88, 91–105, 108, 111, 113–117, 119, 120, 197
participatory action research 97
performativity 23, 101
perspective xxii, 4, 17, 18, 27, 28, 49, 70, 78, 92, 93, 101, 144, 147, 151, 158, 163, 170, 174, 182, 190, 192, 207, 210, 211, 215
postcolonial vii, 42, 144
power xix–xxiv, 5–6, 9, 13, 15, 18–19, 22–23, 27, 31–33, 37, 39, 51, 61, 63–65, 68, 70–71, 78, 92, 95–98, 100, 102–103, 107, 117, 123, 125, 130, 133, 135, 141–143, 146, 148, 152–155, 173–179, 181–182, 184, 190, 199, 207, 212–213, 216
power dynamic 31, 96, 105
power relations 27, 135, 138, 141, 173, 176, 190, 207

privilege 8, 9, 10, 31, 32, 33, 60, 91, 176, 186, 192, 194, 196, 199, 207
public engagement xxi, 93, 125–137

qualitative research 204–217

race vii, 4, 22, 32, 33, 34, 41, 43, 61, 91, 96, 101, 103, 104, 107, 109, 117, 123, 128, 129, 134, 162, 176, 181, 190, 191, 196, 197, 201, 202, 215
racialized 4, 9, 10, 14, 32, 33, 42, 91, 93, 101, 108, 110, 125–138, 191, 196, 200
raciolinguistics 4, 15, 32–33, 37, 40, 41, 43
racism 4, 7, 12, 14, 53, 86, 100, 102, 103, 108, 109, 110, 114, 116, 125, 129, 134, 138, 190, 191, 192, 196, 202
reflexion 5, 6, 13, 14
reflexivity xxiii, 104, 142, 176, 185, 206
research methodology xxii, 165
researcher visibility 177

self-doubt 61, 68, 114, 116
self-reflection 6, 68, 116, 120
social justice xii, 13, 18, 27, 28, 114, 124, 130, 141, 207
social media vii, xix, xxii, xxiii, 77, 78, 88, 107, 110, 125, 126, 128, 130, 132, 134, 137
social transformation 26, 27, 28, 149, 150, 151
stigmatization 103
strategy xxi, 71, 84, 92, 94, 129, 130, 134, 135, 179
support 47, 50, 52, 56–58, 61, 64, 65, 67, 70–71, 180

teacher education 13, 25, 28, 31–43, 123, 167, 206, 207, 217
teacher identity xiv, 33, 39, 91
teaching xix–xxiii, 3, 8, 12–14, 18, 19, 24–27, 33, 34–41, 47, 49, 52, 58, 64–72, 78, 86, 88, 91–93, 97, 99, 100, 102, 107, 122–123, 129, 130, 138, 141, 142, 146, 147, 151, 152, 153, 154, 155, 158, 159–164, 166, 167, 168, 169, 174, 176, 182, 183, 189–202, 204–217

TESOL vii, ix, x, xii, xiii, xiv, 78, 80, 91–105, 108, 109, 110,111, 112, 113, 119, 120, 122–123, 162, 164, 168, 169, 170, 205
testimonio xii, xxii, 1–15, 17–56
theory of performance
thick intersectionality 94
transformation 18, 23, 25, 26, 27, 28, 32, 66, 100, 149, 150, 151, 199, 213
transgressive writing practices 19
translanguaging xii, 79, 82, 84, 85, 101, 114, 119, 128, 129, 169
translingual orientation 131, 132, 134
Turkey 34, 173–187

Twitter/X vii, 77–90, 108–123, 128, 129, 131, 132, 134, 135, 137, 138

underprivileged status 71

voice 41, 45, 55, 57, 58, 65, 78, 80, 82–83, 85, 108, 125–138, 181

Whiteness ix, 4, 11,12, 31–32, 37, 38, 40–42, 93, 103, 109–110,122, 125, 129, 138, 191

Zoom, xxi, 5, 48, 97, 108, 111, 119, 122–124, 131, 152, 166, 170, 209

For Product Safety Concerns and Information please contact our EU Authorised Representative:

Easy Access System Europe

Mustamäe tee 50

10621 Tallinn

Estonia

gpsr.requests@easproject.com